# HOUSTON IS COOKING 2000

## by Ann Criswell

**Nutritionist**
Linda McDonald, M.S., R.D., L.D.

**Wine Consultant**
Denman Moody

**Editor**
Ann Steiner

**Foreword**
Don D. Jordan

**Publisher**
Fran Fauntleroy

HOUSTON
GOURMET

## OUR SPECIAL THANKS TO

Ed Daniels – *Photography*

Mark Ruisinger – *Mark Anthony Florist – Floral Design*

B & C Partners – *Graphic Design*

Nancy Hudgins – *Publicity*

Wetmore Printing Company – Curtis Weeks, Richard Moore

Events – *Table Appointments; China: Rosenthal – Versace
Mottahedeh, Royal Worcester* – Jay Rosenstein

Christofle – *Table Linens* – Glenn Guiler

Wines – *Glazer's* – Sam Clark, Sharon Cooper
*Grand Crew* – Barry Johnson
*Republic Beverage* – Steve Raskin

Rienzi – The Museum of Fine Arts, Houston,
*former home of Mr. And Mrs. Harris Masterson III*

*Rice Epicurean Markets* – Scott Silverman

### SPECIAL FRIENDS WHO HELPED TO MAKE IT ALL HAPPEN:

*Beverly Harris, Lovice Brown, Jackson Hicks, Katherine Howe, Gary Hall,
Arnold Palacios, Yoly Perez, Dan Bulla and The Houstonian*

Houston Gourmet
Houston, Texas

Copyright ©1999 by Houston Gourmet

Printed in the United States of America

ISBN 1-882296-05-2

Library of Congress Cataloging-In-Publication data
Houston Gourmet Publishing Company

All recipes are reprinted with permission of authors.
Photographs printed with permission of Ed Daniels.
LiteFare and nutritional information printed with permission of Linda McDonald.

## FOREWORD BY DON D. JORDAN, CHAIRMAN OF THE BOARD OF RELIANT ENERGY

If there's one thing for certain, it's that I love good food. Even after traveling all over the world, I've learned there are few places that can match Houston for great cuisine!

I've lived in Houston nearly all of my life, and I've worked in the heart of the city for more than 40 years. Just as my own tastes have evolved and changed, so have those of Houston's chefs and diners.

In the 1950s, a famous English novelist named J. B. Priestly visited Houston. In his book, *Journey Down a Rainbow*, he wrote: "[Houston] is bigger than Dallas and supposed to be much rougher and tougher. Somebody up there told me that a gracious-living sort of woman arrived in Houston one evening and asked where she could find a nice restaurant with shaded lights, wine and soft music. 'Sorry, lady,' said the Houstonian. 'This is strictly a whiskey and trombone town.'"

Now Priestly wasn't entirely accurate. Even back in the '50s, Houston had a few fine restaurants. Back then, the selection was limited to just a handful of such establishments – mostly steak and seafood. Today, someone bent on an evening of fine dining is confronted with a myriad of choices...more than enough to satisfy any palette.

There's little doubt that the massive amount of international business conducted from Houston and the influence of immigrants who have come here from every corner of the globe have enhanced the diversity and sophistication of Houston's dining experience. At the same time, the increased variety and quality of restaurants have drawn people out of their homes and into the restaurants, increasing the percentage of time we eat out in this city.

It's all together fitting that Houston has developed into one of the fine dining meccas of the world. Houston is the fourth-largest city in the nation, and its grandeur is apparent in many ways. With the sights and sounds of the Theater District, the city's glittering skyline, the Houston Space Center, the world's largest medical center, the largest rodeo in the world and a multitude of spectacles and outdoor events that we've become famous for, fine dining is just one more way that Houston demonstrates its hospitality and spirit.

We who live here have known for years that there are many wonderful restaurants in our great city. But you don't have to take our word for it. Houston restaurants are repeatedly recognized for their dining experience... from excellent ratings in Zagat Surveys to special editions of Forbes Magazine.

This edition of *Houston Is Cooking* is special because it celebrates the coming of the new millennium. The year *2000* signifies many great things to come – for this city, for its inhabitants and for those visitors we're pleased to welcome to our hometown. The City of Houston is like fine wine – it only gets better with age!

So I raise my glass and offer a toast... to a new century, to a great city and to its people and their passion for fine dining. *Cheers!*

# INTRODUCTION

ANN CRISWELL
Food Editor
The Houston Chronicle

Suppose you wanted some accurate predictions about the millennium. Would you need to consult an economist, computer technologist, a medical wizard, nutritionist, housing specialist, government guru? Perhaps all of these. But we can't ignore a vital link to the next century – the chefs at our favorite restaurants. They have a direct connection to our happiness and well-being in the future.

Chefs know the fluctuations of supply and demand. You want a fish? A tomato with old-fashioned flavor? A home-grown peach? The chef knows if these are available — and so much more. He or she knows that the supply of many of our favorites is finite. Take that concern a step further. The entire field of agriculture is facing monumental changes. Dwindling resources of some products, food safety, food and culture trends, the economy and health-fitness issues are all involved. Experts are looking for definitive answers on hot topics such as genetic engineering of foods; the importance of various nutrients and phytochemicals; food's role in preventing heart problems, cancer and other catastrophic diseases; changes in the Food Pyramid; and irradiation of foods to prevent potentially deadly bacteria such as e-Coli that cause foodborne illnesses.

One thing chefs with vision don't want to see in the new millennium is fruits and vegetables out of season, such as fresh cherries in January, except where they occur naturally. And they want produce with credentials. Local is best. Regional is fine. National is preferable to produce from unknown international growers. Certainly chefs love to import, working with global sources who fulfill their requirement and challenge their creativity. Tony Vallone has long been recognized for flying in the finest ingredients – such as white truffles from Italy in season, olive oils and cheeses – at great effort and expense. Charles Clark of Tasca brings in exotic produce from all over the United States as well as ham, cheese and other specialties from Spain. Gerard Brach of Chez Nous orders lamb raised to his specifications from New Zealand. Robert Del Grande of Cafe Annie has befriended a family in Mexico that produces superior chocolate. Bill Johnson of Sabine searches out local and regional sources for unusual fruits, vegetables, sausages and seafood.

All the best chefs insist on authenticity – Dover sole must come from Dover, England, for example.

More and more food professionals are committed to what is now called sustainable agriculture – foods grown without pesticides or herbicides and processed without preservatives. They support local farmers and often grow many of their own vegetables organically; they maintain compost heaps and recycle paper, glass and metal; they conserve energy by choosing the most efficient power sources; they make it a goal to educate their staffs and customers. These concerned professionals have joined together in an organization called Chefs Collaborative 2000.

We, the diners, are much more knowledgeable today than five or ten years ago, the chefs say. We have been exposed to television and radio food programs, newspapers, magazines, cookbooks and cooking classes. We are computer literate and immersed in new technology. And we've traveled. Consequently our expectations of restaurants are much higher, says Jimmy Mitchell, executive chef of Rainbow Lodge, a member of Chefs Collaborative 2000. Today's customers eat more fish, seafood, game, rice and other grains such as couscous and bulghur. Many customers have environmental concerns and an increasing number of their children and other young people are becoming vegetarians, he says.

Del Grande, also a member of Chefs Collaborative, says: "We've confused the retailing of clothes with the retailing of food. What I like to see is a realistic product that looks like it has been authentically grown, not bred to look beautiful. If you breed for appearance, you don't breed for taste. When you grow and harvest tomatoes yourself, you'll end up with some green tomatoes, some not so good, some perfectly ripe and some overripe. There are good uses for each. If you're going to make a roasted tomato salsa, you don't need a perfect tomato. The more people know about food, the more they demand quality."

Houstonians love to dine out, and do so more frequently than the rest of the country. Our city is so diverse that you can find a food for any mood. Experts agree that our sizable Asian, Black, Hispanic and other ethnic populations will continue to have an impact on local cuisine and that Thai, Vietnamese, Indian, Japanese and Chinese will continue to grow in popularity. Latin, Mediterranean, South American, Middle Eastern, American regional (especially Southern), Caribbean and African – any food that packs a lot of flavor – also is expected to remain in favor in the new century. The increase in consumption of spices in the past 15 years – from one pound to three pounds annually per capita – underscores the flavor trend. So says Victor Gielisse, dean of culinary arts at the Culinary Institute of America (and a former Dallas restaurateur). He believes that America used to be a melting pot, but today the cuisine is better described as multi-national. He says Asian cuisine will continue to be the leader worldwide and that there will be an influx of Moroccan, Tunisian and Indian food. But bizarre fusion combinations – something like Wasabi Risotto – will not be assimilated in our menus. Instead, there will be more emphasis on ethnic cuisine than fusion, Gielisse says.

Because restaurants are increasingly considered entertainment, owners and chefs are constantly challenged. Gazing into the millennium's crystal ball, they see new ideas, new foods and new menus. Our table for the next century is being set.

# TABLE OF CONTENTS

Italian Salad
Shrimp Pasta with Fresh Tomato (Gamberoni el Pomodoro Fresco)
Chicken in Pearl Onions (Pollo en Cacciuclo)
Beef Medallions with Gorgonzola (Fillette el Borgonzo)
Fresh Berries with Meyer Lemon Curd

Creole Onion Soup
Red Snapper Court-Bouillon
Crab Salad Brennan's with (Herb Vinaigrette)
Marbled Fudge Brownies
Chocolate Chip Bourbon Pecan Pie

Double Lamb Chops with Pasilla Chile Mushroom Sauce with (Sautéed Spinach)
Fillet of Beef Roasted with Coffee Beans in (Pasilla Chile Broth) with (Creamy White Grits with Bitter Greens and Wild Mushrooms)
Warm Chocolate Cakes with (Cappuccino Meringue)

Seafood Antipasto (Antipasto di Mare)
Tortellini Pasta with Cream Sauce (Tortellini con Panna)
Linguine with Clam Sauce (Linguine con Vongole)
Eggplant Parmesan (Melanzane Parmigiana)
Fillet of Beef with Brandy Sauce (Filetto de Manzo alla Brandy)
Chicken Marsala (Pollo alla Marsala)

Chilled Cherry Soup
Turbot with Tomatoes and Basil
Alsatian Onion Tart
Chocolate Terrine with (Mocha Vanilla Sauce)

Salad *2000* (Insalata Due Mille) with (Candied Pecans) and (Raspberry Dressing)
Spinach with Orzo and Sun-Dried Tomatoes (Spinaci Carnevale)
Red Baron's Linguine with (Tomato Sauce)(Linguine Barone Russo)
Tuscan Beans (Fagiolo di Toscana)
Braised Lamb Shanks (Agnello al Forno)

Normandy Brie Soup with Black Truffle and (Rosemary Croutons) (Blond Roux)
Summer Swordfish
Mercer's Warm Comfort Strudel (Almond Paste Frangipani)

Smoked Salmon Salad with (Lemon Hazelnut Dressing)
Chicken Pernod Soup
Fillet of Flounder with Dill Sauce
Pork Tenderloin Calvados
Veal Scaloppine with Lemon Butter Sauce
Coquina Cookies

Thai Chicken Curry
The King and I
Putt Thai Korat
Vegetable Musmun
Shuu-Shee Sea Shell by the Sea Shore

Poblano Dip
New World Shrimp with Tomato, Vanilla and Ancho Chili
Venetian Risi e Bisi
Greek Shrimp Salad with (Lemon-Oregano Vinaigrette)
Warm Apple Galette with (Rosemary Syrup) and (Candied Lemon)

Portobello Fries with (Mushroom Tea Vinaigrette)
Pan Seared Tuna Loin with (Shiitake Hoisin Slaw) & (Wonton Crisps)
Grilled Vegetable & Chicken Soup

Hibiscus Salad with (Goat Cheese Cakes) and (Sun-Dried Cherry Dressing)
Smoked Trout Cakes with (Jalapeño Remoulade)
Duck Gumbo
Italian Pear Tart

Gulf Blue Crab Nachos
Frozen Sangria
San Angelo Sauce
King Ranch Casserole
Ribeye Poblano
Chocolate Waffles

# TABLE OF CONTENTS

9

# FRAN FAUNTLEROY

As the turn of the century comes to us all, I am so thankful to have been a small part of our incredible dining arena for so many years. The chefs I know have become such great friends and are a very rewarding part of my life. I have been blessed by each and all of them.

When we began the menu guides in 1979, I had no idea how this concept would take off in our city. Houstonians have always loved to dine out, but many tended to go to the same restaurants each time. Cooking was very important to me and my family but we began to venture out as did many others. The menu guides were a great success and our citizens seemed to truly enjoy them each year.

Then Ann Criswell and I decided to join our love of food and Houston's up and coming dining scene into a cookbook of recipes from our best restaurants. The most frequent question asked of us has been, "Will chefs share their recipes?" We can tell you that the restaurants were delighted! The chefs' camaraderie has become so special. They respect each other, trade ideas and have become a unique group of friends who support each other. We are so proud of this in our work.

Our city is energized, friendly, supportive and caring. We are excited about Houston's accomplishments in every area, but Ann and I are most proud of our fabulous restaurants that have gained so much national recognition in record time. And yet they've shared their talent and energy to help feed our hungry through Share Our Strength and End Hunger.

Ann usually knows the trends in food before they happen, so it has been exciting to see her predictions come true. We are into a lot of fast food and take out; but we will be back in our kitchens more and more in the future. We will be "looking at you" from our cookbooks on your shelves – and you will always have a collector's item of what the food scene was in *2000* when you own our best book yet.

Many blessings and thanks to all who have enjoyed and supported our special endeavor to keep "Houston Cooking." ♥

# LINDA MCDONALD, M.S., R.D., L.D.

Linda McDonald, a food and nutrition consultant to the food industry, is dedicated to helping you enjoy food that tastes great and is good for you. Her restaurant LiteFare tips as well as the Healthy Recipe Modification Tips and Recipe Nutrient Analysis will give you the information you need to make informed decisions about the foods you eat.

Food is a personal and professional passion to Linda. As editor and publisher of SUPERMARKET SAVVY™! Newsletter, a bi-monthly newsletter for health professionals, Linda tracks the latest food trends and reports on new food products. Restaurants also have been a special interest since 1988 when she was honored by the American Heart Association for development of the first Houston Area Dining-Out Guide — Heart Healthy Houston.

Mrs. McDonald holds a Master's Degree from the University of Texas Graduate School of Biomedical Sciences and is an honor graduate of the University of Houston with a degree in Nutrition and Dietetics.

A past president of the Houston Area Dietetic Association and Nutrition Entrepreneurs, a dietetic practice group of the American Dietetic Association, and past director of the Texas Dietetic Association Foundation, Linda now serves on the board of the Houston Culinary Guild and is a member of the International Association of Culinary Professionals, Roundtable for Women in Foodservice, the American Dietetic Association and Les Dames d'Escoffier.

Linda's unique expertise has enhanced menus, food products, educational materials, health professional journals and newsletters. "Houston Is Cooking *2000*" is the tenth book that has benefited from Linda's nutrition knowledge.

Happily married for 38 years, Linda and John McDonald are parents of two married children, Susan who is married to Scott Sorensen, and Scott whose wife is Melissa McDonald. Linda delights in being called "Mema" by four grandchildren — Alexis, Stephen, Julia Rose and Sean.

Food provides the fuel and nutrients that your body needs to stay healthy. To make sure that you eat regularly and desire a variety of foods you are given taste buds and an appetite. Enjoyable dining is a balance of health and taste that satisfies your appetite and nourishes your body. The nutrition component of "Houston Is Cooking *2000*" is provided to help you achieve this needed balance.

# DINING WITH WINE *2000* BY DENMAN MOODY

The major change I sense for dining in the millennium is the increased knowledge and enjoyment of wines of international scope. While many enophiles still have a bias towards French or California wines, consumers are becoming increasingly familiar with wines from Australia, Spain, Italy and even Texas.

After depleting most of my wine repertoire (there are several hundreds of wines listed) I enlisted the aid of three of the most knowledgeable wine wholesalers in Houston: Sharon Cooper of Glazers; Barry Johnson of Grand Crew and Steve Raskin of Republic. Thus, not only do we have a diverse selection of wine producers, but also an interesting variety of views on what types of wines go with different foods.

At least two wines are mentioned with each recipe. The first is usually under $15 (sometimes only $6, like Tyrrell's Long Flat Red (Australia) and Chateau Los Boldos Merlot (Chile). The second usually costs between $15 and $30. If there is a third, it is a wine of great value and will probably cost $50 or more. Wines without a state or country in parenthesis are from California.

Twenty years ago, most people drank white wines. I believe that the increasing interest in red wines is a trend rather than a fad. Also, it is incredible that the true health benefits of moderate wine consumption have been hidden from the public for so long. How many people know for example, that Louis Pasteur said "wine is the most hygienic and healthful of beverages" and Thomas Jefferson said, "No nation is drunken where wine is cheap..."

I would like to dedicate my portion of this book to my friend, Fred Parks, who was one of the very first to bring the notion of dining with fine wines to Houston shortly after the Second World War.

All of us who are involved in the production of this book raise a toast to you and ask for God's blessings in the millennium.

Denman Moody, connoisseur and wine writer, was editor and publisher of "Moody's Wine Review," which the Washington Post said was the "...best publication in this country for tracking the state of rare and exotic wines."

Denman is Regional Provost of the Knights of the Vine as well as a former Host of the Houston Chapter of the International Wine and Food Society. He is also Vice President of Amici della Vite and a member of the Commanderie de Bordeaux.

His wine articles have appeared in numerous publications including: Revue du Vin de France, Paris; International Wine and Food Society Journal, London; International Wine Review; Wine and Spirits; and Texas Monthly.

Denman is Vice President, Client Advisor at Compass Bank.

ITALIAN SALAD
SHRIMP PASTA WITH FRESH TOMATO (GAMBERONI EL POMODORO FRESCO)
CHICKEN IN PEARL ONIONS (POLLO EN CACCIUCLO)
BEEF MEDALLIONS WITH GORGONZOLA (FILLETTE EL BORGONZO)
FRESH BERRIES WITH MEYER LEMON CURD

In the new millennium, Aldo ElSharif will continue to push the envelope of Italian cuisine as he has since opening Aldo's in 1995. At his intimate restaurant many Houstonians have had their first taste of Tufino truffle cheese, truffle oil, San Daniele prosciutto from Friuli (which is aged 600 days), smoked eel from Holland and exotic fish and seafood from Australia, New Zealand, Hawaii, Italy, Spain and other European waters.

What does this inventive chef predict for the next century? Not a revolution, but he sees a trend taking shape. There will be fewer one-course meals – the standard meat, vegetable and starch – on one plate. He thinks his menus will be made up of three or four courses or a celebratory seven-course meal; they will feature "the best variety of foods and wines from global markets."

Quality is his main concern, he says. Since he has been in Houston he has tried to educate diners on the finest foodstuffs. Early on, he displayed a huge round of Parmigiano-Reggiano, the classic Parmesan cheese of Italy, and carved off chunks for complimentary servings for guests. Later he did the same with Grana Padano, so diners could taste the difference in the cheeses and develop their palates.

"I want people to experience the quality," he says. He can't resist proffering a bite of some new find such as tree-ripened olives, Porchetta Rognatti ham or a sip of truffle grappa to challenge the taste buds. The olives are grown in specific groves like wines from designated vineyards. The feta he imports from Greece is packed in wooden barrels. To broaden diners' experience, Aldo has a complimentary chef's tasting table in the kitchen where guests can sample wines and anything on the dinner menu. He also has opened a wine bar, Osteria D'Aldo, downtown at 301 Main Street and a delicatessen, Salumeria D'Aldo, at 306 Main where people can buy fine-quality oils, vinegars, cheeses and other imported specialties.

Aldo thinks Italian food will remain popular in the next century although it will develop in new directions. It will perhaps focus on simpler and more stylish regional cuisines such as wild game and wild birds from Tuscany and liqueurs and liquors in sauces typical of Milan. And he notes there will be more from Sicily than spaghetti and meatballs such as unique pastas and wild mushrooms. He thinks people will be more health conscious and more aware of the importance of moderation – even in a seven-course meal.

The two-story wood-frame house on lower Westheimer has been refurbished and renovated but because there are less than a dozen tables, it is still like dining in someone's home. The wine list features more than 800 selections and inspires wine dinners in the upstairs party room that accommodates 60. Aldo loves to cook and his varied background – Egyptian, Italian, French, Greek, English and American – influences his style. He delights in preparing special dishes coordinated with complimentary wines.

─────────── *LITE FARE* ───────────

Chef Aldo's menu features fresh vegetables and herbs, lean meats and fish and pastas galore. Choose a lycopene-rich Pomodoro Sauce prepared with no added oil served over a choice of appetizer or entrée pasta portion. Choosing a smaller portion is an effective method for controlling calories. Special requests are encouraged – from vegetarian meals to sauces on the side.

*Aldo's*
*219 Westheimer*
*Houston, Tx 77006*
*713-523-2536*

# ITALIAN SALAD

| | |
|---|---|
| 1 | pound arugula, cut in half |
| 3/4 | pound frisée, cut in half |
| 2 | heads fresh fennel, sliced |
| 2 | heads radicchio, sliced |
| 1/3 | cup roasted pine nuts |
| 1/4 | cup extra-virgin olive or truffle oil |
| 2 | tablespoons aged balsamic vinegar |
| | Salt and freshly ground black pepper to taste |
| 1/4 | pound thinly shaved Parmigiano-Reggiano cheese |
| 6 | wedges Roma tomato |
| 12 | endive leaves |

Mix arugula, frisée, fennel, radicchio and pine nuts in a large chilled bowl. Combine oil and vinegar; toss with greens. Add salt and pepper. Arrange greens on individual plates. Scatter Parmesan on top of salad and garnish each with a tomato wedge placed between 2 endive leaves. Serves 6.

 Dark greens are loaded with vitamins A and C. To balance the fat, reduce Parmesan to 2 ounces (about 1/2 cup), oil to 2 tablespoons and pine nuts to 3 tablespoons.

# SHRIMP PASTA WITH FRESH TOMATO (GAMBERONI EL POMODORO FRESCO)

| | |
|---|---|
| 1 | pound dry linguine |
| 1/3 | cup extra-virgin olive oil |
| 24 | (10/15 count) shrimp, peeled and deveined |
| 16 | garlic cloves, thinly sliced |
| 1 1/2 | cups dry white wine |
| 12 | Roma tomatoes, chopped |
| 1/2 | cup chopped fresh basil |
| 1 | tablespoon chopped fresh Italian parsley |
| | Salt and freshly ground black pepper to taste |

Cook pasta in large pot of boiling water until al dente. Drain; set aside and keep warm. Heat oil in medium skillet; sauté shrimp with garlic until shrimp are pink. Remove shrimp and keep warm. Deglaze pan by adding wine and stirring up any brown bits from bottom of pan. Add tomatoes, basil and parsley; reduce slightly. Season with salt and pepper. Return shrimp to pan. Add pasta; toss to combine. Serves 6.

 Besides containing vitamins A and C, tomatoes are a good source of the antioxidant lycopene. This recipe is tasty and healthy. Enjoy!

 Folonari Orvieto (Italy); Fontanassa Gavi di Gavi (Italy).

# CHICKEN IN PEARL ONIONS (POLLO EN CACCIUCLO)

| | |
|---|---|
| 6 | (5- to 6-ounce) natural free-range chicken breast halves |
| | Salt and freshly ground black pepper to taste |
| 1/2 | cup all-purpose flour |
| 1/4 | cup extra-virgin olive oil |
| 3 | tablespoons unsalted butter |
| 2 | cups chicken stock |
| 1 | cup brown sauce (see Special Helps section) |
| 1/2 | cup whipping cream |
| 1 | cup Madeira wine |
| 1 | cup dry sherry |
| 2 | cups sliced exotic mushrooms |
| 1 | cup pearl onions |
| 1 | tablespoon chopped fresh rosemary |
| 1 | tablespoon chopped shallots |
| 2 | tablespoons Key lime juice |

Dust chicken with salt, pepper and flour. Heat oil in a large sauté pan over medium heat. Sauté chicken in oil until golden brown. Remove excess oil from pan; add butter, stock, brown sauce, cream, Madeira, sherry, mushrooms, onions, rosemary and shallots to pan all at once. Simmer until reduced by half. Add lime juice, salt and pepper. Serves 6.

Remove skin from chicken. Reduce oil to 2 tablespoons for sautéing. Use a low-sodium and fat-free chicken broth and substitute half-and-half for cream. Balance with plain rice and steamed vegetables.

Barbera d'Asti Michele Chiarlo (Italy); Iron Horse Sangiovese.

# BEEF MEDALLIONS WITH GORGONZOLA (FILLETTE EL BORGONZO)

| | |
|---|---|
| 1 | tablespoon unsalted butter |
| 6 | (5-ounce) medallions of beef tenderloin |
| 1 | tablespoon chopped shallots |
| 1/2 | cup brandy |
| 1 1/2 | cups demi-glace (see Special Helps section) |
| 1 | cup whipping cream |
| 6 | ounces Gorgonzola cheese, crumbled |
| 1 | tablespoon fresh green peppercorns |
| 12 | leaves fresh sage, cut in half |
| 1 1/2 | teaspoons fresh thyme leaves |
| | Salt and freshly ground black pepper to taste |
| 2 | tablespoons truffle oil |

Heat butter in medium skillet; sauté tenderloins on each side with shallots. Deglaze with brandy; add demi-glace, cream, Gorgonzola, peppercorns, sage and thyme. Cook to medium-rare; add salt and pepper. Drizzle with oil. Accompany with truffle mashed potatoes and a leafy green. Serves 6.

Beef tenderloin is not only a lean cut of meat but also a good source of iron. To control added fat, substitute half-and-half for cream, reduce Gorgonzola to 3 ounces and eliminate oil for drizzling.

Tyrrell's Long Flat Red (Australia); Kendall-Jackson Grand Reserve Zinfandel.

# FRESH BERRIES WITH MEYER LEMON CURD

| | |
|---|---|
| 5 | Meyer (see Note) or regular lemons, about 1 cup juice |
| 1/2 | cup sugar |
| 1 | teaspoon cornstarch |
| 2 | eggs, beaten |
| 8 | egg yolks, beaten |
| 1 1/2 | cups unsalted butter |
| 3 | cups mixed berries: strawberries, blueberries, raspberries and golden raspberries |
| | Mint sprigs for garnish |

Wash lemons and finely grate zest (see Special Helps) from 2 lemons into a glass or stainless steel bowl. Juice all lemons and add to zest with sugar and cornstarch; mix. Add eggs and egg yolks. Place bowl over a pot of simmering water. Stirring periodically, cook until mixture thickens enough to coat the back of a spoon. Whisk in butter, 1 tablespoon at a time, until all is incorporated. Transfer lemon curd to another chilled bowl. Cover tightly with plastic wrap and chill 2 to 3 hours. Serve in martini glasses, lace cookie baskets or wine glasses garnished with berries and mint sprigs. Makes 3 cups lemon curd. Serves 6.

*Note:* Meyer lemons are sweeter, milder lemons grown in California; they are available only for a brief season.

Berries are a good source of fiber and vitamin C. Double the berries and halve the Lemon Curd.

Quady Elysium (1/2 bottle); Graham's Six Grape Port (Portugal).

FACING PAGE, FROM LEFT: *Mark Oster, Silas Rushton, Marco Wiles, Aldo and Lisa ElSharif, Aldo's.*

FOLLOWING PAGE, FROM LEFT: *Mark Holley, Melissa Piper, Alex Brennan-Martin, Carl Walker, Chris Shepherd, Brennan's.*

# HOUSTON IS COOKING
## *2000*

CREOLE ONION SOUP
RED SNAPPER COURT-BOUILLON
CRAB SALAD BRENNAN'S *with Herb Vinaigrette*
MARBLED FUDGE BROWNIES
CHOCOLATE CHIP BOURBON PECAN PIE

A different Brennan's in the year 2000? Mais non! "The longer I'm in this business, the more reverence I have for the way things used to be." That comforting message for Brennan's devotees comes from Alex Brennan-Martin, who carries forth the New Orleans family restaurant traditions of the legendary Commander's Palace. "One of the things I learned about dining I learned from the masters – our parents: There is a balance between the classics and what is in the memories, minds and hearts of our customers." Rest assured that signature Creole Classics will remain on the menu – Turtle Soup, Shrimp Creole, Shrimp Remoulade, Pecan-Crusted Fish, Bread Pudding Soufflé and Bananas Foster.

The formula is timeless, but it does leave the door open for progress. Brennan-Martin and executive chef Carl Walker enjoy updating tradition. "Nothing makes me happier than taking an old dish and giving it new life," says Brennan-Martin. They seek out produce and fresh herbs from local farms, and fresh seafood, meats and game from near and far. The result is Texas-Creole cuisine, a marriage made in culinary heaven. Indulge in crawfish or wild game enchiladas with tomatillo salsa, Texas Barbecue Shrimp with Jalapeño Corn Pudding, Louisiana Fried Oysters on Chili-Corn Sauce, Louisiana Crab Cakes with Tequila Beurre Blanc, Bananas Foster Croissant Bread Pudding and Chocolate Chip Bourbon Pie. New desserts are constantly being introduced by talented executive pastry chef Melissa Piper.

For the restaurant's 31st anniversary in 1998, Brennan's expanded the dining room, built a new kitchen and a new Kitchen Table, where 10 guests can dine while watching all the action and drama of the chefs at work. The Wine Table in the dining room offers guests a six-course dinner with five wines; menus are coordinated by Walker and Martin Korson, Brennan's Wine Guy. "We want people to enjoy the whole experience. We now have the luxury of doing some things we couldn't do before," says Brennan-Martin. Currently, instead of grilling, they are concentrating on old-fashioned roasts – meat cooked on the bone, tied and roasted, such as stuffed breast of veal or whole fish. "My dream is not to do grilled veal chops but to roast them. Our new oven racks are set so you can roast individual pieces. It is less convenient for us, but the food tastes better."

And taste is the thing. "Food is so much better than it used to be," said Brennan-Martin. The major trend he sees is that customers are increasingly knowledgeable. Proving that eating is clearly an adventure, Brennan's Chef for a Day program allows an individual – it could be you – to experience a chef's routine. The person arrives early in the morning, meets with the purchasing agent, is introduced to the cooks, plans the menu with the chef and goes to work. During the day, the "chef" also chooses the wines; in the evening he removes his apron and becomes host to five previously invited guests.

─────────── *LITE FARE* ───────────

Brennan's menu includes Creole classics that are higher in fat and sodium due to the preparation methods and sauces. But the menu also features lean meats, fresh vegetables, grains and legumes that are prepared with a lighter touch. Look for a spectacular vegetarian entrée under Seasonal Specials. Brennan's Spoon Desserts are a dieter's delight – teaspoon-size portions of their famous desserts such as Crème Brûlée, Pecan Pie and Chocolate Decadence.

*Brennan's*
*3300 Smith St.*
*Houston, TX 77006*
*713-522-9711*

# CREOLE ONION SOUP

1/4 cup vegetable oil
4 cups julienned yellow onions
1/4 cup all-purpose flour
5 cups beef broth
2 tablespoons brandy
2 tablespoons Louisiana hot sauce
2 tablespoons Worcestershire sauce
Salt and freshly ground black pepper to taste

Heat oil in a large stockpot over high heat. When it just starts to smoke, add onions and sauté until caramelized or browned. Remove from heat, add flour and stir well. Add broth, brandy, hot sauce and Worcestershire. Bring to a medium simmer; let simmer 5 to 10 minutes. Add salt and pepper. Serves 6.

*Note:* Use Texas 1015 onions when available.

Onions contain a powerful antioxidant, quercetin that can fight cancer, lower cholesterol and thin your blood. Be sure to use yellow onions because white onions do not contain quercetin. To reduce fat, cut oil to 1 tablespoon. To reduce sodium, choose a low-sodium Worcestershire sauce.

Beringer White Zinfandel; Trimbach Gewürztraminer (France).

# RED SNAPPER COURT-BOUILLON

3/4 cup peeled, seeded and julienned tomatoes
1/3 cup julienned onion
1/2 cup julienned mixed roasted red, green and yellow bell peppers
2 small garlic cloves, thinly shaved
1/3 cup thinly cut (diagonally) celery
1/2 teaspoon Louisiana hot sauce
1/2 teaspoon Worcestershire sauce
2 tablespoons red wine
2 drops liquid crab boil (don't use more)
2 to 4 bay leaves
1/4 teaspoon salt
1/8 teaspoon finely ground black pepper
2 lemon wedges
2 (5-ounce) red snapper fillets
6 (16/20 count) shrimp, peeled and deveined
2 to 3 teaspoons Creole seafood seasoning

In a glass or stainless steel bowl, mix tomatoes, onion, peppers, garlic, celery, hot sauce, Worcestershire, wine, crab boil, bay leaves, salt, pepper and lemon; set aside.

Preheat oven to 350 degrees. Place an 18-inch square of heavy-duty foil flat on work surface. Season fish and shrimp with Creole seasoning. Place fish on foil and arrange three shrimp on top of each fillet. Spoon generous amount of vegetable mixture on top of fish and shrimp; cover with another 18-inch square sheet of foil. Fold edges of foil tightly two to three times on each side. Then turn each corner of foil down to create a small triangle shape. This helps lock in more heat during cooking. Place foil packet on cookie sheet and bake 20 minutes. Foil will puff up when finished cooking. Carefully cut around edges of foil to avoid escaping steam; remove bay leaves and spoon contents into a bowl or onto a plate. Accompany with potatoes, rice or other favorite starch. Serves 2.

*Note:* Recipe also can be prepared in large extra-heavy duty Reynolds foil Hot Bags or a casserole dish.

This healthful recipe contains plenty of vitamins A and C in the peppers and quercetin in the onion. To reduce sodium, eliminate added salt.

Kendall-Jackson Vintner's Reserve Chardonnay; Ferrari-Carano Chardonnay.

# CRAB SALAD BRENNAN'S *with Herb Vinaigrette*

| | |
|---|---|
| 2 | medium-size red bell peppers |
| 4 | cups sliced button mushrooms or a mixture of shiitake and oyster mushrooms |
| 2 | tablespoons vegetable oil |
| 1 | teaspoon Creole seasoning |
| 1 | cup hearts of palm |
| 2 | medium avocados |
| | Juice of 1 lemon |
| 2 | cups jumbo lump crabmeat, cleaned and picked over |
| 3/4 | cup Herb Vinaigrette, divided (recipe follows) |
| 6 | cups baby greens |
| 6 | chives, cut in 1-inch pieces |

Roast peppers under the broiler until they are heavily blistered. Place in brown paper or plastic bag and let sit 10 minutes (fold top of bag over so heat isn't lost). Scrape skin off peppers with a small knife. Rinse peppers under running water to remove any seeds. Lay peppers on cutting board and cut into 1/4-inch dice. Refrigerate until needed.

Toss mushrooms with oil; sprinkle with Creole seasoning. Mushrooms may be grilled, broiled or sautéed until tender. Refrigerate until needed.

Slice hearts of palm into 1/4-inch crescents. Refrigerate until needed. Peel avocado and cut into 1/2-inch dice; toss with lemon juice. In large bowl, toss peppers, mushrooms, hearts of palm, avocado, crabmeat and 2 tablespoons vinaigrette.

Toss greens with remaining vinaigrette in large bowl. Divide among 6 plates. Top greens with crab mixture; garnish with chives. For showy presentation, press crab mixture into a small cup and invert on top of greens. Serves 6.

## HERB VINAIGRETTE

| | |
|---|---|
| 4 | teaspoons diced yellow bell pepper |
| 4 | teaspoons diced green bell pepper |
| 4 | teaspoons diced red bell pepper |
| 2 | teaspoons dry mustard powder |
| 1 | teaspoon dried oregano |
| 1 | teaspoon salt |
| 1/2 | teaspoon freshly ground black pepper |
| 1/2 | teaspoon minced garlic |
| 3/4 | cup cottonseed oil |
| 1/4 | cup red wine vinegar |

### Herb Vinaigrette
Combine peppers, dry mustard, oregano, salt, pepper, garlic, oil and vinegar in a jar with tight-fitting lid. Shake well before use. This vinaigrette is better if it sits 24 hours at room temperature before using. Makes about 1 1/4 cups.

Crab is a good source of vitamin B12 and contains some omega-3 oils. To reduce fat content, eliminate oil for coating mushrooms and instead use a nonstick cooking spray. Use 1 avocado. Reduce oil to 1/2 cup in the Herb Vinaigrette; use 6 tablespoons of vinaigrette.

Fall Creek Chenin Blanc (sweet – Texas); Zaca Mesa Roussanne.

# MARBLED FUDGE BROWNIES

1    cup semisweet chocolate chips, divided
5    tablespoons unsalted butter at room temperature, divided
1    (3-ounce) package cream cheese, softened
1    cup sugar, divided
3    eggs, divided
1/2    cup plus 1 tablespoon all-purpose flour, divided
1 1/2    teaspoons vanilla extract, divided
1/2    teaspoon baking powder
1/4    teaspoon salt
1/4    teaspoon almond extract
1/2    cup chopped pecans

Melt 1/2 cup chocolate chips and 3 tablespoons butter in top of a double boiler over simmering water on very low heat or in the microwave (see Special Helps section). Stir until smooth; remove from heat and set aside.

Cream remaining 2 tablespoons butter with cream cheese. Gradually add 1/4 cup sugar; cream until light and fluffy. Blend in 1 egg, 1 tablespoon flour and 1/4 teaspoon vanilla; set aside.

Preheat oven to 350 degrees. In large electric mixer bowl, beat remaining 2 eggs until light in color. Gradually add remaining 3/4 cup sugar, beating until thickened. Add baking powder, salt and remaining 1/2 cup flour. Blend in cooled chocolate mixture, remaining 1 1/4 teaspoons vanilla, almond extract and pecans. Fold in remaining 1/2 cup chocolate chips. Spread half of brownie mixture in a greased 9-inch square pan. Then spread cream cheese batter over top. Spoon remaining brownie mixture gently over cream cheese layer. Zig zag a spatula through batter one time in each direction to create marble effect. Bake 30 minutes, or until top springs back when lightly pressed in the center. Let cool and cut into 9 squares.

🍎 Chocolate is a mood enhancer so indulge just a bit!

🍇 Commandaria St. John (Cypress); Rosenblum Black Muscat.

# CHOCOLATE CHIP BOURBON PECAN PIE

3    eggs
1    cup sugar
1    cup light corn syrup
1/4    cup bourbon
2    tablespoons melted butter
1    teaspoon vanilla extract
1 1/2    cups pecan pieces
1    cup semisweet chocolate chips
1    (9-inch) unbaked pastry shell

Preheat oven to 350 degrees. Beat eggs and sugar in medium bowl until smooth. Add corn syrup, bourbon, butter and vanilla; mix until well incorporated; set aside. Scatter pecans and chocolate chips in bottom of pastry shell. Pour custard mixture over top. Bake 50 to 55 minutes, or until custard has set. Serves 8.

🍎 Pecans are a good source of fiber and minerals. Use restraint with this delicious dessert. Share a sliver with a friend.

🍇 KWV Ruby Port (South Africa); Chambers Muscat (Australia).

DOUBLE LAMB CHOPS WITH PASILLA CHILE MUSHROOM SAUCE *with Sautéed Spinach*
FILLET OF BEEF ROASTED WITH COFFEE BEANS *in Pasilla Chile Broth with Creamy White Grits with Bitter Greens and Wild Mushrooms*
WARM CHOCOLATE CAKES *with Cappuccino Meringue*

Robert Del Grande, award-winning chef/co-owner of Cafe Annie, is such a presence in the restaurant community Houstonians might expect him to be a trailblazer in the new millennium as he was in Southwestern Cuisine. But he has a more philosophical approach. Cafe Annie, one of Houston's premier restaurants, will be closed New Year's Eve of 2000, and Del Grande hopes customers will join him in reflection. "I think people should pause and ask themselves if they're happy with the direction they're going. If not, they should consider what makes them happy and what they want to do about it."

Rather than develop something startlingly new, Del Grande hopes to continue seeking out the best regional products and cooking in his own style. His innovative, complex Southwestern dishes brought him national attention. He pioneered the use of many chilies, exotic ingredients such as huitlacoche (a Mexican corn fungus used like mushrooms) and herbs such as epazote (a Mexican weedlike herb). He now values simplicity, he says. "But not just how simple something can be – how great it can be. If you have a great piece of fish, you can just put sea salt on it and nothing else." Because of overfishing and environmental problems, Del Grande is concerned about supplies of high-quality fish in the future. He also hopes for improvements in American products, particularly butter and cream.

The pairing of wines and foods will continue to be a major focus, he says. "I am always interested in seeing new things, but we're looking at refining our cooking and giving it a local identity. I like dishes that never wear out even if you have them on your menu for 10 years." An example is Cafe Annie's Black Bean Terrine with Goat Cheese. Customers would howl if that and other signature dishes disappeared from the menu. Del Grande and Cafe Annie have won almost every major culinary award. Although he has no formal training as a chef (he holds a Ph.D. in biochemistry from the University of California at Riverside), Del Grande seems to have an infallible ability to combine flavors and textures – chicken is dusted with cocoa and roasted, then served with caramelized pumpkin seeds. Roast pheasant with pecans is flavored with cinnamon and served with Red Chile Sauce and huitlacoche. Even as simple a thing as salt gets his attention. There are many beyond sea and kosher salts to compliment each dish. A current favorite is fleur de sel, a French salt harvested from sea foam.

Del Grande encourages input from his staff and is always experimenting in the kitchen, says Cafe Annie's chef de cuisine, Ben Berryhill, who attended the Culinary Institute of America. The restaurant is a family operation. Del Grande and his wife, Mimi, are co-owners with her sister and brother-in-law, Candy and Lonnie Schiller. They also co-own Cafe Express, Rio Ranch and Taco Milagro.

———————————————— LITE FARE ————————————————

Although Cafe Annie does not specialize in light fare, Robert Del Grande and chef de cuisine Ben Berryhill strive to produce well-balanced plates. Overuse of any ingredient whether fat, salt or chilies is avoided. Emphasis is placed on subtlety, fragrance and harmony of flavors. Special attention is paid to anyone with dietary preferences or restrictions. Vegetarian plates are viewed as a welcome challenge and are available upon request.

*Cafe Annie*
*1728 Post Oak Blvd.*
*Houston, Tx 77056*
*713-840-1111*

# DOUBLE LAMB CHOPS WITH PASILLA CHILE MUSHROOM SAUCE *with Sautéed Spinach*

| | |
|---|---|
| 4 | double lamb chops or 1 rack of lamb, cut into 4 double chops |
| 1 | teaspoon coarse salt |
| 1/2 | teaspoon freshly ground black pepper |
| 2 | teaspoons virgin olive oil |
| 1/2 | yellow onion (about 4 ounces), coarsely chopped |
| 4 | garlic cloves |
| 6 | pitted prunes, chopped |
| 2 | pasilla chilies (1/2 ounce), stemmed, seeded and coarsely chopped |
| 8 | ounces portobello mushroom, stemmed and cap cut into small cubes |
| 1 | tablespoon chopped fresh tarragon |
| 3 | cups chicken stock |
| 2 | tablespoons whipping cream Sautéed Spinach (recipe follows) |

Season chops with salt and pepper. Heat oil in skillet over high heat until very hot. Place chops in pan; reduce heat to medium-high and sear chops on both sides until nicely browned, about 2 minutes per side. Remove chops from pan and reserve.

Place same skillet over medium-high heat and add onion, garlic, prunes and pasillas. Stirring frequently, sauté until onion is well browned, about 5 minutes. Add mushroom and sauté until browned, about 8 minutes. Take care not to burn ingredients. Reduce heat to medium and place chops over mushroom mixture. Cover and cook 8 to 10 minutes, adding tarragon the last 5 minutes. Chops should be rosy pink in center at this point. Remove chops from pan and reserve on platter; keep warm.

Preheat oven to 400 degrees. Add stock to same skillet. Bring liquid to a boil then reduce heat and simmer 5 minutes. Cool mixture to warm. Transfer mixture to a blender and puree. Return puree to same skillet, bring to a boil, then reduce heat to simmer. Add cream and season with a pinch of salt and pepper. Transfer sauce to a smaller container and keep warm. Rinse out skillet and wipe dry to prepare spinach. To serve, warm chops 2 to 3 minutes in oven. Divide spinach between two plates. Arrange chops over spinach, spoon some of the sauce over each chop and serve. (Alternatively, each chop may be split in half between the bones. In this case, arrange single chops on each plate.) Serves 2 to 4.

## SAUTÉED SPINACH

| | |
|---|---|
| 2 | teaspoons virgin olive oil |
| 1/2 | yellow onion, cut into thin slices |
| 2 | garlic cloves, minced |
| 8 | ounces fresh spinach, stemmed and cleaned well Generous pinch of salt and freshly ground black pepper |

**Sautéed Spinach**

Heat oil in skillet over high heat. Add onion and garlic; sauté very quickly until onion just starts to caramelize (see Special Helps section). Add spinach all at once and stir until completely wilted. Add salt and pepper. Serves 2.

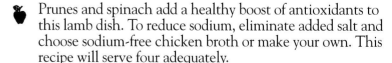 Prunes and spinach add a healthy boost of antioxidants to this lamb dish. To reduce sodium, eliminate added salt and choose sodium-free chicken broth or make your own. This recipe will serve four adequately.

 Bogle Petite Sirah; Zaca Mesa Syrah.

# FILLET OF BEEF ROASTED WITH COFFEE BEANS *in Pasilla Chile Broth with Creamy White Grits with Bitter Greens and Wild Mushrooms*

| | |
|---|---|
| 2 | pounds fillet of beef (preferably cut from large end of whole fillet) |
| 1 | teaspoon coarse salt |
| 1 | teaspoon freshly ground black pepper |
| 2 | tablespoons virgin olive oil |
| 2 | tablespoons finely ground coffee beans |
| 1 | tablespoon unsweetened cocoa powder |
| 1/8 | teaspoon ground cinnamon |
| | Pasilla Chile Broth (recipe follows) |
| | Creamy White Grits with Bitter Greens and Wild Mushrooms (recipe follows) |
| | Watercress sprigs for garnish |

## PASILLA CHILE BROTH

| | |
|---|---|
| 1 | tablespoon unsalted butter |
| 1/2 | large white onion (8 ounces), coarsely chopped |
| 4 to 8 | garlic cloves |
| 2 | pasilla chilies (about 1/2 ounce), stemmed, seeded and torn into large pieces |
| 1 | thick white corn tortilla (about 3/4 ounce), torn |
| 2 1/2 | cups chicken stock |
| 1/4 | cup whipping cream |
| 1 | teaspoon coarse salt |
| 1 | teaspoon brown sugar |

## CREAMY WHITE GRITS WITH BITTER GREENS AND WILD MUSHROOMS

| | |
|---|---|
| 4 | cups water |
| 1 1/2 | teaspoons salt |
| 1 1/4 | cups stone-ground regular white grits |
| 1 | tablespoon unsalted butter |
| 1/2 | yellow onion, chopped |
| 2 | garlic cloves, chopped |
| 3/4 | pound shiitake mushrooms, stemmed and caps cut into quarters |
| 4 | ounces arugula or other bitter greens, coarsely chopped |

Tie fillet of beef with butcher twine at 1/2-inch intervals. Rub fillet well with salt and pepper, then with oil. Combine ground coffee, cocoa powder and cinnamon; mix well. Spread mixture over a work surface and roll fillet in mixture to evenly coat the beef. Marinate about 30 minutes at room temperature.

Prepare Pasilla Chile Broth; reserve. Prepare grits and bitter greens; reserve. Preheat oven to 400 degrees. Place fillet on a rack in roasting pan; roast 10 minutes. Immediately reduce heat to 250 degrees. After 20 minutes, check internal temperature of fillet (125 degrees for medium rare and 135 degrees for medium). If more cooking is necessary, return beef to 250-degree oven and slowly roast to desired temperature. Remove fillet from oven and keep warm. Remove string before carving. Slice fillet into 1/4-inch medallions. Spoon some of the grits in the center of each plate. Arrange medallions around grits. Ladle some of the Pasilla broth over fillet. Garnish with watercress sprigs. Serves 4 to 6.

**Pasilla Chile Broth**

Melt butter in medium saucepan over medium-high heat. Add onion and garlic; sauté until nicely browned. Add pieces of chilies and tortilla. Slowly sauté until golden brown. Reduce heat to medium-low if necessary. Add stock and bring to a boil, then simmer lightly covered 10 minutes. Remove from heat and let cool. Transfer mixture to blender and puree about 1 minute, or until smooth. Strain sauce in a sieve. Add cream, salt and sugar; blend. Sauce should be the consistency of cream. If too thick, add more stock or water to correct to a very light consistency; reserve. Makes about 2 cups.

**Creamy White Grits with Bitter Greens and Wild Mushrooms**

Bring water and salt to a boil in a heavy-bottom 2-quart saucepan. Whisk in grits; bring water back to a boil. Reduce heat to a very low simmer. Cover pan and cook, whisking every 2 to 3 minutes until grits are thick, about 20 minutes. If grits become too thick, whisk in water to adjust consistency.

Melt butter until foaming in a skillet over medium-high heat. Add onion and garlic; sauté until onion is translucent. Add mushrooms; sauté until lightly cooked. Add greens; briefly sauté until wilted. Remove from heat. Stir greens mixture into grits and keep warm. Serves 4 to 6.

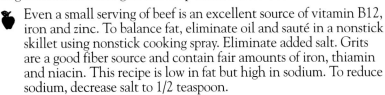 Even a small serving of beef is an excellent source of vitamin B12, iron and zinc. To balance fat, eliminate oil and sauté in a nonstick skillet using nonstick cooking spray. Eliminate added salt. Grits are a good fiber source and contain fair amounts of iron, thiamin and niacin. This recipe is low in fat but high in sodium. To reduce sodium, decrease salt to 1/2 teaspoon.

Condado de Haza (Spain); any Amarone Recioto della Valpolicella (Italy).

25

# WARM CHOCOLATE CAKES *with Cappuccino Meringue*

6 ounces semisweet chocolate, chopped or semisweet chocolate chips
1/2 cup whipping cream
1/2 cup unsalted butter
2 tablespoons unsweetened cocoa powder
4 eggs
1/2 cup sugar
1 teaspoon vanilla extract
1/4 cup all-purpose flour, sifted
Cappuccino Meringue (recipe follows)

Combine chocolate, cream, butter and cocoa powder in large bowl. Place bowl over a pot of simmering water and slowly melt chocolate and butter. Or, microwave on medium (50 percent) 3 minutes. Stir until smooth. Remove from heat and cool to room temperature.

In electric mixer bowl, beat eggs, sugar and vanilla at high speed until mixtures forms a thick pale ribbon, about 5 to 8 minutes. The mixture will triple in volume.

Preheat oven to 350 degrees. Gently fold whipped eggs into chocolate mixture; then gently fold in flour. Chill batter about 20 minutes. Spoon batter into 4 (1-cup) buttered ramekins. Bake about 25 minutes, until just firm (should be moist in center). Let cool about 30 minutes. Tops of the cakes will settle and create a depression. Gently turn cakes out of cups and arrange, top side up, on a sheet pan, reserve until ready to serve. Prepare meringues.

Heat oven to 400 degrees. Fill depressions in cake tops with meringue; bake 5 minutes. Serve immediately while meringue is soft. Serves 4.

## CAPPUCCINO MERINGUE

4 large egg whites
1 cup sugar
1/4 cup water
1 teaspoon coffee extract or powdered espresso coffee
1 teaspoon unsweetened cocoa powder

**Cappuccino Meringue**

Whip egg whites until they hold soft peaks. While whites are whipping, combine sugar and water in a small saucepan and bring to the soft ball stage (234 to 240 degrees on a candy thermometer). Slowly pour hot syrup mixture in a steady stream into egg whites; continue whipping until glossy and cool (until bottom of bowl is cool). Fold in coffee extract and cocoa powder.

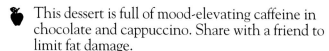 This dessert is full of mood-elevating caffeine in chocolate and cappuccino. Share with a friend to limit fat damage.

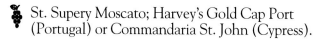 St. Supery Moscato; Harvey's Gold Cap Port (Portugal) or Commandaria St. John (Cypress).

FACING PAGE: *Robert, Mimi and daughter Tessa Del Grande, Cafe Annie.*

FOLLOWING PAGE, SITTING: *Hessni Malla, La Tour d'Argent;*
STANDING: *Gregory Torres, Cavatore.*

SEAFOOD ANTIPASTO (ANTIPASTO DI MARE)
TORTELLINI PASTA WITH CREAM SAUCE (TORTELLINI CON PANNA)
LINGUINE WITH CLAM SAUCE (LINGUINE CON VONGOLE)
EGGPLANT PARMESAN (MELANZANE PARMIGIANA)
FILLET OF BEEF WITH BRANDY SAUCE (FILETTO DE MANZO ALLA BRANDY)
CHICKEN MARSALA (POLLO ALLA MARSALA)

**C**avatore has been a 15-year feast for Houstonians who love Italian food – and that includes almost all of us. We never seem to tire of Fettuccine Alfredo, Veal Milanese, Chicken Rosemary and Eggplant Parmigiana. These are the rich classics, prepared by chefs who follow honored culinary traditions. And it takes that kind of basic knowledge to meet the challenge of providing the lighter fare that many customers now prefer. Such is the case with Chef Greg Torres, who thoughtfully offers low-calorie, low-fat, low-cholesterol daily specials.

Torres, who says the restaurant kitchen is his second home, also strives to please customers who are looking for indulgence. His repertoire of desserts includes 15 cakes and 15 kinds of cheesecake. In addition, the dessert tray presents an array of Italian sweets made in-house – cannoli, spumone and tiramisu – as well as chocolate and white chocolate mousses served in chocolate shells. There is enough variety to send a customer into a frenzy of indecision. But it is easy to select a compatible wine from Cavatore's lengthy list, which is especially strong in Italian wines including Barolos and Chianti Riservas.

The origin of the restaurant is oft-told: How the owners found a rustic 100-year-old barn in Bastrop, had it disassembled, carefully numbered the boards and moved it to Houston to a site across the street from their other restaurant, La Tour d'Argent off Loop 610. The barn was painstakingly reassembled around a new frame. Co-owner Sonny Lahham located enough metal panels for the roof by advertising in the newspaper for rusty metal. It opened in November 1984. Customers are presented with an entertaining history lesson as they peruse the walls and beams lavishly decorated with vintage photographs, paintings, old movie posters (including originals of Fellini's "8 1/2"), flags, yellowed newspaper advertisements, family mementos, tools, utensils and even strings of garlic.

The overall effect lends an air of a party in the making. Loyal customers come time and again for business lunches and meetings, drinks after work, dinner, wedding rehearsals, birthdays, anniversaries and other celebratory occasions. A pianist plays nightly.

The restaurant is named for the co-owner, Giancarlo Cavatore, who comes from a small medieval village in northern Italy; his family coat of arms dates back more than 800 years. Looking ahead to the millennium, co-owner Sonny Lahham says the restaurant will continue its most popular specials including pasta, seafood, veal and chicken. But there is a trend to lighter, fresher sauces instead of those painstakingly simmered 15 or 16 hours. Lahham says the challenge is to maintain flavors without adding fat and calories. Their goal is to provide a satisfying casual dining-out experience that makes guests feel comfortable and happy and want to come again.

### LITE FARE

Cavatore is an Italian restaurant with a healthy conscience. Look for the Low Calorie Chef's Specialties, which include lean proteins and pasta dishes with light sauces. Regular pasta dishes come in two sizes for those who are portion conscious – appetizer and entrée. Pastas also are divided into "fresh," which usually contain eggs and oil and "dry" that are relatively fat-free.

*Cavatore*
*2120 Ella Blvd.*
*Houston, Tx 77008*
*713-869-6622*

# SEAFOOD ANTIPASTO (ANTIPASTO DI MARE)

6   (12/15 count) shrimp, peeled and deveined
6   medium sea scallops
4   ounces cleaned squid
10  mussels
3   garlic cloves, minced
1/4 cup white wine
1/2 cup chopped fresh basil
1/2 cup chopped fresh parsley
1/4 cup pitted black olives, chopped
1/4 cup pitted green olives, chopped
2   tablespoons fresh lemon juice
    Salt and freshly ground black pepper to taste

Bring salted water to a boil in a large saucepan; add shrimp, scallops, squid and mussels. Cook 6 minutes; drain water and reserve seafood. In a bowl, combine garlic, wine, basil, parsley, black and green olives, lemon juice, salt and pepper. Add seafood; chill before serving. Serves 2.

This is a deliciously healthful low-fat recipe but it is high in sodium. Reduce sodium by using a total of 1/4 cup olives.

Lungarotti Pinot Grigio (Italy); Fiano di Avellino Feudi di San Gregorio (Italy).

# TORTELLINI PASTA WITH CREAM SAUCE (TORTELLINI CON PANNA)

8   ounces fresh veal-stuffed tortellini pasta
2   tablespoons unsalted butter
6   tablespoons whipping cream
    Salt and freshly ground black pepper to taste
1/4 cup chopped fresh parsley
1/3 cup freshly grated Parmesan cheese

Cook tortellini in a large pot of boiling water 5 minutes; drain and set aside. Melt butter in a hot skillet. Add cream; season with salt and pepper. Add parsley and tortellini; heat thoroughly. Mix in cheese. Serves 2 as an appetizer.

Balance fat in this dish by substituting low-fat marinara sauce for cream sauce and reducing Parmesan to 2 tablespoons.

Pieropan Soave (Italy); Biodi-Santi Rivolo (Italy); Jermann Vintage Tunina (Italy).

# LINGUINE WITH CLAM SAUCE (LINGUINE CON VONGOLE)

1  pound dried linguine
3  dozen fresh small clams or
   2 (6-ounce) cans clams
2  tablespoons extra-virgin olive
   oil
3  garlic cloves, chopped
6  tablespoons clam juice
6  tablespoons white wine
   Pinch of crushed red pepper
   Pinch of dried oregano
1  tablespoon chopped fresh basil
1  tablespoon chopped parsley
   Salt and freshly ground black
   pepper to taste
   Fresh basil for garnish

Cook pasta in large pot of boiling water until al dente. Drain; set aside and keep warm. Steam clams just until opened. Reserve 4 clams for presentation and remove remaining clams from shells; discard shells.

Heat oil in skillet and sauté garlic until golden. Add clams, their juice and wine. If using canned clams, omit wine. Cook 6 minutes; mix with pasta. Add red pepper, oregano, basil, parsley, salt and pepper; toss to combine. Divide among four bowls; garnish each with fresh basil and a reserved clam. Serves 4 as an entrée.

🍎 Enjoy this healthful recipe – fat calories are only 16 percent and sodium is really low.

🍇 Sartarelli Castello di Jesi Verdicchio (Italy); Schiopetto Sauvignon Colli (Italy).

# EGGPLANT PARMESAN (MELANZANE PARMIGIANA)

1  (12- to 14-ounce) eggplant,
   peeled and sliced 1/4-inch thick
   Salt and freshly ground black
   pepper to taste
3  eggs, beaten
   All-purpose flour
1/2  cup olive oil
1/2  cup prepared pasta sauce
1/2  cup chopped fresh basil leaves
4  slices Mozzarella cheese

Season eggplant with salt; let stand one hour. Preheat oven to 350 degrees. Drain excess liquid. Dip eggplant in egg then heavily coat with flour. Heat oil in nonstick skillet; sauté eggplant 3 minutes on each side. Place in a 1 1/2-quart casserole and top with salt, pepper, pasta sauce and basil. Arrange cheese on top; bake 3 minutes, or until cheese melts. Accompany with angel hair pasta dressed with garlic and olive oil. Serves 2 as an entrée.

🍎 To reduce fat, substitute egg whites or fat-free egg substitute for eggs and reduce oil to 1 tablespoon. Choose skim milk Mozzarella and use two slices.

🍇 Santo Stefano Ripasso Boscaini (Italy); Antinori Marchese Chianti Classico Riserva (Italy).

# FILLET OF BEEF WITH BRANDY SAUCE (FILETTO DE MANZO ALLA BRANDY)

6    tablespoons unsalted butter
2    (8-ounce) beef fillets
1    cup sliced mushrooms
3    tablespoons brandy
6    tablespoons brown sauce (see Special Helps section)
2    tablespoons whipping cream
     Salt and freshly ground black pepper to taste

Heat skillet 2 minutes. Melt butter in skillet and cook steaks to preferred doneness. Remove steaks from skillet and keep warm. In same skillet, sauté mushrooms 2 minutes. Return meat to skillet; add brandy. Flambé (see Special Helps section), lighting carefully with a taper match. Add brown sauce and cream; simmer 2 minutes. Add salt and pepper. Accompany with sautéed vegetables. Serves 2.

Beef is an excellent source of iron and other minerals. To reduce fat, eliminate butter and use a nonstick skillet with nonstick cooking spray. This recipe adequately serves 4.

Sebastiani Cask Cabernet Sauvignon; Raymond Cabernet Sauvignon Reserve.

# CHICKEN MARSALA (POLLO ALLA MARSALA)

3    tablespoons margarine
2    (4- to 6-ounce) boneless, skinless chicken breast halves
     All-purpose flour
     Salt and freshly ground black pepper to taste
2    garlic cloves, minced
1    cup sliced mushrooms
3    tablespoons Marsala wine
1/4  cup brown sauce (see Special Helps section)
2    tablespoons whipping cream
     Rosemary sprigs for garnish

Heat skillet; melt margarine. Dust chicken lightly with flour; season with salt and pepper. Cook chicken 3 minutes on each side. Add garlic and mushrooms; sauté 2 minutes. Add Marsala, brown sauce and cream; simmer 5 minutes over medium heat. Garnish with rosemary sprigs. Serves 2.

For low-fat preparation, reduce margarine to 1 tablespoon and substitute evaporated skim milk for cream. Serve with plain rice and grilled vegetables.

Illuminati Riparoso (Italy); Badia Chianti Classico Roberti Stucchi (Italy); Hoffstaetter Pinot Nero Cru Saint Urbano (Italy).

CHILLED CHERRY SOUP
TURBOT WITH TOMATOES AND BASIL
ALSATIAN ONION TART
CHOCOLATE TERRINE *with Mocha Vanilla Sauce*

Rack of lamb, fresh foie gras, fresh Dover sole, Muscovy duck, Steak Marchand du Vin, soufflés. These are among the classics at the award-winning Chez Nous restaurant, and owner Gerard Brach and chef Stephen Gasaway don't expect the constants to change in the new millennium. But the chefs will continue to pique customers' curiosity with inventive specials such as quail stuffed with portobello mushrooms, dried apricots, foie gras and ground veal. Or the five-course Chef's Table dinner — two appetizers, two entrées and dessert.

Chez Nous has loyal customers. Some drive 100 miles or more to dine at this small, highly acclaimed restaurant in Humble because they can count on an exceptional experience. Many come for the Rack of Lamb, which Brach has raised to his specifications in New Zealand. It remains the most popular menu item; Brach sells about 5,000 a year. Duck also is a best seller whether it is the grilled breast with orange Grand Marnier sauce and fresh berries, confit made from the leg meat or Duck Shepherd's Pie. The right side of the menu features classics such as Tournedos Rossini, two beef medallions wrapped in bacon, topped with fresh foie gras and napped with Madeira sauce. But the left side of the menu is like an artist's palette to the chefs. Today it might feature Normandy Duck Mousse with Plum Wine and Pickled Cherries; tomorrow, Blue Crab Salad with lump crab tossed with homemade lemon mayonnaise, avocado, mango, tomato and basil.

Brach was born in Alsace and trained in Europe and North Africa before coming to America in 1961. He helped organize the restaurants at Sharpstown Shopping Center, the first food court in a Houston mall. Gasaway is a graduate of the culinary program at Houston Community College. He has worked for one-star restaurants in France, which inspired some of his creations at Chez Nous. He thinks Mediterranean cuisine will be increasingly popular in the new century. It fits in well here, he says, because of the focus on fish and seafood, herbs and tomato and basil sauces. And it includes specialties of France, Italy and the Riviera. At Chez Nous they butcher their own meat, make sausage, pâtés and terrines and prepare all the desserts. Only fresh ingredients are used; if fresh fish isn't available, fish isn't served.

Who would guess that this small country restaurant was once a Pentecostal church? Brach and his wife, Sandra, transformed it into a French-style farm cottage with blue wainscoting, lace curtains, paintings, photographs and copper and dusty rose accents. They intend to keep it a small, personal family operation. Brach's daughter, Danielle Noble-Brach, is the maitre d.' Chez Nous has received the DiRoNA award for distinguished restaurants of North America and the Best of the Best Five Star Diamond Award from the National Academy of Restaurants and Hospitality Sciences among other honors.

--- *LITE FARE* ---

Researchers for years have tried to determine why the French have fewer heart attacks than U.S. citizens. Is it the red wine, olive oil or northern fish high in omega-3 oils that counter the high-fat sauces? Chez Nous' menu celebrates the French Paradox but also offers a grilled vegetable plate with a southwestern twist and grilled fish with a mango-lime salsa. Special requests are encouraged and taken seriously.

*Chez Nous*
*217 S. Ave. G.*
*Humble, Tx 77338*
*281-446-6717*

# CHILLED CHERRY SOUP

| | |
|---|---|
| 2 1/2 | pounds cherries*, washed and pitted |
| 1 | cup water |
| 1/2 | cup sugar |
| 1 | scant cup fresh orange juice |
| 1/4 | cup fresh lemon juice |
| 1/4 | cup honey |
| | Fresh mint for garnish |

**\*Preferably Bigareaux or Burlat. Bing also may be used. If fresh aren't available, frozen or canned may be substituted.**

Place cherries in a heavy saucepan with water and sugar. Cover and cook over medium heat. While cherries are cooking, combine orange and lemon juices in a medium bowl; whisk in honey. When cherries start to boil, remove pan from heat. Reserve cooking juices from cherries; set aside. Using a slotted spoon, transfer cherries to bowl with juice and honey; stir well to combine. Reserve about 3/4 cup cherries for garnish.

Place half of cherry-citrus mixture in blender or food processor and pulse to a coarse puree, adding a little of the cooking juices to blend. Soup should have the consistency of thick syrup. Remove from blender; transfer to bowl. Repeat with remaining cherry-citrus mixture. Refrigerate several hours or until well chilled. Soup should be a deep pink. To serve, place 1 tablespoon reserved cherries in center of a 6-ounce bowl; pour soup on top. Garnish with mint and 1 tablespoon cherries. Serves 6.

*Note:* Can also be served as dessert with vanilla ice cream. Or mixture can be used for cherry sorbet. Whip 3 egg whites until stiff, fold into mixture and make sorbet according to manufacturer's directions for ice cream maker.

Cherries contain pectin, a fiber that can lower your cholesterol. This is a healthful way to start or end a meal.

# TURBOT WITH TOMATOES AND BASIL

| | |
|---|---|
| 3 | tablespoons olive oil |
| 6 | (4- to 6-ounce) turbot or flounder fillets, preferably with skin |
| 1/3 | cup all-purpose flour |
| | Salt and freshly ground black pepper to taste |
| 2 | plum tomatoes, peeled, seeded and chopped |
| 1/2 | cup chopped fresh basil or opal basil |
| 1/2 | cup sliced blanched almonds |
| 1/2 to 1 | cup dry white wine |
| 1/2 to 1 | cup fish stock (see Special Helps section) |
| 1/2 | cup whipping cream |
| | Basil or opal basil sprigs for garnish |
| | Tomato rose for garnish (optional) |

Preheat oven to 400 degrees. Heat oil in one large or two medium skillets, large enough to hold fillets in single layer. Dust fillets with flour, shaking off excess. Put fillets, skin-side-up, into pan; season with salt and pepper. Sauté over medium heat 1 to 2 minutes per side. Remove fillets to a lightly oiled oven-proof pan and place in oven to finish cooking, 6 to 8 minutes.

Add tomatoes, basil and almonds to same skillet(s) with as much of the wine, stock and cream as needed to make about 3/4 cup of thickened pan sauce. Simmer until thickened. If you cook fillets in one pan, less liquid will be needed than for 2 pans. Tilt pan back and forth, cooking over medium-high heat to evaporate and thicken sauce.

Transfer fillets to a warm plate; spoon some of the pan sauce over top. Garnish with basil sprigs and tomato rose. Serve with steamed Yukon potatoes or new potatoes dressed with parsley. Serves 6.

Fish is a great source of heart-healthy omega-3 oils. To keep fat content under control, reduce oil to 1 tablespoon for sautéing, substitute evaporated skim milk for cream and reduce almonds to 1/4 cup.

Napa Ridge Chardonnay or Macon-Villages Jadot (France); Meursault Olivier LeFlaive (France); Chartron Trebuchet, Bonneau du Martray or Bouchard Pere et Fils Corton Charlemagne (France).

# ALSATIAN ONION TART

**Pastry Shell**

| | |
|---|---|
| 2 1/2 | cups all-purpose flour, chilled |
| 1 | teaspoon salt |
| 1/2 | cup chilled unsalted butter, cut into pieces |
| 1/2 | cup chilled margarine, cut into pieces |
| 1/2 | cup ice water |
| 1 | egg |
| 1 | tablespoon whipping cream |

## ONION FILLING

| | |
|---|---|
| 2 | tablespoons vegetable oil |
| 5 | medium-size yellow onions, cut in half then into thin slices |
| 4 | eggs |
| 1 | cup milk |
| 1 | cup whipping cream |
| 1/8 | teaspoon nutmeg |
| | Salt and freshly ground black pepper to taste |

In bowl of electric mixer with paddle attachment, mix flour, salt, butter and margarine on low speed just until mixture resembles coarse meal. Add ice water very slowly with mixer running; mix just until dough comes together. (Dough should not be mixed too long or it will toughen. Make sure dough is not too sticky at this point. If it is too wet, remove dough from mixer, place on a lightly floured surface and lightly knead in a small amount of flour to eliminate stickiness. Never use too much flour with pie or tart dough or it can cause toughness and dryness. Also, any excess flour on surface will burn in oven.) Place dough in center of large piece of plastic wrap. Wrap well and refrigerate about 3 hours, which makes it easier to roll out.

When dough is chilled, lightly dust surface with flour and roll dough into a 16-inch diameter circle. Wrap dough around rolling pin and carefully roll into a 10-inch tart pan or quiche dish. Gently pick up sides of dough circle and fit dough into pan, placing flush with bottom of pan. (The sides will hang over.) Carefully roll rolling pin over top of pan, shaping and trimming scalloped edges clean of excess dough. Prick bottom with a fork to ensure even baking. Combine egg and cream; brush over pastry shell. Refrigerate about 1 hour. Preheat oven to 350 degrees. Bake 12 to 15 minutes until partially cooked (bottom of crust turns a pale golden color and dough in center is no longer raw). Set aside.

**Onion Filling**
Heat oil in large skillet over medium heat. Add onions and sauté until soft and browned, stirring to prevent sticking. Remove from heat and let cool slightly before placing in bottom of tart shell. Lightly beat eggs with a whisk in medium bowl. Add milk and cream; whisk until well combined. Add nutmeg, salt and pepper; pour over onions. Bake 20 to 25 minutes, or until custard is set and crust is golden brown. Serves 6.

Studies on onions suggest that they may raise the good HDL cholesterol and lower blood pressure. But use moderation; this tart has a high level of saturated fat.

Rutherford Hill Gewürztraminer; Hugel or Trimbach Gewürztraminer (France); Domaine Zind Humbrecht Gewürztraminer (France).

# CHOCOLATE TERRINE *with Mocha Vanilla Sauce*

6 ounces bittersweet chocolate
1 ounce unsweetened baking chocolate
3 tablespoons unsweetened cocoa powder
3 tablespoons unsalted butter
5 egg yolks
10 tablespoons powdered sugar, divided
10 egg whites at room temperature
1/8 teaspoon salt
6 tablespoons whipping cream
Mocha Vanilla Sauce (recipe follows)

Line a 9x5x3-inch bread pan or terrine with parchment paper, cutting paper at corners to fit smoothly. In a medium bowl, combine chocolates; add cocoa powder and butter. Cover bowl with aluminum foil; set aside. Bring a medium saucepan of water to a boil and remove from heat. Make a double boiler by placing bowl with chocolate on top of saucepan until chocolate melts. Or, melt in microwave (see Special Helps).

In another bowl, whisk egg yolks and 6 tablespoons powdered sugar. Continue whisking until well blended; set aside. In clean electric mixer bowl with clean beaters, whip egg whites and salt until stiff but not dry. Meanwhile, pour cream into a medium bowl and whisk until light and fluffy; set aside. Increase speed on mixer and add remaining 4 tablespoons powdered sugar to egg whites. Beat until whites are quite stiff.

Stir chocolate mixture into egg yolk mixture; blend well. Fold half the egg whites into chocolate mixture to lighten it. Fold in remaining egg whites, working quickly to avoid deflating mixture. Fold in cream. Pour mixture into prepared mold. Cover with plastic wrap; refrigerate until chocolate sets up, at least 6 hours but preferably overnight.

Prepare Mocha Vanilla Sauce. Unmold terrine by inverting onto a flat surface; remove paper. Dip thin knife blade into hot water between each slice and slice terrine into 16 pieces. Cover center of each of 8 dessert plates with 2 to 3 tablespoons of sauce. Place two slices of terrine on top. Serves 8.

## MOCHA VANILLA SAUCE

2 egg yolks
6 tablespoons sugar
1 tablespoon powdered instant coffee
1 cup milk
1/4 cup whipping cream
1 vanilla bean

### Mocha Vanilla Sauce

Put egg yolks into a medium bowl, add sugar and whisk until mixture is smooth and lemon-colored. Whisk in coffee and set aside. Combine milk and cream in a small saucepan. Add vanilla bean and bring mixture to a boil. Pour a little of the hot milk mixture into the egg mixture, whisking constantly to prevent eggs from curdling. Return all the egg mixture to saucepan and cook over medium heat, stirring constantly, until thickened enough that mixture coats the back of a spoon. Strain sauce through a mesh strainer. Set aside. Makes about 1 1/2 cups.

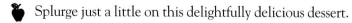 Splurge just a little on this delightfully delicious dessert.

Ficklin Port; Seppelt Muscat (Australia) or Disznoko Tokaji Aszú 4 or 5 Puttonyos (500 ml – Hungary).

FACING PAGE FROM LEFT: *Gerard Brach, Stephen Gasaway, Danielle Noble-Brach, Chez Nous.*

FOLLOWING PAGE FROM LEFT: *Tommy Leman, Napoleon Palacios, Damian's.*

SALAD *2000* (INSALATA DUE MILLE) *with Candied Pecans and Raspberry Dressing*
SPINACH WITH ORZO AND SUN-DRIED TOMATOES (SPINACI CARNEVALE)
RED BARON'S LINGUINE *with Tomato Sauce* (LINGUINE BARONE RUSSO)
TUSCAN BEANS (FAGIOLO DI TOSCANA)
BRAISED LAMB SHANKS (AGNELLO AL FORNO)

Damian's has its eye on the future but its roots are in the past. One of Houston's enduring favorites, the restaurant has made a celebration of Italian family cooking. But it is updated often after the owners, Joseph "Bubba" Butera and Frank B. Mandola, and chefs, Jose Napoleon Palacios and Tommy Leman, make periodic trips to Italy. There they seek out new dishes as well as new techniques and styles of cooking. For the new millennium, they hope to introduce authentic ingredients that are unknown or unfamiliar in Italian-American fare such as the herb nepitella. From Tuscany, it tastes like a cross between marjoram and thyme. Leman has built relationships with several small producers in Italy to bring in fresh truffles in season, truffle oil, porcini mushrooms, fine olive oils and some lesser-known pastas. One addition to the menu that has proved extremely popular is fresh sardines, alici, from the Italian Riviera. They are marinated in lemon juice, olive oil and capers. Insalata due Mille (Salad *2000*), created for the millennium, already has established a prominent place on the menu.

Leman, who graduated from the Culinary Institute of America, worked in Florence, Italy for a year at Ristorante La Giostra owned by Dimitri Kunz d'Asburgo Lorena, the last of the royal Hapsburg line, and his two sons. For Damian's, Leman adapted the Linguini Barone Rosso and Veal Piemontese from his mentor's repertoire. Bistecca alla Fiorentina, another popular addition to the menu, is a 2-inch thick, 32-ounce Porterhouse steak done in Florentine tradition. No butter, no heavy sauces.

Damian's also is going back to basics – fresh, seasonally appropriate foods, simply prepared without unnecessary embellishments. The emphasis is on big flavors. "People are not in the mood for fats and sauces," says Leman. "We use olive oil on the table, not butter, and serve low-salt Tuscan bread and a low-rise focaccia. Grilled vegetables accompany many entrées and the chefs buy local organic greens when possible. Although the grilled 16-ounce veal chop is the menu best seller, red snapper is consistently popular – Damian's often sells 150 pounds of snapper at lunch and requires three deliveries a day. Whenever possible, they use Gulf Coast fish and seafood. A new item is farm-raised clams from Clearwater, Florida. They are harvested and brought to a farm to purge, then flown to Houston. Sea bass is a big seller. Cappuccino, espresso or coffee and dessert is the perfect ending to any meal. Damian's Lemon Tart, Panna Cotta and Sicilian Bread Pudding with Whiskey Hard Sauce are among many diners' favorite dessert memories.

Damian's was founded by Houston restaurateur Damian Mandola, and many of the menu items are longtime Mandola family specialties – Snapper Nino Jr., Shrimp Damian's, Involtini di Pollo, Gamberoni Vincenzo. The current owners, Mandola's cousins, bought the restaurant in 1993.

**Damian's
Cucina Italiana**

---
*LITE FARE*
---

Damian's menu contains the basics for healthful dining – lean meats and seafood with complex carbohydrates in pasta, breads and fresh vegetables. Look for interesting sauces that are natural vegetable purees – asparagus, carrot and tomato. Start your meal or make a meal of the low-fat soups – Minestrone or Pasta e Fagioli. This restaurant thrives on special requests and will help with dietary needs.

*Damian's
3011 Smith St.
Houston, Tx 77006
713-522-0439*

# SALAD *2000* (INSALATA DUE MILLE)

Candied Pecans
(recipe follows)
3/4    cup Raspberry Dressing
(recipe follows)
4    cups arugula, cleaned and dried
6    ounces goat cheese, cut into 8
(1/4-inch) slices
1/2    cup fresh raspberries

CANDIED PECANS
3/4    cup pecan halves
1    egg white
1/2    cup sugar

RASPBERRY DRESSING
1    pint fresh raspberries
1/4    cup sugar
1/2    cup red wine
1/4    cup balsamic vinegar
2    tablespoons honey
3/4    cup vegetable oil
Salt and freshly ground black
pepper to taste

Prepare Candied Pecans; reserve. Prepare Raspberry Dressing; reserve. Combine arugula and dressing; toss. Garnish with pecans, cheese and berries. Serves 4.

Candied Pecans

Preheat oven to 300 degrees. In a medium bowl, toss pecans with egg white. Sprinkle with sugar and toss to fully coat each pecan. Discard extra sugar. Place pecans on a parchment-lined 12x18-inch cookie sheet. Bake 7 to 10 minutes, turning pecans over about halfway through cooking to evenly roast. Watch as pecans tend to burn easily. Makes 3/4 cup.

Raspberry Dressing

Combine raspberries, sugar and wine in a 2-quart saucepan; bring to a boil. Mash with potato masher as mixture cooks, Cook about 10 to 12 minutes, or until sauce thickens. Strain through a fine mesh strainer; let cool. Combine strained sauce, vinegar and honey; whisk until smooth. Whisking constantly, slowly add oil until fully incorporated. Add salt and pepper. Makes about 2 1/2 cups.

 To balance fat in this otherwise healthy recipe, reduce dressing to 4 tablespoons, pecans to 1/4 cup and cheese to 3 ounces.

# SPINACH WITH ORZO AND SUN-DRIED TOMATOES (SPINACI CARNEVALE)

1    pound fresh spinach, stemmed
and well washed
2    tablespoons olive oil
2    garlic cloves, chopped
1/4    cup chopped sun-dried
tomatoes
1    cup cooked orzo (rice-shaped
pasta)
Salt and freshly ground black
pepper to taste

Briefly blanch cleaned spinach in salted boiling water to cover. Plunge into ice water to stop cooking process. Drain thoroughly in colander by pressing spinach against sides; reserve.

Heat oil in a 10-inch skillet. When a haze appears, add garlic and tomatoes; briefly sauté in order to infuse flavors into oil. Add spinach; toss to heat through. Add orzo, salt and pepper. Serves 4.

 Spinach is high in iron but less than two percent of it is bioavailable. Both spinach and tomatoes are high in antioxidants, nutrients that fight cancer. Enjoy this healthful recipe.

# RED BARON'S LINGUINE (LINGUINE BARONE RUSSO)

2 cups Pomodoro Sauce (recipe follows)
Salt to taste
1 pound imported linguine (preferably De Cecco)
1/2 cup pine nuts (pignoli), toasted
1/2 cup fresh basil leaves
1/2 cup grated Parmigiano-Reggiano cheese
1 cup cubed fresh mozzarella

## TOMATO SAUCE (POMODORO SAUCE)

2 (28-ounce) cans imported San Marzano canned Roma tomatoes (preferably Cento brand)
2 ribs celery, chopped
1/2 large yellow onion, chopped
1 medium carrot, peeled and chopped
3 garlic cloves, crushed
1/2 cup extra-virgin olive oil
1/2 cup water, if needed
1 teaspoon sugar
Salt and freshly ground black pepper to taste
1/2 cup chopped fresh basil

Prepare Pomodoro Sauce; reserve. Bring water to a rolling boil in an 8-quart stockpot. Add salt, stirring until fully dissolved. Cook pasta until al dente; drain and keep warm. Place pine nuts, basil and Parmesan in a food processor. Pulse until coarsely chopped; reserve.

Put Pomodoro Sauce into a 12-inch preheated skillet; add pine nut mixture. Cook on high until bubbling; add mozzarella. Add pasta and toss until all pasta is coated evenly and mozzarella begins to melt. Accompany with Parmesan if desired. Serves 4.

**Tomato Sauce (Pomodoro Sauce)**

Combine tomatoes, celery, onion, carrot, garlic and oil in a 4-quart saucepan. Stirring constantly, slowly bring to a simmer. Continue to simmer uncovered 2 1/2 to 3 hours, to a medium consistency. Add water if sauce begins to stick or becomes too thick. Process in a food mill or blender until smooth. Return to heat and add sugar, salt and pepper. Add basil and remove from heat to cool; reserve. Makes about 2 quarts.

Tomatoes contain lycopene, an antioxidant that protects against some cancers. To reduce fat, eliminate added oil in the Pomodoro Sauce, reduce pine nuts to 1/4 cup, Parmesan to 1/4 cup and Mozzarella to 1/2 cup.

Farnetella Colli Sensei or Nozzole Chianti Classico (Italy); Fontodi Chianti Classico Riserva (Italy); Argiano Solengo (Italy).

# TUSCAN BEANS (FAGIOLI DI TOSCANA)

1 pound dried cannellini or white kidney or navy beans
1 gallon water, divided
5 garlic cloves, whole, divided
5 sprigs sage, divided
Salt and freshly ground black pepper to taste
2 tablespoons extra-virgin olive oil
1 Roma tomato, chopped or diced
1/4 pound roasted red bell peppers
1/2 cup finely chopped red onion
1 tablespoon chopped fresh oregano

Rinse beans, removing any pebbles and grit. Soak in 8 cups cold water overnight in large stockpot. Drain water and add remaining 8 cups fresh water. Add 3 garlic cloves, 3 sage sprigs, salt and pepper. Simmer 40 minutes or until tender.

Preheat oven to 400 degrees. Drain beans; discard garlic and sage. Mix beans with oil, tomato, peppers, onion, oregano, remaining 2 sprigs sage and remaining 2 garlic cloves, crushed. Adjust salt and pepper if needed. Transfer to a 2-quart glass or earthenware baking dish; bake 10 to 15 minutes. Serves 4.

*Note:* This dish can be served hot, room temperature or cold. By omitting the baking, use this as a bean salad or antipasto.

This healthy recipe might also lower your cholesterol. Dr. David Jenkins at the University of Toronto found that a daily regimen of beans depressed cholesterol an average of 7 percent in men with high cholesterol who were already on a low-fat diet.

D'Angelo Aglianico del Vulture (Italy); Terrabianca Campaccio (Italy); Ornalaia (Italy).

# BRAISED LAMB SHANKS (AGNELLO AL FORNO)

4  (about 1 pound) lamb hind
   shanks
   Salt and freshly ground black
   pepper to taste
   All-purpose flour
2  tablespoons unsalted butter,
   divided
2  tablespoons extra-virgin olive
   oil, divided
1  medium onion, chopped
1  medium leek, cleaned, trimmed
   and chopped
1  medium carrot, chopped
1  rib celery, chopped
2  shallots, chopped
3  garlic cloves, crushed
5  Roma tomatoes, quartered
2  thyme sprigs
2  rosemary sprigs
1  bay leaf
6  cups high quality stock
   (see Note)
1/2  cup dry white wine

Preheat oven to 350 degrees. Season lamb with salt and pepper; dredge in flour, shaking off excess. Set a 3-quart roasting pan over medium-high heat. Add 1 tablespoon each butter and oil. When haze appears, add lamb shanks and sear evenly on all sides, turning as needed. When fully browned, remove pan from heat and set lamb shanks aside. Blot excess fat from casserole with paper towel, leaving food particles on bottom of pan intact.

Return pan to heat with remaining 1 tablespoon each butter and oil. Add onion, leek, carrot, celery and shallots, stirring often until they are caramelized. Add garlic and sauté briefly; stir in tomatoes. Add thyme, rosemary and bay leaf; cook 4 to 5 minutes until tomatoes render juices. Return shanks to pan; add stock and wine until shanks are almost covered. Bring to a simmer on range top, cover with aluminum foil and cook in oven 2 to 2 1/2 hours.

Test meat for doneness with a fork. When meat is tender, remove and set aside. Strain braising liquid, pushing against side of strainer to extract all flavors from aromatic vegetables. Skim all visible fat off surface with ladle. Reduce sauce by half over high heat. Adjust salt and pepper. Ladle sauce over shanks and garnish as desired. Serves 4.

*Note:* 4 cups chicken stock and 2 cups veal stock or 6 cups chicken if veal is not available.

Serving suggestion: This hearty peasant style dish is beautiful served over herbed mashed potatoes or a creamy polenta.

Eliminate butter and oil by braising lamb shanks in a nonstick pan using nonstick cooking spray. To reduce sodium, use sodium-free stock.

Rosemount Shiraz (Australia); Ratti Barbera d'Alba Torriglione (Italy); Carretta Barolo Cannubi (Italy).

NORMANDY BRIE SOUP WITH BLACK TRUFFLE *and Rosemary Croutons*
SUMMER SWORDFISH
MERCER'S WARM COMFORT STRUDEL

La Réserve is consistently one of Houston's favorite choices for fine dining. We go there for special occasions or holidays or just to be pampered in an elegant setting while enjoying cutting-edge cuisine and wines. Mercer Mohr, a graduate of the Culinary Institute of America, joined the Omni in November 1998 as executive chef. He came from San Francisco where he was executive chef at the award-winning Clift Hotel and was named San Francisco's Chef of the Year in 1998 by the Chefs Association of the Pacific Coast.

He praises the creative atmosphere in Houston. People love to try new things here, he says. "The more people read and learn about food, the more they are concerned about how it affects their health."

Mohr, who says he reads every food magazine and cookbook he can find, says you have to keep up with the trends. "A menu is successful based on how well you offer what people are looking for, and tastes change all the time. Twenty years ago butter was the main seasoning. I would start the day by making a five-gallon pot of clarified butter. Years ago, some cooks added baking soda to vegetables as they cooked to preserve the color and avoid the appearance of overcooking. Now people want fresh vegetables lightly steamed, roasted or grilled, generally without butter. If I sent out overcooked vegetables I would really hear about it."

The Omni, one of three Texas hotels to receive AAA's highest Five-Diamond rating, is committed to revitalizing the concept of fine dining in hotels, Mohr says. La Réserve is traditionally French but without the old-style cream sauces. "We thicken sauces with juice from parsnips, or vegetable purees, so no flour or other starch is needed." A little beet juice or roasted red bell pepper juice might be used for color or a touch of jalapeño, lemongrass or ginger juice to pick up the flavor. People are eating much more fish and seafood, says Mohr, who flies fresh fish in from Hawaii twice a week. He is always on the alert for new items – an organic vegetable (pea shoots are a favorite find), locally produced herbs or sausages.

American cuisine is the food of the future, he says. American chefs are pioneers and have overcome the perception that they are young, inexperienced and untrained, he says. "We were in the forefront of doing lighter cuisine. American chefs now have respect for quality. They have a reason for what they're doing – they're not just taking shortcuts. "More people will be looking for a late-night dessert or aperitif, after the theater, a movie or a business dinner. It would be nice to have a glass of champagne or a Cognac and share a small soufflé, miniature chocolate gâteau, a fresh fruit sorbet or a cheese plate.

Mohr predicts that Fusion will continue – elements of Asian and other ethnic cuisines will be combined. But he thinks traditional spices, seasonings and condiments will be used in new ways. Chutneys are a case in point. They are spin-off of salsas, he says, and their popularity should carry over into the new millennium. Cuban and Caribbean may not reach the major trend stage, "but they will always be out there because they're fun."

---

*LITE FARE*

Notice the profusion of fresh vegetables and grains that grace La Réserve's menu. A four-course Vegetarian Sampler is available on request; a vegan version is also available but advance notice is required. Seasonal vegetables are featured with many grown locally. This kitchen is fully prepared to customize food to your specifications and to make it taste great as well.

*La Réserve*
*Omni Houston Hotel*
*Four Riverway*
*Houston, Tx 77056*
*713-871-8177*

# NORMANDY BRIE SOUP WITH BLACK TRUFFLE *and* *Rosemary Croutons*

Rosemary Croutons (recipe follows)
1 (10-inch) wheel Brie cheese
Blond Roux (recipe follows)
10 shallots, chopped
4 tablespoons clarified butter
4 tablespoons white truffle oil
4 cups dry white wine
4 cups strong chicken stock
4 cups whipping cream
1 cup freshly grated Parmesan cheese
Ground white pepper and salt to taste
White truffle oil for garnish
8 to 10 slices black truffle
Chopped chives

## ROSEMARY CROUTONS
2 tablespoons garlic oil
8 to 10 (2x6-inch) slices thin rosemary focaccia

## BLOND ROUX
3/4 cup all-purpose flour
3/4 cup melted unsalted butter

Prepare Rosemary Croutons; set aside. Remove rind from Brie and cut into cubes; set aside. Prepare Blond Roux; set aside. Sauté shallots in butter and oil in a stockpot over medium heat. Add wine and simmer until reduced to 1 cup. Add stock, bring to a boil, then add roux. Bring cream just to a boil in a medium saucepan; add to soup. Reduce heat to low. Adjust thickness by adding stock or cream if necessary. Add Brie and Parmesan, stirring until all ingredients are incorporated. Strain soup; adjust consistency and season to taste with pepper, salt and oil. Ladle into bowls and garnish each with a black truffle slice, chives and crouton. Serves 8 to 10.

### Rosemary Croutons
Preheat oven to 350 degrees. Brush oil on focaccia. Place in baking cups and form into "U" shape to hang over edge of soup bowl as a garnish. Set cups on a baking sheet and bake until golden brown, about 4 minutes; cool.

### Blond Roux
Whisk flour into butter in a small saucepan over medium heat. Simmer slowly until it smells nutty or turns a pale golden color. Do not brown. Makes about 1 1/2 cups.

Enjoy a cup of this high-fat cheese soup and balance it with a low-fat entrée.

Weinbach Gewürztraminer (France); Trimbach Gewürztraminer Reserve Personnelle (France).

# SUMMER SWORDFISH

1 pint yellow cherry tomatoes
1 pint red cherry tomatoes
5 (12-ounce) bunches fresh spinach or 3 cups cooked spinach
1 tablespoon chopped garlic, divided
3/4 cup pure olive oil, divided
Salt and freshly ground black pepper to taste
Juice of 2 lemons
6 (5- to 6-ounce) swordfish steaks or favorite grilling fish
6 jumbo shrimp or prawns
6 jumbo sea scallops or bay scallops
1 1/2 cups dry white wine
30 to 40 fresh purple basil leaves
Basil sprigs for garnish (optional)

Remove stems and cut tomatoes in half; set aside. Thoroughly wash and stem spinach; drain well on paper towels and pat dry. Lightly sauté spinach in large skillet with 2 teaspoons garlic and 1 tablespoon oil. Season with salt and pepper; set aside.

Thirty minutes before cooking, pour a little lemon juice over swordfish, shrimp and scallops; season with salt and pepper. Before cooking, brush each fish steak with 1 teaspoon oil; charcoal grill or sear swordfish in a hot skillet, turning when seared, about 3 minutes per side. When swordfish is turned, grill shrimp and scallops for garnish. Slightly under-cook seafood so it can be held in an oven a few minutes. Remove all seafood from grill and place on a cookie sheet in a warm oven while finishing recipe.

Reheat spinach. Heat another large skillet; add remaining oil, remaining 1 teaspoon garlic and wine. (Do not brown garlic.) Add tomatoes; toss a couple of times. Be careful; if pan is very hot, it will flame. Just heat tomatoes; do not cook. Add basil leaves, salt and pepper.

To serve, place a mound of sautéed spinach in middle of each of 6 large heated bowls. Spoon tomato mixture around it. Place fish on top of spinach and garnish each with 1 shrimp and 1 scallop. Garnish with a sprig of fresh basil. Serves 6.

*Notes:* If more liquid is needed with tomatoes (for sauce broth), add some additional water, white wine and lemon juice. Readjust seasoning. Olive oil, garlic and wine mixture works well with pastas, mussels, chicken or vegetables.

Spinach and tomatoes in this recipe are full of antioxidants and vitamins A and C. Tomatoes are a good source of lycopenes, which protect against some cancers. To keep fat content in balance, reduce oil to 3 tablespoons.

Chateau Woltner Napa Howell Mountain Chardonnay; Louis Latour Chassagne-Montrachet (France).

# MERCER'S WARM COMFORT STRUDEL

Almond Paste Frangipani
(recipe follows)
20 (12x18-inch) sheets filo dough
1 cup clarified butter, divided
4 medium Granny Smith apples,
  cored and peeled
1/4 cup sugar
2 teaspoons ground cinnamon
1/4 teaspoon ground nutmeg
  Favorite ice cream
  Fresh berries for garnish

Prepare Frangipani; set aside. Brush each sheet of filo with butter and stack 5 layers. Repeat three times. With a sharp knife cut each stack in half to make 2 (6x9-inch) rectangles. Preheat oven to 400 degrees.

Spread about 3 tablespoons of Frangipani over each filo rectangle. Cut apples in half; diagonally slice 1/8-inch fans out of each half. Fan one-half apple on top of each rectangle. Combine sugar, cinnamon and nutmeg in a small bowl; sprinkle over top of apple; roll up tight like a burrito. Brush with remaining butter; let sit at least 10 minutes.

Place strudels on greased baking sheet and bake until golden brown, about 10 minutes. Remove from oven and cut off each end so it will stand up. Slice strudels diagonally in half and stand two pieces on end on each plate. Accompany with a scoop of favorite ice cream and fresh berries. Serves 8.

*Note:* Add raisins or dried cherries to apple. Just about any seasonal stone fruit, such as peaches, plums and nectarines work well.

## ALMOND PASTE FRANGIPANI

1 (7-ounce) package almond
  paste
1/2 cup all-purpose flour
2 tablespoons sugar
1 egg
1/4 teaspoon vanilla extract
1/4 cup milk

### Almond Paste Frangipani
Blend almond paste with flour and sugar by hand or in a food processor. Add egg, vanilla and milk; blend. Consistency should be like wet sand. Makes about 1 3/4 cups.

Splurge on just a small sliver of this rich dessert.

Durban Muscat Beaumes-de-Venise (France); Joseph Phelps Late Harvest Riesling; any German Beerenauslese (Germany).

SMOKED SALMON SALAD *with Lemon Hazelnut Dressing*
CHICKEN PERNOD SOUP
FILLET OF FLOUNDER WITH DILL SAUCE
PORK TENDERLOIN CALVADOS
VEAL SCALOPPINE WITH LEMON BUTTER SAUCE
COQUINA COOKIES

Sonny Lahham, co-owner of La Tour d'Argent, says inspiration often comes to him because delicious aromas waft up to his office from the kitchen below. The scent of lamb roasting or rosemary perfuming the air has led Lahham and Hessni Malla, chef and catering director, to create or refine items on the menu. They travel to France periodically to study trends. As La Tour d'Argent moves into the new millennium, Lahham says they will continue to do what they do best — serve French classics, such as chateaubriand, tournedos, duck, foie gras, escargot, sweetbreads and rack of lamb. But the classics are often updated in lighter, more healthful ways to please today's diners. Malla uses no butter and very little cream; the refined sauces are based on stock reductions. He is happy to poach, grill or steam items on request. Lahham thinks fresh fruit, especially exotic tropical fruits, will be used more extensively with entrées in the new century.

Guests expect the best at La Tour d'Argent, which is known for its fine food and wines, attentive service and relaxing atmosphere. It features Russian service, and several flambé dishes and other specialties are prepared or carved tableside. Dover sole is flown in from Europe within 48 hours after it is caught; wild game from New Zealand comes in twice weekly. The wine list features an in-depth collection of Bordeaux and Burgundies and such treasures as a $5,000 bottle of 1952 Chateau Petrus and a $12,000 bottle of 1899 Chateau d'Yquem.

Considered one of Houston's most romantic restaurants, La Tour d'Argent has several cozy dining nooks and three "proposal" tables, so named because of the number of marriage proposals made there. It also is a favorite location for business and corporate lunches, private parties, wine dinners and red-letter occasions. The restaurant started life as a log cabin; it was built in 1917 and is said to be the oldest log cabin in Harris County. It was moved to its current site in 1981, but was almost destroyed by fire just before it opened. Lahham, his wife and friends scraped and renovated the burned logs, one by one, and the restaurant opened after only a short delay. Lahham is a hands-on owner and built one beautifully appointed dining room himself. Co-owner Giancarlo Cavatore procures most of the art works from Europe; in Greece he found the cast iron fountain of Bacchus, a focal point of the restaurant entrance.

La Tour d'Argent makes the most of its setting on the wooded banks of White Oak Bayou where birds, raccoons, quail, squirrels and other wild life provide a continuing show. Inside, the elegance of leaded glass doors and windows, crystal chandeliers, fine paintings and hand-carved reproductions of Queen Anne chairs contrasts with the rustic hunting lodge ambiance created by beamed ceilings, wooden tongue-in-groove floors, and stone fireplaces. Several walls are almost covered by more than 2,000 hunting trophies (including tiger skins and rhinoceros heads).

--- LITE FARE ---

Classic French cuisine features lean meats prepared with tasty but often high-fat sauces. To keep fat and sodium to moderate amounts, ask for sauces to be served on the side and add just enough for enjoyment. Daily Specials always contain a deliciously prepared Heart Healthy entrée. A grilled vegetable is available on request.

*La Tour d'Argent*
*2011 Ella Blvd.*
*Houston, Tx 77008*
*713-864-9864*

# SMOKED SALMON SALAD *with Lemon Hazelnut Dressing*

Lemon Hazelnut Dressing
(recipe follows)
12 ounces smoked salmon
1 head radicchio, sliced
4 Belgium endive, sliced
1 heart of romaine, chopped
1 bunch watercress

Prepare dressing; reserve. Slice salmon (make sure there are no bones); place in medium bowl. Add radicchio, endive, romaine and watercress; toss with salmon. Pour dressing over salad; toss. Serves 4.

## LEMON HAZELNUT DRESSING

Juice of 2 medium lemons,
about 2 tablespoons
5 tablespoons hazelnut oil
2 teaspoons dry white wine or
sherry
1/2 teaspoon Dijon mustard
Salt and freshly ground black
pepper to taste

**Lemon Hazelnut Dressing**
In a small bowl, combine lemon juice, oil, wine, mustard, salt and pepper. Whisk ingredients until blended. Makes about 1/2 cup.

Salmon, a fatty fish, is high in omega-3 oils that may protect against heart disease, cancer, arthritis and high blood pressure. To reduce total fat, decrease dressing to 4 tablespoons.

Domaine Ste. Michelle Extra Dry Sparkling Wine (Washington); Dr. Loosen or Kunstler Riesling Kabinett (Germany).

# CHICKEN PERNOD SOUP

2 teaspoons olive oil
2 teaspoons finely chopped shallots
2 teaspoons finely chopped celery
2 (4-ounce) boneless, skinless
chicken breasts, finely ground
2 teaspoons all-purpose flour
4 teaspoons Pernod (anise liqueur)
4 cups chicken stock
2 bay leaves
Salt and freshly ground black
pepper to taste
1/2 cup whipping cream
2 teaspoons snipped chives

Heat oil in large skillet over medium heat. Sauté shallots and celery about 2 minutes. Add chicken; cook 3 minutes. Sprinkle on flour; add Pernod, stock, bay leaves, salt and pepper. Cook 7 minutes; add cream and chives. Remove bay leaves and adjust seasoning. Serves 4.

Keep fat low by eliminating oil and sautéing vegetables in 1/4 cup stock. Choose low-sodium, low-fat chicken broth or make your own (see Healthy Recipe Modifications). Substitute evaporated skim milk for cream.

King Estate Pinot Gris (Oregon); Cossart-Gordon Verdelho Madeira (Portugal).

# FILLET OF FLOUNDER WITH DILL SAUCE

1/2 cup vegetable oil
4 (6- to 7-ounce) flounder fillets
  Salt and freshly ground black pepper to taste
1 tablespoon chopped shallots
1 cup sliced mushrooms
1/2 teaspoon all-purpose flour
4 teaspoons dry white wine
1/2 cup fish stock (see Special Helps section)
1 teaspoon unsalted butter
  Juice of 1 lemon
1 tablespoon chopped fresh dill
5 teaspoons whipping cream
  Watercress sprigs and lemon slices for garnish

Heat oil in large skillet over medium heat. Season flounder with salt and pepper; cook about 2 minutes on each side. Remove from skillet; set aside on platter. Discard grease from skillet. In same skillet, add shallots and mushrooms; cook about 2 minutes. Sprinkle on flour; add wine, stock, butter and lemon juice. Simmer about 5 minutes. Add dill and cream; simmer 2 minutes. Pour over flounder. Garnish with watercress and lemon slices. Serves 4.

Fish is lean and healthy. Keep total fat low by sautéing flounder in a nonstick skillet with a nonstick cooking spray.

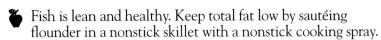 Hüpler Grüner Veltliner (Austria); Joseph Phelps or Iron Horse Viognier.

# PORK TENDERLOIN CALVADOS

1 tablespoon vegetable oil
4 (6- to 7-ounce) pork tenderloins
1 cup peeled, julienned portobello mushroom caps
1 tablespoon chopped shallots
1/4 cup Calvados (applejack brandy)
1/2 cup brown sauce (see Special Helps section)
1/2 cup peeled and julienned apple

Heat oil in large skillet over medium heat. Remove silver skin from tenderloins and sauté pork on all sides, about 10 to 12 minutes for medium. In same skillet add mushrooms and shallots. Add brandy; flambé (see Special Helps section), lighting carefully with a taper match. Add brown sauce and reduce 2 minutes. Remove pork from skillet, slice and arrange on serving plate. Add apple to sauce, cook 1 minute and pour over pork. Serves 4.

Pork is an excellent source of thiamin, with generous amounts of other B vitamins and infection-fighting zinc. Enjoy this low-fat, low-sodium entrée.

Ravenswood Zinfandel; Rosenblum Napa Zinfandel.

# VEAL SCALOPPINE WITH LEMON BUTTER SAUCE

1/4   cup vegetable oil
14   ounces boneless veal, thinly
      sliced and tenderized
      Salt and freshly ground black
      pepper to taste
      All-purpose flour
1/2   cup sliced shiitake mushrooms
1   tablespoon chopped shallots
1/2   cup dry white wine
      Juice of 1 1/2 lemons
1/2   cup unsalted butter

Heat oil in medium skillet over medium heat. Season veal with salt and pepper; dust with flour. Sauté veal on both sides until light brown. Remove veal from skillet; discard oil. In same skillet, add mushrooms and shallots; sauté 2 minutes. Add wine, lemon juice and butter; cook 2 minutes. Pour sauce over veal. Serves 2.

The American Heart Association recommends limiting the total amount of meat to 6 ounces per day. To stay within that guideline, limit veal to 12 ounces and sauté in a nonstick skillet with nonstick cooking spray. Reduce butter to 1 tablespoon.

Fall Creek Granite Reserve (Texas); Bonny Doon Ca Del Solo Big House Red; Tignanello (Italy).

# COQUINA COOKIES

1   cup unsalted regular margarine
2   cups all-purpose flour
2   tablespoons powdered sugar
1   teaspoon baking powder
2   teaspoons vanilla extract
1 1/2   cups chopped pecans
1   cup granulated sugar
2   teaspoons ground cinnamon

In electric mixer bowl, beat margarine on medium speed until softened. Add flour, powdered sugar, baking powder, vanilla and pecans; mix about 2 minutes. Let dough sit 1 hour on counter.

Preheat oven to 325 degrees. Scoop out silver dollar size pieces of dough and place on ungreased baking sheet. Bake until light brown, about 15 to 16 minutes. Remove from pan. In separate bowl, mix granulated sugar and cinnamon. Dust cookies while still warm with sugar mixture. Makes about 30.

Can you eat just one of these treats?

Quady Essencia (1/2 bottle); Sandeman Founders Reserve Port (Portugal).

Thai Chicken Curry
The King and I
Putt Thai Korat
Vegetable Musmun
Shuu-Shee Sea Shell by the Sea Shore

If you made a blueprint for the ideal food of the future, it might well be Thai. Traditionally a balance of five flavors – hot, bitter, sweet, sour and salty – Thai is essentially low-fat and rich in healthful complex carbohydrates. It delivers superb textures and flavors from small amounts of meat, poultry and fish. Think of the smooth and crunchy contrast of chicken or pork with peanut sauce, roasted hot peppers and chili paste with steamed rice or chicken soup in which lemon grass, coconut milk and fresh herbs create a symphony on the palate. Think garlic, ginger, sweet basil, chile peppers, kaffir lemon leaves, galangal (Thai ginger), Thai curry and cilantro.

Alice Vongvisith, owner, has seen the popularity of Thai food mushroom since Nit Noi opened in June 1987 in the Rice Village; she has helped make Thai one of Houston's favorite ethnic cuisines. The restaurant soon expanded around the corner to Nit Noi II, and Nit Noi on Woodway opened in 1999. The restaurants are a family endeavor for Alice; her husband Sam, an engineer at Kellogg and Co.; her son, Doi Heckler; and his wife, Malisa. The menu features specialties of Alice's homeland, especially Korat, a vegetable- and rice-growing area that is the center of rice noodle manufacturing in Thailand, she says. The menu changes to reflect what Alice discovers on periodic trips to Thailand. "Just like in America, my friends and family say they are cooking less and less; there's lots of take-out and more focus on vegetable and vegetarian dishes."

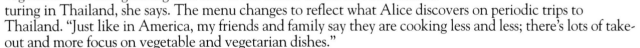

*Nit Noi*

Looking ahead to the millennium, Alice has moved Nit Noi about half a block east to a larger space on the same street at 2426 Bolsover and closed Nit Noi II. The new restaurant seats about 125 and has a full-service bar with television. Walls are enhanced with murals by Phyllis Bowman and Elva Stewart, who did the murals in the original Nit Noi. Brass elephants and other art objects from Thailand are decorative attention-getters.

The menu at the new restaurant covers a range of regional Thai foods from fiery and spicy to mild. It emphasizes fish and seafood, noodle and rice dishes, salads, soups, vegetable and vegetarian dishes. Sunday brunch has been added with new specialties every week – four main dishes, three salads, a couple of stir-fries and rice.

Putt-Thai Korat, one of Thailand's national dishes, made with beef, chicken or pork, egg, assorted vegetables and spices, continues to be a best seller. So is Alice's Delight, a combination of brown and wild rice, chicken, a variety of fresh vegetables, oyster sauce and Thai fish sauce (nam pla). Regulars have made specials from the Off-the-Menu menu among the most-requested dishes. Alice also hopes to acquaint Houstonians with more authentic Thai dishes, such as Prik Num, a fiery-hot dish of young chilies, shallots and garlic.

*Nit Noi*
*2426 Bolsover*
*Houston, Tx 77005*
*713-524-8114*

*6395 Woodway*
*Houston, Tx 77057*
*713-789-1711*

———————————— LITE FARE ————————————

Thai Cuisine is light and healthy if you avoid fried items. You can derive special health benefits from many vegetarian dishes that contain tofu. Soy contains isoflavones that can protect against cancer, osteoporosis, menopausal symptoms and heart disease. Stir-fried dishes can be prepared with little or no oil. Avoid dishes prepared with coconut milk, which is high in saturated fat. Accompany entrées with vegetables and plain rice.

# THAI CHICKEN CURRY

1 (4-ounce) boneless, skinless
  chicken breast
1 tablespoon Thai chili paste
1 cup coconut milk (not cream
  of coconut)
1 medium red potato, cooked
1/2 cup fresh green beans
1/2 cup snow peas
1/2 cup pineapple chunks
1 tablespoon brown sugar
1 tablespoon fish sauce (nam pla)
  or to taste
5 sweet basil leaves, chopped
5 whole cherry tomatoes

Cut chicken into bite-size pieces. Put into heated medium skillet or wok with chili paste and milk. Cook about 3 minutes over medium heat. Cut potato into quarters and add to chicken with beans, snow peas, pineapple, sugar, fish sauce, basil and tomatoes. Cook, stirring midway, about 5 minutes, or until chicken is done. Serve with steamed rice. Serves 2.

Snow peas, green beans and pineapple are high in vitamins A and C. Coconut Milk has 97% fat calories with 90% of those in the form of saturated fat. To reduce fat content, substitute low-fat milk for coconut milk.

Chateau Moncontour Vouvray Demi-Sec (France); Wehlener Sonnenuhr Riesling Spätlese (Germany).

# THE KING AND I

3 garlic cloves, crushed
4 small tomatoes, crushed
2 shallots, chopped
4 mushrooms, sliced
2 tablespoons vegetable oil
1 tablespoon Thai fish sauce
  (nam pla)
1 tablespoon honey
2 cups steamed Jasmine rice
1/2 cup lump crabmeat, cleaned
  and picked over
1 cup crushed pineapple, drained
1 (8-ounce) red snapper fillet,
  steamed
  Sliced mushrooms, tomatoes
  and carved Thai chilies for
  garnish (optional)

In a medium bowl, combine garlic, crushed tomatoes, shallots and mushrooms. Heat oil in large skillet over medium-high heat. Add garlic mixture and sauté until shallots are translucent. Stir in fish sauce and honey; set aside.

In a medium bowl, mix rice with crabmeat and pineapple. Arrange on a large plate and top with snapper. Pour sautéed vegetable sauce over top and garnish with mushrooms, tomatoes and chilies. Serves 2.

Prepare this low-fat dish without fish sauce to decrease sodium.

Alderbrook Gewürztraminer; Brancott Gewürztraminer Patutalin Estate (New Zealand).

# PUTT THAI KORAT

*One of Thailand's national dishes, done in the style of Alice Vongvisith's hometown, Korat.*

| | |
|---|---|
| 2 | tablespoons peanut oil |
| 1 | egg |
| 1 | cup diced skinless, boneless chicken |
| 1 1/2 | tablespoons brown sugar |
| 2 | tablespoons rice wine vinegar |
| 2 | tablespoons soy sauce |
| 2 | cups rice noodles, soaked in cold water 30 minutes; drained |
| 2 | tablespoons shrimp sauce (from Asian market) |
| 3 | green onions, chopped |
| 1 | cup bean sprouts |
| 2 | tablespoons crushed roasted peanuts |
| 1 | lime wedge |

Heat oil in skillet. Stir in egg, then chicken. Add sugar, vinegar and soy sauce; stir-fry until chicken is cooked. Add drained noodles and stir-fry a minute or two. Add shrimp sauce, onion and sprouts. Cook about 5 minutes. Sprinkle with peanuts and squeeze lime over top. Serves 2.

🍎 This recipe is low in fat but high in sodium. To reduce sodium, eliminate fish sauce and use low-sodium soy sauce.

🍇 Castell Blanch Extra Dry Cava (Spain); Beringer Founders Chardonnay.

# VEGETABLE MUSMUN

| | |
|---|---|
| 1 1/2 | cups mixed fresh vegetables, cut in chunks (such as kabocha squash or mini pumpkin, yellow squash, zucchini, carrots, unpeeled eggplant, green beans and cauliflower) |
| 1 | cup new red potatoes, cooked and drained |
| 1 | cup cherry tomatoes |
| 1 | (14-ounce) can coconut milk (not cream of coconut) |
| 1 | tablespoon musmun paste (Thai herb seasoning) |
| 1 1/2 | tablespoons brown sugar |
| 2 | tablespoons shrimp sauce (from Asian market) or 1 teaspoon salt |
| 1 | cup pearl onions |
| 2 | tablespoons chopped peanuts |

Cook vegetables in boiling water, just until tender crisp. Start with those that take the longest, such as kabocha squash and carrots. Add potatoes and cherry tomatoes; finish cooking. Drain and set aside.

Combine coconut milk and musmun paste in a medium saucepan; bring to a boil, reduce heat and add sugar and shrimp sauce. Add onions and all reserved vegetables; simmer until tender, about 8 to 10 minutes over low heat. Top with chopped peanuts. Serve plain or over rice or noodles. Serves 2.

🍎 This recipe is packed with nutrients in the fresh vegetables. Decrease fat content by substituting low-fat milk for coconut milk. One tablespoon of fish sauce has more sodium than 1 teaspoon of salt. To reduce salt content, eliminate fish sauce.

🍇 Chateau Ste. Michelle Johannisberg Riesling (white – Washington); Villa Mt. Eden Pinot Noir (red).

# SHUU-SHEE SEA SHELL BY THE SEA SHORE

3   garlic cloves, crushed
1   tablespoon sliced lemon grass
3   Thai red chilies
1   tablespoon finely sliced kaffir lemon leaves, plus 1 leaf for garnish (see Note)
2   tablespoons Thai red curry paste
1   cup coconut milk (not cream of coconut)
1   teaspoon sugar
1   tablespoon Thai fish sauce (nam pla)
1   (8-ounce) fillet fresh red snapper
6 to 8   (21/25 count) shrimp, peeled and deveined
6   spears asparagus

Place garlic, lemon grass, chilies, lemon leaves and curry paste in a blender; blend until finely chopped. In a 1-quart saucepan, bring coconut milk just to a boil over medium-high heat. Stir in garlic mixture, sugar and fish sauce.

Steam or poach snapper and shrimp about 5 minutes; do not overcook. Drain and set aside. Snap off tough ends of asparagus and steam spears about 3 minutes. Arrange snapper fillet on plate and top with shrimp. Pour sauce over top and arrange asparagus spears to the side; garnish with remaining lemon leaf. Accompany with steamed rice. Makes 2 servings.

*Note:* Lemon grass and other Thai ingredients are available at Asian markets and some specialty supermarkets. If kaffir lemon leaves are not available fresh or frozen, add grated lemon rind to taste.

Contrary to popular belief there is no evidence that chilies can cause ulcers. Chilies do contain a bioflavonoid, capsaicin, which may prevent blood clots. To reduce fat content, substitute low-fat milk for coconut milk and to reduce sodium, eliminate fish sauce.

Hanna or St. Supery Sauvignon Blanc; Caymus Conundrum.

FACING PAGE, FROM LEFT: *Mercer Mohr, La Réserve at the Omni; Alice Vongvisith, Nit Noi.*

FOLLOWING PAGE: *Jim Mills, Olivette at The Houstonian.*

OLIVETTE

POBLANO DIP
NEW WORLD SHRIMP WITH TOMATO, VANILLA AND ANCHO CHILI
VENETIAN RISI E BISI
GREEK SHRIMP SALAD *with Lemon-Oregano Vinaigrette*
WARM APPLE GALETTE *with Rosemary Syrup and Candied Lemon*

When Jim Mills, award-winning executive chef of The Houstonian Hotel, Club & Spa, gazes into the crystal ball of the millennium he sees issues of the culinary future. "I don't see food changing instantaneously just because the calendar rolls over to 2000." But there are many changes on the horizon, he says.

Limited meat eating probably makes the most sense from health, economic and supply points of view, Mills says. "The right plate for today and the coming millennium is about four ounces of concentrated protein, a bit of carbohydrate and lots of vegetables." Accustomed as we are to standardized, mass-produced food, Mills notes a growing movement for specialty items such as boutique cheeses, new varieties of vegetables and fresh herbs. "At the Houstonian we are trying to provide choices that make sense and encourage people to make good choices. We want to entertain our guests, spark their imaginations and stimulate their taste buds." Anticipating the future, the Houstonian revamped the Café in 1998 and renamed it Olivette. There Mills focuses on Mediterranean and New World cuisine. Mediterranean Cuisine is being touted as a healthful way to eat, and the eclectic menu offers the flavor-packed specialties of Italy, France, southern Spain, Greece, Morocco and Mediterranean Africa. Along with beef, pork, chicken and pasta dishes, diners find exciting options such as Grilled Salmon and Sweet Corn Risotto with Red Bell Pepper Pesto, Seven Vegetable Tagine with Couscous, Chick Peas and Harissa (the spicy hot sauce of chilies, garlic and spices from Tunisia) and a side dish of Broccoli Rabe with Grilled Lemon. A complimentary basket of artisan breads is accompanied by chickpea dip and a customized mix of olives, Holland peppers, lemon, oil and herbs. Santa Barbara Olive Company cures the olives especially for the Houstonian.

olivette
AT THE HOUSTONIAN

Mills' new menus and plans reflect changing attitudes, he says. "The changes are driven by science, economics and supply. In the '60s and '70s a lot of people started to realize that resources were finite and that if we don't want them to disappear we have to change. I think people will continue to exercise more care about what they eat. It really is a sign of maturity to be more concerned about quality than quantity."

Looking deeper in the crystal ball, Mills predicts a growing momentum behind food safety issues. Because of overfishing, depleted natural resources and environmental concerns, Mills says aquaculture will become increasingly important and most fish will come from farmed sources. In the immediate future, Mills is anticipating the completion of a new kitchen, banquet kitchen, pastry shop and store room. A new display kitchen is located at the back of Olivette where diners can observe the chefs in action. The Houstonian is a luxury hotel that appeals to health- and fitness-minded guests. It is frequently host to executive conferences, corporate meetings and charity events.

——————————— LITE FARE ———————————

Chef Jim Mills continues a long tradition of healthful cuisine with great taste. Forty percent of the lunch items and fifteen percent of the dinner items are touted as healthful and specify calories and fat grams. Proteins take a back seat to carbohydrates. The menu is divided into "tiny," "small" and "large" plates. What a great way to control portions and limit calories!

*Olivette*
*The Houstonian*
*111 N. Post Oak Lane*
*Houston, Tx 77024*
*713-685-6713*

# POBLANO DIP

|       |                                                           |
|-------|-----------------------------------------------------------|
| 3     | poblano peppers                                           |
| 1/2   | yellow onion                                              |
| 3     | garlic cloves (skin on)                                   |
| 1     | teaspoon olive oil                                        |
| 2     | ounces cream cheese, softened (can use reduced fat)       |
| 2     | ounces Monterey Jack cheese                               |
| 3/4   | cup sour cream (can use light)                            |
| 2     | teaspoons milk                                            |
|       | Juice of 1/2 lime                                         |
| 3     | tablespoons coarsely chopped cilantro leaves             |
| 1/2   | teaspoon salt                                             |
| 1/4   | teaspoon black pepper                                     |

Preheat oven to 475 degrees. Place peppers, onion and garlic on a cookie sheet. Lightly coat with oil. Roast about 5 minutes, removing garlic when soft. Remove peppers when charred and wrinkled, about 13 more minutes. Place in a plastic bag to steam. When onion is soft and golden, remove and cool.

Let peppers stand 10 minutes, remove skins, stems and seeds. Peel garlic and remove outer layer of onion if it is dark. Combine vegetables when cool in the work bowl of a food processor fitted with the steel blade. Add cream cheese, Monterey Jack cheese, sour cream, milk, lime juice, cilantro, salt and pepper; puree until smooth. Correct seasoning and transfer to serving bowl. Cover and chill. Makes about 2 cups.

Choose reduced fat cream cheese and light sour cream to decrease fat.

Karly Pokerville Zinfandel; Silverado Sangiovese.

# NEW WORLD SHRIMP WITH TOMATO, VANILLA AND ANCHO CHILI

|       |                                                              |
|-------|--------------------------------------------------------------|
| 20    | (10/15 count) shrimp (fresh if possible)                     |
| 3     | ancho chilies, stems and seeds removed                       |
| 1/3   | cup hot water                                                |
| 2     | tablespoons olive oil                                        |
| 1/4   | cup diced red onion                                          |
| 3     | tablespoons minced garlic                                    |
| 2     | cups Roma tomatoes, peeled, seeded and chopped               |
| 1 1/2 | cups chicken stock                                           |
| 1     | vanilla bean, quartered and scraped (essential)              |
| 1/4   | teaspoon kosher salt                                         |
| 3     | tablespoons roasted pepitas (Mexican pumpkin seeds)          |
| 4     | sprigs cilantro for garnish                                  |
| 4     | wedges lime for garnish                                      |

Rinse shrimp, peel and devein, leaving tails on. Cover and refrigerate until needed. Wash anchos in hot water, chop coarsely and place in a small bowl with hot water. Let stand 25 minutes before use.

Heat oil in a large skillet. When smoking, carefully add shrimp and sauté 1 minute, shaking pan often. Add onion and cook 30 seconds more, then add garlic. When garlic is golden, add tomatoes. Cook 30 seconds, then add chilies, squeezing out most of the soaking liquid. Add stock, vanilla bean and salt. Bring mixture to a rapid boil, then reduce heat and cook until shrimp turn pink. The liquid should be reduced by two-thirds at this point. Remove shrimp and divide among 4 warmed dishes; top each serving with sauce. Place a vanilla stick on top of each serving, then garnish with pepitas and cilantro sprigs. Garnish each serving with a lime wedge. Serves 4.

The lycopene in tomatoes and capsaicin in peppers contribute many healthful benefits. To keep total fat under control, reduce oil for sautéing to 1 tablespoon.

Kendall Jackson Vintner's Reserve Chardonnay (white); Daniel Gehrs Syrah (red).

# VENETIAN RISI E BISI

| | |
|---|---|
| 1 | tablespoon olive oil |
| 1 1/2 | cups Arborio rice |
| 1 | tablespoon minced shallot |
| 1 | teaspoon salt |
| 1 | quart heated chicken stock, divided |
| 1 3/4 | cups fresh green peas, blanched (or early June frozen, thawed) |
| 1/4 | cup grated Parmigiano-Reggiano cheese |
| | Cracked black pepper to taste |

Heat oil in a medium saucepan. Add rice and sauté until golden, then add shallot and salt. Add stock, about 1 cup at a time, stirring occasionally while rice cooks. Add more stock as it is absorbed, until rice is cooked, about 17 minutes. Mash peas slightly with a fork and stir into rice towards end of cooking. Rice should be firm, not mushy, but not crunchy. Stir in cheese; add pepper. Serves 4.

This is a great low-fat recipe. To reduce sodium, eliminate added salt and use low-sodium chicken broth.

Pietra Santa Dolcetto; Fabiano Amarone (Italy).

# GREEK SHRIMP SALAD *with Lemon-Oregano Vinaigrette*

| | |
|---|---|
| 1 | quart water |
| 1 | tablespoon salt |
| 1/2 | tablespoon black pepper |
| 1 | rib celery, leaves removed, diced |
| 1/2 | yellow onion, diced |
| 4 | lemons, divided |
| 1/2 | bay leaf, broken |
| 20 | (16/20 count) shrimp, washed |
| | Lemon-Oregano Vinaigrette (recipe follows) |
| 1/3 | (15-ounce) can chickpeas, drained |
| 1/2 | cucumber, peeled and sliced 1/4-inch thick |
| 1/2 | red onion, cut into slivers |
| 2 | ripe tomatoes, cut into sixths |
| 1/4 | cup pitted kalamata olives |
| 1 | (6-ounce) jar artichoke quarters, drained |
| 1 | head Romaine lettuce, torn, reserve outer leaves for garnish |

## LEMON-OREGANO VINAIGRETTE

| | |
|---|---|
| 3 | tablespoons fresh lemon juice |
| 1 | minced shallot |
| 2 | garlic cloves, minced |
| 1/3 | cup extra-virgin olive oil |
| 2 | teaspoons shredded fresh oregano |
| 1/2 | teaspoon salt |
| 1/2 | teaspoon black pepper |

Combine water, salt, pepper, celery, yellow onion, 1 lemon (cut in half) and bay leaf in a medium saucepan over high heat. Bring to a boil, then reduce heat and simmer 15 minutes. Increase heat so water is boiling; add shrimp and allow water to return to a boil. Cook 30 seconds or until shrimp turn pink. Remove pan from heat; drain shrimp. Refresh under cold water, shell, remove tails and devein. Split shrimp in half lengthwise.

Prepare vinaigrette; set aside. In a large bowl, combine shrimp, chickpeas, cucumber, red onion, tomato, olives, artichokes and romaine. Toss with vinaigrette and correct seasoning. Place reserved romaine leaves on each of 4 plates; top with salad mixture. Decorate with wedges of 3 remaining lemons. Serves 4.

### Lemon-Oregano Vinaigrette

Place lemon juice, shallot and garlic in a small bowl. Whisk in oil, then stir in oregano, salt and pepper. Makes 1/2 cup.

Chickpeas are one of the richest sources of anti-cancer compounds called protease inhibitors, which also can help lower cholesterol. Eliminate added salt in boiling water and dressing. Reduce dressing to 4 tablespoons.

Chateau Julia Chardonnay (Greece); Amethystos Fume (Greece).

# WARM APPLE GALETTE *with Rosemary Syrup* *and Candied Lemon*

| | |
|---|---|
| 3 | apples (such as Granny Smith or Jonathan), peeled, cored and cut in 3/4-inch dice |
| 3 | tablespoons unsalted butter |
| 2/3 | cup sugar |
| | Unbaked pastry for single-crust 9-inch pie |
| 1 | tablespoon milk |
| 1 | tablespoon sugar |
| | Rosemary Syrup (recipe follows) |
| | Candied Lemon (recipe follows) |
| | Rosemary sprigs for garnish |

## ROSEMARY SYRUP

| | |
|---|---|
| 1/2 | cup sugar |
| 2/3 | cup water |
| 2 | sprigs fresh rosemary |

## CANDIED LEMON

| | |
|---|---|
| 1/2 | cup sugar |
| 1/3 | cup water |
| 1 | lemon, thinly sliced and seeded |

Preheat oven to 350 degrees. Place a large skillet over medium-high heat. When hot, add apples, butter and sugar. Cook quickly, but don't shake pan or stir too much so that apples will color. When apples are softened, golden and glazed, remove from heat and cool.

Place pastry on a lightly floured surface; roll out for a 9-inch pie plate. Place pastry on a nonstick baking sheet. Pile cooled apples in center, leaving a 2-inch space around the edge. Fold up exposed dough all around, leaving apples in center uncovered. Brush pastry with milk and sprinkle with sugar. Bake until browned and bubbly, about 35 minutes. Let stand until cool.

Prepare syrup; cool. Prepare lemon; reserve. Cut apple galette into 4 pieces; place a wedge on each plate. Drizzle with syrup; garnish with lemon and a rosemary sprig. Serves 4.

**Rosemary Syrup**

Mix sugar and water; bring to a boil in a small saucepan. Cook 1 minute, remove from heat, add rosemary and cool.

**Candied Lemon**

Mix sugar and water in a small skillet; bring to a boil. Cook until sugar mixture is thick, then add lemon slices; toss well to coat. Return to a boil; cook 1 minute. Use tongs to remove to a plate and drain. Reserve.

What a treat to find a dessert recipe with only 30 percent of calories from fat. But calories are high so divide this recipe into eight slices.

Geyser Peak Late Harvest Riesling (1/2 bottle); Zaca Mesa Late Harvest Viognier; Schloss Johannisberg Beerenauslese (Germany).

PORTOBELLO FRIES *with Mushroom Tea Vinaigrette*
PAN SEARED TUNA LOIN *with Shiitake Hoisin Slaw & Wonton Crisps*
GRILLED VEGETABLE & CHICKEN SOUP

Fusion, with more Latin American influences, is the future Richard Pignetti foresees for food in the millennium. An inventive chef, Pignetti opened his casual bistro in July 1998 with a menu fusing Southwestern, Continental and Asian flavors and techniques. Even the architecture and décor are eclectic with lots of natural woods, stone and bright mosaic accent walls.

NEW AMERICAN CUISINE

"Our tastes are changing. The trend is to Latin American with a mixture of Asian and Italian. I don't think any food will ever be as popular as Italian has been in the past, but I don't think Italian will be the major influence in the future. Perhaps the lighter Mediterranean fare will take that honor," he says. Pignetti is of Italian heritage (he is a cousin to the Mandola and Carrabba restaurant clan) and has lived in St. Croix where he became a certified scuba diver. He says a cook on his grandparents' ranch in Wyoming has been his greatest influence. The native Houstonian spent six weeks on the ranch for five summers beginning when he was 11. As he followed the cook, Lena Brown, around the bunkhouse kitchen, he learned to pick the freshest vegetables, smoke meat, catch trout and cook out on the range, he says.

Other cooking experiences have given him a strong foundation in Italian cooking. He was a chef at Buttarazzi's on FM 1960, the chef who opened Ciro's, a member of the group that launched the Original Pasta Co. and corporate chef for Corelli's in Houston and Sugar Land. For his namesake restaurant, which he describes as a New American Bistro, he takes a melting pot approach. He might fry lobster tempura-style and serve it on smoked corn risotto with plum essence. Or he might bake the lobster tail and drizzle it with white truffle oil or "lacquer" baked lobster with a glaze of Thai Sirachi hot sauce. By cooking balsamic vinegar down almost to syrup consistency, he created an Italian agri-dolce (sweet-sour) glaze for roast lamb. The glaze also is brushed on the plate for presentation.

In the future he thinks some of the things seen in authentic tacarias will become mainstream in America. Entrées will be fruitier, with glazes, salsas and chutneys incorporating fresh fruit, particularly tropical and exotic fruits. "There are already a lot of Americanized flavors coming from Latin countries," he says. That is true of one of his signature dishes, Pollo San Juanita, created and named for a lost love. Chicken breast is dusted with cumin, pan-seared with fire-roasted onion and peppers, then finished with tequila, lime and cilantro.

There's a camaraderie among professional chefs in Houston, Pignetti says, and he hopes his restaurant will be a "home away from home" for chefs. He invites friends as guest chefs on Friday and Saturday nights, and diners never know who might be at the stove from time to time during the week.

---

*LITE FARE*

Pignetti's menu highlights engaging combinations of lean proteins such as fish, chicken and seafood, intriguing vegetables – stir-fried purple cabbage, eggplant ratatouille and confetti vegetables – and interesting starches such as glazed yams, orzo pasta and corn risotto. For a sampling of these delicious carbohydrates, request the Vegetable Plate that can also be prepared Vegan, without any animal products. Special requests are honored and taken seriously.

*Pignetti's*
*414 West Gray*
*Houston, Tx 77019*
*713-522-8488*

# PORTOBELLO FRIES *with Mushroom Tea Vinaigrette*

| | |
|---|---|
| 8 | large portobello mushrooms |
| 1 | cup Mushroom Tea (see Note) |
| 1/2 | cup Mushroom Tea Vinaigrette (recipe follows) |
| 2 | cups all-purpose flour |
| 4 | eggs, slightly beaten |
| 2 | cups dry bread crumbs |
| 2 | cups peanut oil |
| 1/2 | cup arugula, well washed and drained |
| 1 | cup prosciutto, cut into 1/8-inch strips and rendered until crispy |
| 4 | ounces shaved Parmigiano-Reggiano cheese |
| 1 | tablespoon coarsely ground black pepper |

Remove stems and gills from mushrooms; use to prepare Mushroom Tea. Prepare vinaigrette; reserve. Slice mushroom caps into 1/2-inch strips. Dredge in flour, then egg, then bread crumbs. Heat oil in a deep saucepan. Place mushrooms in hot oil and cook until golden brown, about 3 minutes. To serve, stack mushrooms in a crisscross fashion on plate. Drizzle vinaigrette over top. Garnish with arugula, prosciutto cracklings, Parmesan and pepper. If desired, additional vinaigrette may be served on the side for dipping. Serves 6.

*Note:* To make mushroom tea, steep stems and gills in 2 cups boiling water 10 minutes. Strain and reserve liquid.

## MUSHROOM TEA VINAIGRETTE

| | |
|---|---|
| 1 | cup Mushroom Tea (see Note above) |
| 3/4 | cup extra-virgin olive oil |
| 1/2 | cup balsamic vinegar |
| 1/4 | cup honey |
| 1 | teaspoon each, chopped: garlic and shallots |
| 1/2 | teaspoon each, chopped fresh: thyme, oregano, mint and parsley Salt and freshly ground black pepper to taste |

**Mushroom Tea Vinaigrette**

Combine Mushroom Tea, oil, vinegar, honey, garlic, shallots, thyme, oregano, mint, parsley, salt and pepper in a 1-quart glass jar with tight-fitting lid. Shake until ingredients are emulsified. Makes 2 1/2 cups. Store covered in refrigerator up to 2 weeks.

Use moderation with this recipe.

Roccadella Macie Chianti Classico (Italy); Frescobaldi Pomino (Italy).

# PAN SEARED TUNA LOIN *with Shiitake Hoisin Slaw &* *Wonton Crisps*

Shiitake Hoisin Slaw (recipe follows)
3 pounds No. 1 sushi-grade yellowfin tuna
2 tablespoons kosher salt
2 tablespoons coarsely ground black pepper
1/4 cup peanut oil
Wonton Crisps (recipe follows)

Prepare slaw; set aside and keep warm. Preheat oven to 350 degrees. Cut tuna into 6 (8-ounce) portions. Combine salt and pepper; coat tuna on all sides. Heat oil in a large skillet. Carefully place tuna in pan and cook 45 seconds on each side. Transfer to a baking pan and bake in oven until desired doneness, about 7 minutes for medium rare (recommended.)

Prepare Wonton Crisps; set aside. Place tuna on plate and serve with slaw and wontons; drizzle with wasabi sauce. Serves 6 to 8.

## SHIITAKE HOISIN SLAW

3 medium-size red onions, cut into 1/4-inch strips
1/4 cup peanut oil
2 tablespoons chopped shallots
1 tablespoon chopped garlic
1 pound shiitake mushrooms, stemmed and coarsely chopped
1/2 cup dry sherry (gold or cream)
1/2 cup hoisin barbecue sauce (available at Asian markets)

**Shiitake Hoisin Slaw**

Grill onions 5 to 10 minutes. Heat oil in a saucepan; add shallots and garlic. Cook until shallots are translucent. Add mushrooms and sherry; cook 2 minutes. Add grilled onions and hoisin sauce; combine. Serves 6.

## WONTON CRISPS

3/4 cup peanut oil
6 wonton skins, cut into triangles
2 tablespoons balsamic vinegar
1 teaspoon wasabi powder (available at Asian markets)
1/4 cup water

**Wonton Crisps**

Heat oil in deep saucepan and fry wonton skins until golden brown. Brush vinegar on wontons after they are fried. Combine wasabi powder and water for sauce; mix well. Serves 6.

Tuna is a high-fat fish full of health-giving nutrients. It is loaded with niacin and vitamins A and B12 that help build healthy red blood cells and an effective immune system. In addition, tuna is a good source of omega-3's that help protect against heart disease. To control fat, eliminate Wonton Crisps, use just 1 tablespoon oil to sauté fish and 1 tablespoon oil to sauté vegetables in slaw. Also, eliminate added salt for tuna.

Columbia Crest Chardonnay (Washington); Freemark Abbey or Vine Cliff Chardonnay.

# GRILLED VEGETABLE & CHICKEN SOUP

| | |
|---|---|
| 1 | medium size yellow squash |
| 1 | medium zucchini |
| 1 | medium carrot |
| 2 | tablespoons chopped garlic |
| 2 | tablespoons canola oil |
| | Salt and freshly ground black pepper to taste |
| 1/4 | cup chopped shallots |
| 1 | tablespoon virgin olive oil |
| 1 1/2 | pounds smoked chicken breast, shredded |
| 2 | cups marinara sauce (jarred such as Classico or Five Brothers) |
| 4 | cups low-sodium chicken broth |
| 2 | teaspoons chopped fresh basil |
| 1 | teaspoon each, chopped fresh: thyme, oregano and mint |
| 1 | teaspoon each: kosher salt and black pepper |
| 6 to 8 | toasted bread triangles for garnish |

Use a melon baller to cut balls of yellow squash, zucchini and carrot. Blanch carrot balls in boiling water 1 1/2 minutes. Combine garlic and canola oil in a small bowl. Brush yellow squash, zucchini and carrot balls with mixture; sprinkle with salt and pepper. Grill outside over wood or indoor grill until fork tender; set aside.

Sauté shallots in olive oil until golden brown in a medium saucepan. Add chicken, marinara sauce and broth; bring to a boil, reduce heat and simmer 5 minutes. Add basil, thyme, oregano, mint, salt and pepper. Ladle into bowls and garnish each with bread and reserved vegetables. Serves 6 to 8.

To reduce fat in this healthy soup, eliminate oil to grill vegetables and use nonstick cooking spray.

Mont Gras or Chateau Los Boldos Merlot (Chile); St. Francis Merlot.

FACING PAGE, FROM LEFT:  *Richard Pignetti, Adam Gonzalez, Greg Chopin, Jeff Hilson, Pignetti's.*

FOLLOWING PAGE:  *Jimmy Mitchell, Donnette Hansen, Rainbow Lodge.*

HIBISCUS SALAD *with Goat Cheese Cakes and Sun-Dried Cherry Dressing*
SMOKED TROUT CAKES *with Jalapeño Remoulade*
DUCK GUMBO
ITALIAN PEAR TART

A prolific garden grows alongside the kitchen of Rainbow Lodge, which nestles in a picturesque setting on Buffalo Bayou. Here executive chef Jimmy Mitchell nurtures herbs, peppers, nine different heirloom tomatoes, four types of basil and squash (which provides the squash blossoms for a popular menu item, fried squash blossoms). The garden is being expanded so he can produce even more. Mitchell takes a hands-on approach to "bring the garden to the table."

Owner Donnette Hansen, niece of the original owner, set the restaurant on its course toward contemporary American cuisine, and Mitchell fits right in. Environmentally conscious, he maintains a compost heap for the garden and is an avid recycler. In 1997, Rainbow Lodge was the only restaurant to receive the environmental award from the Houston Corporate Recycling Council. He is a member of Chefs Collaborative 2000, which promotes sustainable agriculture.

Mitchell's Contemporary American Cuisine covers a lot of territory. Flavors of the West and Southwest show up in game, chipotles, jalapeños and other chilies, corn and cilantro. There's a touch of Louisiana in duck gumbo and crawfish fritters with Creole mustard. You'll find Asian Fusion in soy- and ginger-marinated scallops on Asian cabbage salad; sunflower seed-encrusted trout fillets with ginger grilled shrimp and sunflower sprouts; and rack of lamb with Asian cabbage and sesame salad. Mitchell's training with noted California chef John Ash shows up in West Coast specialties. Texas is well represented on the menu with such dishes as Hibiscus Salad assembled with local greens and Texas goat cheese as well as sun-dried cherries and hibiscus leaf dressing. Venison, elk, buffalo, quail, pheasant and other wild game star on the menus along with beef, pork, lamb, chicken, lobster, salmon and other fish. A large selection of fine wines is available to compliment any dish – Rainbow Lodge has been recognized by the Wine Spectator with its Award of Excellence.

Mitchell says he will continue to go back to basics for the millennium although menus are upscale. Fresh ingredients are constantly improving, says Mitchell, who supports local farmers' markets and small, independent growers of organic heirloom greens, tomatoes and herbs. He credits travel, a growing interest in gardening (now the Number 1 leisure time activity in America), exposure to cookbooks, cooking magazines, television cooking shows and the availability of recipes on the Internet for the sophistication of today's diners.

In addition to the food and wine, the rustic hunting lodge with its eclectic collection of antiques, fishing and hunting trophies has long made Rainbow Lodge one of Houston's favorite destinations for special occasions. The romantic ambiance makes it a favored location for engagements, weddings and anniversaries. The restaurant is located on the wooded banks of Buffalo Bayou. On park-like grounds, it offers ever-changing views of the Bayou; resident birds and wild life provide entertainment.

--- LITE FARE ---

Rainbow Lodge specializes in wild game and birds that are naturally lean and can be prepared low fat. Chef Jimmy Mitchell features seasonal organic produce that is grown in the restaurant garden or purchased from local organic farmers. Look for Jimmy's Garden Pick, which is a selection of these organic vegetables. Special requests are encouraged and honored.

*Rainbow Lodge*
*No. 1 Birdsall*
*Houston, Tx 77007*
*713-861-8666*

# HIBISCUS SALAD *with Goat Cheese Cakes and Sun-Dried Cherry Dressing*

1    cup plus 2 tablespoons Sun-Dried Cherry Dressing (recipe follows)
     Goat Cheese Cakes (recipe follows)
1 1/2   pounds mixed lettuces
1    medium-size yellow tomato, diced
1/2   cup shelled pistachios
1/4   cup sun-dried cherries

Prepare dressing; set aside. Prepare cheese cakes; set aside. Place lettuce in large bowl; toss with dressing. Arrange on chilled plates. Place 2 cheese cakes on each side of plate and tomato on each side of plate. Sprinkle top of salad with pistachios and cherries. Serves 6.

## SUN-DRIED CHERRY DRESSING

1/4   cup sun-dried cherries
3/4   cup hibiscus vinegar (see Note)
1/4   cup red Zinfandel wine
3/4   cup olive oil
     Salt and freshly ground black pepper to taste

**Sun-Dried Cherry Dressing**

Puree cherries with vinegar and wine until smooth in a blender. Slowly incorporate oil until it is emulsified and smooth. Add salt and pepper. Makes about 2 cups.

*Note:* To make hibiscus vinegar, combine 2 ounces of dried hibiscus blossoms (Jamaican sorrel; available in Mexican markets) and 1 cup white wine vinegar. Heat to boiling in a small pan; reduce heat and simmer 10 minutes. Cool and strain.

## GOAT CHEESE CAKES

6    sun-dried tomatoes
2    tablespoons red wine
1    garlic clove
4    ounces goat cheese (such as Yellow Rose from Texas)
4    large fresh basil leaves, chiffonade (see Special Helps section)
2    cups plain dry bread crumbs

**Goat Cheese Cakes**

Puree tomatoes, wine and garlic until smooth in a blender. In a medium bowl, combine cheese and tomato mixture; fold in basil. Form cheese mixture into 12 half-dollar size cakes. Coat with bread crumbs. Spray a medium nonstick skillet with nonstick cooking spray; heat over medium heat. Place cheese cakes in pan; cook until light brown, about 1 minute, on each side. Serves 6.

Balance fat by including just one Goat Cheese Cake per serving, reducing dressing to 1 tablespoon per serving and eliminating pistachios.

Fall Creek Sauvignon Blanc (Texas); Sancerre Domaine de Rossignol Vieille Vignes (France).

# SMOKED TROUT CAKES *with Jalapeño Remoulade*

| | |
|---|---|
| 3/4 | cup Jalapeño Remoulade (recipe follows) |
| 2 | tablespoons plus 1/4 cup pomace olive oil, divided |
| 1 | red bell pepper, diced |
| 1 | green bell pepper, diced |
| 1 | yellow bell pepper, diced |
| 1 | jalapeño pepper, seeded and finely diced |
| 1 | yellow onion, diced |
| 1/2 | bunch green onions, diced |
| 4 | ribs celery, diced |
| 3 | garlic cloves, minced |
| 2 | tablespoons chopped fresh cilantro leaves |
| 1 | tablespoon chopped fresh sage |
| 1 | tablespoon chopped fresh thyme |
| 2 | pounds boneless smoked trout, skin removed |
| 4 | eggs, beaten |
| 3 | cups dry bread crumbs, divided |

## JALAPEÑO REMOULADE

| | |
|---|---|
| 1/4 | red onion, finely chopped |
| 1/4 | cup chopped fresh cilantro leaves |
| 1 to 2 | green onions, finely chopped |
| 2 | tablespoons chopped capers |
| 1/2 | rib celery, finely chopped |
| 1/2 | jalapeño pepper with seeds, finely chopped |
| 1 | pint mayonnaise (can use light) |
| 2 | tablespoons whole-grain mustard |
| | Juice of 1 lime |
| | Lemon pepper to taste |
| | Worcestershire sauce to taste |
| | Hot red pepper sauce to taste |
| | Salt to taste |

Prepare Jalapeño Remoulade; reserve. Heat 2 tablespoons oil in medium skillet; sauté red, green, yellow and jalapeño peppers; yellow and green onions, celery, garlic, cilantro, sage and thyme; cool. Add trout to cooled mixture. Add eggs and 2 cups bread crumbs to mixture; mix with large wooden spoon. Form 12 half-dollar size cakes and coat in remaining 1 cup crumbs. Pan fry in nonstick skillet in remaining 1/4 cup oil until golden brown. Serve immediately and accompany with Jalapeño Remoulade. Serves 6 (2 cakes each).

### Jalapeño Remoulade

Mix red onion, cilantro, green onion, capers, celery, jalapeño, mayonnaise, mustard and lime juice in a medium bowl. Season with lemon pepper, Worcestershire, pepper sauce and salt. Cover and refrigerate. Keeps about 1 week. Makes about 3/4 quart.

🍎 Trout is a great source of vitamin B12, with added benefits of body-building protein, niacin, iron, potassium and omega-3 oils. To reduce fat and cholesterol, decrease oil to 3 tablespoons – 1 tablespoon to sauté vegetables and 2 tablespoons to pan-fry trout cakes. Substitute 1 cup fat-free egg substitute or 8 egg whites for eggs and reduce Jalapeño Remoulade to 6 tablespoons.

🍇 Wildman or Chapin – Landais Vouvray (France); Chateau Moncontour Vouvray (France).

# DUCK GUMBO

| | |
|---|---|
| 1 | (6-pound) or 2 (3-pound) duck(s) |
| | Salt and freshly ground black pepper to taste |
| 2 | tablespoons paprika, divided |
| 3 | quarts water |
| 6 | tablespoons olive oil |
| 1 | large yellow onion, diced |
| 1 | red bell pepper, diced |
| 1 | green bell pepper, diced |
| 1 | yellow bell pepper, diced |
| 4 | ribs celery, chopped |
| 1/2 | bunch green onions, chopped |
| 2 | garlic cloves, minced |
| 1 | pound andouille sausage, sliced 1/4-inch thick |
| 1/2 | cup vegetable oil |
| 1/2 | cup all-purpose flour |
| 2 | tablespoons filé powder |
| 1 | (28-ounce) can diced tomatoes, including liquid |
| 1 | tablespoon dried thyme |
| 1 1/2 | teaspoons freshly ground black pepper |

Allow two days preparation. Prepare duck on the first day and make gumbo on the second day. Preheat oven to 350 degrees. Season duck with salt, pepper and 1 tablespoon paprika. Cook covered in a roasting pan 3 hours, or until done. When cool, remove skin. Debone meat and dice. Combine bones and water in a large stockpot; simmer 3 hours. Strain.

Heat olive oil in an 8-quart stockpot. Add yellow onion, peppers, celery, green onion, garlic and sausage; cook until soft. Add duck stock and simmer 20 minutes. Add duck meat.

Combine vegetable oil and flour in a small skillet. Stirring constantly with a wooden spoon, cook slowly until light brown. Or prepare in microwave (see Special Helps section). Add filé. Add roux to gumbo, stirring over low heat until it thickens. Add tomatoes, remaining 1 tablespoon paprika, thyme, pepper and salt; simmer about 20 minutes. Serves 12 to 16.

- Eliminate oil by sautéing vegetables in chicken broth. Choose low-sodium, fat-free chicken broth or make your own (see Healthy Recipe Modifications).

- Chateau Montfaucon Côtes du Rhone (France); Coudoulet de Beaucastel (France); Côte-Rôtie Guigal (France).

# ITALIAN PEAR TART

| | |
|---|---|
| 2 | medium firm-ripe pears without blemishes, such as Bosc |
| 1/4 | cup unsalted butter |
| | Favorite pie crust dough for a single 10-inch pie |
| 1 | (7-ounce) package almond paste |
| 4 | large eggs |
| 1/3 | cup sugar |
| 1 | tablespoon vanilla extract |
| 1 | teaspoon ground allspice |
| | Pinch of salt |
| 1/2 | cup whipping cream |
| | Fresh berries and brandy-flavored whipped cream for garnish |

Peel pears, halve vertically and core. Cut each half into 4 slices. Heat butter in small skillet until foamy. Add pear slices and sauté until browned on both sides, turning as needed. Remove from heat and cool.

Preheat oven to 350 degrees. Roll out dough and fit into a 10-inch tart pan with removable bottom. Work from center to edge to avoid trapping air. Roll rolling pin across top to remove excess dough. Arrange pear slices in a circle, reserving 3 pieces for center of tart.

Break almond paste into pieces and combine with eggs, sugar, vanilla, allspice and salt in food processor; process until smooth. Add cream; blend. Pour custard into center of tart pan, letting custard flow out to edges. Some edges of pear slices will not be covered. Place tart on baking sheet and bake 30 minutes. Tart is done when an even light brown. Cool tart thoroughly before removing from pan. Cover and refrigerate 1 hour or as long as overnight before cutting. Accompany with fresh berries and brandy-flavored whipped cream. Serves 8 to 10.

- This does not count towards your 5-A-Day of fruits and vegetables but delight in a tiny morsel anyway!

- Michele Chiarlo Nivole (Italy); Chateau Rieussec or Chateau Suduiraut (France).

GULF BLUE CRAB NACHOS
FROZEN SANGRIA
SAN ANGELO SAUCE
KING RANCH CASSEROLE
RIBEYE POBLANO
CHOCOLATE WAFFLES

Houston may grow ever more sophisticated in tastes but occasionally you get hungry for home cooking – chicken fried steak and gravy, mashed potatoes, beans, a Texas T-bone, Mexican food, cornbread and pecan pie. That's when you head for Rancho Tejas to indulge your appetite for ribs, seafood, enchiladas, fajitas, King Ranch Casserole, venison, quail or fried catfish. Owner Pat McCarley doesn't expect drastic changes in the new millennium, but he does think the large immigration of Vietnamese to the Gulf Coast will influence Texas cuisine. "The Vietnamese will leave their mark on Texas cooking because there are so many similarities in the food – a lot of fish and seafood, rice, chilies and spices. The Asian influence came about in Texas because some really talented and noteworthy chefs were looking for new influences. Vietnamese is a natural." It may take its place beside Mexican, German and Cajun, he says.

The family tradition of hospitality was established in 1836 when McCarley's great-great-great grandfather, Samuel McCarley, accommodated General Sam Houston and 2,500 of his troops when they stopped at the McCarley farm near present-day Hempstead. Today, Rancho Tejas is a must stop when you have guests from out of town or when you're entertaining friends and family.

The restaurant is a little more casual now than when it opened in 1995, and the atmosphere is more steakhouse and Texican grill than ranch house. McCarley has updated the menu and created several sauces, which can be mixed and matched with steaks and fish. He added a Sunday brunch buffet filled with Mexican egg dishes, migas, chiliquiles, quesadillas, tamales and Jalapeño Pie with a cornbread crust. Guests also can opt for regular breakfast fare including egg dishes and pecan waffles as well as chocolate waffles for dessert.

McCarley says customers are eating more fish and seafood. Seafood Enchiladas are the menu best seller, followed by Chicken Fried Steak. He improves on tradition with CFS: Round steak is tenderized in a buttermilk marinade then breaded with light sourdough "wash" and served with Cream Gravy. Hand-made tamales are a Rancho Tejas tradition; McCarley even teaches children's classes in tamale-making periodically. Pecan Pie is transformed into a rich cobbler and topped with Blue Bell Homemade Vanilla ice cream. The cobbler is a popular gift item. It is baked and shipped in a Texas-shaped cast aluminum pan.

The urban ranch house is in view of Loop 610. It owes its atmosphere to a ceiling-high sepia-toned mural wall depicting historic food scenes and regions of Texas, open-trussed ceilings of natural pine (the ceiling peaks at 26 feet), massive wood-burning stone fireplaces, murals and metal art. Architect Stephen A. Lucchesi researched West Texas forts built with native materials before designing the building. His wife, Amy, painted the mural and McCarley's wife, Chris, helped with the interiors.

--- LITE FARE ---

Rancho Tejas specializes in mesquite grilling of meats, poultry, fish, seafood and vegetables. Mesquite grilling can add flavor to foods and preserve nutritional value while allowing fat to drain. Choose lean meats such as beef tenderloin, venison or chicken breast. Accompany these with grilled vegetables and plain rice. Enjoy the special sauce toppings in moderation.

*Rancho Tejas*
*4747 San Felipe*
*Houston Tx 77056*
*713-840-0440*

# GULF BLUE CRAB NACHOS

| | |
|---|---|
| 1 | (.9-ounce) package Knorr hollandaise sauce mix |
| 1 | cup milk |
| 1/4 | cup unsalted butter |
| 5 | ounces fresh lump crabmeat, cleaned and picked over |
| 2 | tablespoons chopped cilantro leaves |
| 2 | tablespoons chopped green onion |
| 2 | strips bacon, cooked crisp and chopped |
| 2 | teaspoons chopped pickled jalapeños |
| 8 | tostada shells (such as Old El Paso) |
| 1 | cup mixed, shredded: Cheddar and Monterey Jack cheese Whole pickled jalapeños, guacamole, pico de gallo and sour cream for garnish |

Prepare hollandaise sauce according to package directions using milk and butter; reserve. Preheat broiler. Mix crabmeat, cilantro, onion, bacon and chopped jalapeño in a bowl. Combine hollandaise and crab mixture in a medium skillet; heat until bubbling, stirring constantly. Remove from heat, spread mixture over tostada shells with a spatula and sprinkle with cheese. Place under broiler just to melt cheese. Garnish with whole jalapeños, guacamole, pico de gallo and sour cream; serve immediately. Serves 8.

Prepare hollandaise sauce with skim milk and no butter. Eliminate bacon and substitute low-fat cheese for regular.

Domaine Ste. Michelle Extra Dry Sparkling Wine (Washington); Chateau Moncontour Vouvray (France).

# FROZEN SANGRIA

| | |
|---|---|
| 2 | cups Burgundy or other dry red wine |
| 1 | cup water |
| 1/2 | cup fresh orange juice |
| 1/4 | cup fresh lime juice |
| 1/4 | cup sugar |
| 1/4 | cup grenadine |
| 1/4 | cup brandy |
| 1/4 | cup Triple Sec Orange and lime cartwheels, cherries and cinnamon sticks for garnish |

This recipe can be prepared in several ways: *Ice Cream Freezer:* Combine wine, water, orange and lime juices, sugar, grenadine, brandy and Triple Sec in ice cream maker and churn until slushy according to manufacturer's directions. *Freezer:* Combine above ingredients in bowl and place in freezer. Stirring occasionally, freeze a couple of hours. Because of alcohol content, mixture will never freeze solid in a home freezer. *Blender:* Eliminate water and pour remaining ingredients over ice in a blender; process. *Punch Bowl:* Eliminate water, combine remaining ingredients and pour over ice ring in a punch bowl.

To serve: Garnish with orange and lime cartwheels, cherries and cinnamon sticks. Makes 4 1/2 cups, 6 (3/4-cup) servings.

This drink is loaded with vitamin C and calories. Sip slowly.

# SAN ANGELO SAUCE

| | |
|---|---|
| 1 | cup finely chopped bacon |
| 1 1/2 | cups finely chopped mushrooms |
| 1/2 | cup finely chopped onion |
| 1/4 | cup all-purpose flour |
| 1 | (12-ounce) can evaporated milk |
| 2 | teaspoons salt |
| 1/4 | teaspoon white pepper |
| 2 | cups whipping cream |
| 3 | cups halved medium mushrooms |
| 1 | teaspoon hot red pepper sauce |
| 1 | teaspoon Worcestershire sauce |
| 1/2 | cup sherry |

Sauté bacon in a medium skillet over medium heat until half done. Add chopped mushrooms and onion; sauté until onion is soft, about 5 minutes. Sprinkle in flour and cook 2 minutes, stirring constantly. Mix in milk, salt and pepper, stirring constantly. Return to a simmer. Add cream, halved mushrooms, pepper sauce, Worcestershire and sherry; simmer 3 minutes, stirring constantly. Immediately pour sauce over steak, fish or chicken and divide halved mushrooms equally. Serves 4, about 1 cup each.

 For a low-fat version, substitute evaporated skim milk for regular, half-and-half for cream and turkey bacon for regular. Skip added salt. Plan on 8 (1/2 cup) servings.

# KING RANCH CASSEROLE

| | |
|---|---|
| 2 | tablespoons vegetable oil |
| 1 | cup chopped yellow onion |
| 3/4 | cup chopped green bell pepper |
| 3/4 | cup chopped roasted red bell pepper |
| 3/4 | cup chopped roasted poblano pepper |
| 1 1/4 | cups chopped mushrooms |
| 3/4 | cup drained pico de gallo |
| 1 | quart prepared cream sauce (see Note and Special Helps section) |
| 1 | tablespoon freshly ground black pepper |
| 1 | teaspoon chili powder |
| 1/2 | teaspoon ground cumin |
| 2 | teaspoons minced garlic |
| 2 | teaspoons hot green pepper sauce |
| 3/4 | cup roasted corn kernels |
| 1/2 | cup chopped green onion |
| 12 | corn tortillas, softened in broth |
| 1 1/2 | cups diced smoked or baked chicken |
| 1 1/2 | cups grated sharp Cheddar cheese |

Heat oil in a medium skillet over medium heat. Add yellow onion, green, red and poblano peppers, mushrooms and pico de gallo; sauté until soft, about 5 minutes. Set aside. Place cream sauce in a saucepan and whisk in pepper, chili powder, cumin, garlic and pepper sauce. Heat to a simmer, stirring constantly; remove from heat and set aside. Mix corn and green onion in a small bowl; set aside.

Preheat oven to 350 degrees. Layer ingredients in a 13x9x2-inch casserole in the following order: 4 tortillas, 1/2 cup chicken, 1 cup vegetable mixture, 1 cup sauce, 1/2 cup cheese and 1/3 cup corn mixture. Repeat layers two more times. Spread remaining 1 cup sauce on top with a spatula, pressing down slightly to cover entire casserole. Bake 30 minutes. We serve this as a side dish. To serve as a main dish, double the chicken. Serves 6 to 8 as a side dish.

*Note:* Packaged cream sauce mixes and prepared sauces in a jar are available. You can even use an Alfredo sauce.

For low-fat preparation, eliminate oil by sautéing in a low-sodium, low-fat chicken broth. Use skim milk in preparing cream sauce. Substitute low-fat Cheddar for regular. Divide into 8 servings.

Fall Creek Chenin Blanc (white – Texas); Joseph Phelps Le Mistral (red).

# RIBEYE POBLANO

| | |
|---|---|
| 3 | poblano peppers |
| 1 | quart chicken stock, divided |
| 1/2 | tablespoon chicken seasoned stock base |
| 1/2 | cup corn oil |
| 1/2 | cup all-purpose flour |
| 1/2 | teaspoon garlic powder |
| 1/2 | teaspoon salt |
| 1/4 | teaspoon black pepper |
| | Pinch of cayenne pepper |
| 6 | tablespoons whipping cream |
| 1/2 | cup grated Monterey Jack cheese |
| 4 | (14-ounce) ribeye steaks |

Roast poblanos over an open flame until skins begin to blister and turn black. Immediately place peppers in a covered container and let cool slightly. Remove all skin, seeds, stems and veins; discard. Puree poblanos in blender with 1 cup stock; set aside. Pour remaining 3 cups stock into a medium saucepan, add chicken base and bring to a simmer; reserve.

Heat oil in a medium skillet over medium-high heat. Whisk in flour and make a blond roux (see Special Helps section), about 5 minutes. Whisk in poblano puree, garlic powder, salt, black and cayenne peppers; simmer 1 minute. Gradually stir in remaining simmering stock and simmer 10 minutes, stirring constantly. Whisk in cream; add cheese, whisking until melted. Keep warm while grilling steaks. Serves 4, about 1 cup each.

*Note:* To serve, pour onto warm plates and place grilled ribeye steaks on top of sauce. For this recipe, grill steaks as desired. We think mesquite works best.

 Beef is an excellent source of protein, iron, vitamin B12 and zinc. But current recommendations are for 6 ounces of meat per day. So divide this recipe into 8 servings and reduce Poblano Sauce to 1/4 cup per serving.

Cline Mourvèdre; Fife Petite Sirah.

# CHOCOLATE WAFFLES

| | |
|---|---|
| 1/2 | cup unsalted butter |
| 3/4 | cup chocolate syrup |
| 6 | tablespoons water, divided |
| 1 | cup sugar |
| 1/2 | cup chocolate milk |
| 6 | eggs, lightly whisked |
| 1 2/3 | cups pancake/waffle mix |
| 1 | tablespoon vanilla extract |
| | Vanilla ice cream, chopped pecans and favorite fruit syrup for garnish |

Melt butter with chocolate syrup and 2 tablespoons water in a small saucepan over medium heat. Stir in sugar until dissolved; remove from heat. Combine remaining 4 tablespoons water and milk in mixer; pour in eggs and beat on medium speed 1 minute. Add pancake mix; beat on low speed 2 minutes. Add butter mixture and vanilla slowly; beat on low speed 3 minutes until smooth. Let mixture sit 5 minutes before cooking in a preheated waffle iron. Serve hot with ice cream, pecans and syrup. Makes 6 to 8 waffles.

These delicious waffles weigh in at just 33 percent fat calories. Serve with sliced fruit, berries or fat-free or low-fat ice cream or yogurt.

Pour a little Pedro Ximenez Sherry over the vanilla ice cream.

FACING PAGE, FROM LEFT: *Pat McCarley, Rancho Tejas.*

FOLLOWING PAGE: *Tony Rao, Michelle LeBleu, River Oaks Grill.*

JUMBO LUMP CRAB CAKES *with Mango Salsa and Avocado Cream*
ORANGE SCENTED CHICKEN
BLACKENED DUCK BREAST WITH GINGERED PEA SHOOTS AND FRIZZLED CARROTS
EGGPLANT SANDWICH

River Oaks Grill anticipates the new millennium by going "back to basics," according to owner Tony Rao and executive chef Michelle LeBleu. "There are only so many basic types of food, so we are searching for big-time flavors," he says. "It's all about spices and flavors," says LeBleu, whose bywords are "fresh," "quality" and "moderation." Rao, a chef and longtime Houston restaurateur, bought the Grill in February 1998. He quickly updated the River Oaks neighborhood restaurant by relaxing the dress code to "country club casual" and adding more contemporary dishes and fine wines. In addition to great food, loyal customers are drawn to the Grill by the music in the Piano Bar and periodic wine tastings. The private wine room can accommodate 40. Rao says they also can cater parties for as many as 500.

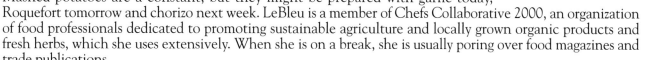

LeBleu, a native Houstonian and graduate of Texas A&M University and the Culinary Institute of America, streamlined the menu, and says it is now "a celebration of the evolution of American contemporary cuisine." The world is her supermarket. Real Dover sole comes from England, boutique cheeses from Europe and California and meats, fish and specialty products from other global markets. Mashed potatoes are a constant; but they might be prepared with garlic today, Roquefort tomorrow and chorizo next week. LeBleu is a member of Chefs Collaborative 2000, an organization of food professionals dedicated to promoting sustainable agriculture and locally grown organic products and fresh herbs, which she uses extensively. When she is on a break, she is usually poring over food magazines and trade publications.

"America is an 'ethnic' nation," says Rao and that allows a lot of leeway in menus. LeBleu does her own version of fusion cuisine, creatively melding the exotic flavors of Asia, the Mediterranean and Europe with the more familiar flavors of America, particularly the American South. As starters, one menu lists Ginger Risotto with a Medley of Sautéed Vegetables and a Drizzle of Cardamom Mustard, Southern Fried Quail with Creamy Buttermilk Gravy and Apricot Ancho Sauce, and Baked Brie with Basil Oven Roasted Tomatoes, Petite Salad and Crusty French Bread. LeBleu uses various techniques – poaching, roasting, boiling, grilling and broiling – to bring out the best in each dish.

People are eating more fish today, a trend she thinks will continue. She offers six fish dishes daily as well as shrimp, crab and other shellfish specialties. Chilean Sea Bass is a customer favorite, and soft-shell crabs are a bestseller when they're in season. The most popular menu item continues to be butterflied Rack of Lamb with garlic and caramelized fennel. Because people seem to be incorporating more vegetables in their meals, LeBleu also focuses on creative uses of vegetables, particularly "under-appreciated" root vegetables (Beet Risotto is a standout). Most desserts are made in-house. The dessert tray holds a tempting assortment of bread pudding, carrot cake, fresh fruit tarts, Chocolate Framboise Layer Cake with chocolate ganache, Crème Brûlée, Carrot Cake with Cream Cheese Icing and Tiramisu.

---

*LITE FARE*

---

The menu at River Oaks Grill features several vegetarian and healthful choices. Start with Roasted Vegetable Napoleon or the House Salad with a Balsamic or Raspberry Vinaigrette served on the side or prepared by special request with no oil. Best entrée choices are Grilled Blackened Snapper with a Carrot-Curry Sauce or Vegetable Plate Special, on request. Special requests are encouraged.

*River Oaks Grill*
*2630 Westheimer*
*Houston, Tx 77098*
*713-520-1738*

# JUMBO LUMP CRAB CAKES *with Mango Salsa*

|       | Mango Salsa (recipe follows) |
|-------|------------------------------|
| 3/4   | cup unsalted butter |
| 1     | each, cut in small dice: red, green and yellow bell peppers |
| 1     | green jalapeño, seeded and finely chopped |
| 1     | teaspoon chopped garlic |
| 1     | teaspoon chopped shallots |
| 1/2   | teaspoon cayenne pepper |
| 2     | teaspoons paprika |
| 1/2   | cup all-purpose flour plus more for dredging |
| 3     | green onions, chopped |
| 1     | bunch cilantro (leaves only), chopped |
| 3 1/2 | cups Japanese bread crumbs (Panko, see Note), divided |
| 1 3/4 | cups jumbo lump crabmeat, cleaned and picked over |
| 4     | eggs, beaten |
|       | Clarified butter (see Special Helps section) |
|       | Avocado Cream (recipe follows) |
| 1/2   | cup sour cream |

## MANGO SALSA

| 1   | mango, seeded and peeled, cut in medium dice |
|-----|----------------------------------------------|
| 1/2 | red jalapeño, seeded and chopped |
| 2   | teaspoons finely diced red onion |
| 1   | tablespoon chopped cilantro leaves |
|     | Fresh lime juice and salt to taste |

## AVOCADO CREAM

| 2   | large ripe avocados |
|-----|---------------------|
|     | Juice of 1 lime |
| 1/4 | cup chicken stock or water |

Prepare salsa; cover and refrigerate. Melt butter in large skillet; sauté bell peppers, jalapeño, garlic, shallots, cayenne and paprika. Add 1/2 cup flour and blend well. Remove mixture and place in a bowl. Blend in onion, cilantro and 1 1/2 cups bread crumbs; mix in crabmeat. Let mixture cool until you can form it into 8 (3-inch by 1/2-inch-thick) patties.

Preheat oven to 350 degrees. Dust each patty with flour; dip in beaten eggs, then in remaining 2 cups bread crumbs. Wipe out skillet from above procedure. Sauté patties in skillet in clarified butter until lightly browned; flip, sauté other side. Transfer to baking pan and bake 7 minutes until golden brown.

Prepare Avocado Cream. Spread a little Avocado Cream in a design in middle of each of 4 plates. Set 2 crab cakes on top. Garnish with Mango Salsa and drizzle sour cream over top. Serves 4.

*Note:* Panko may be purchased at Asian markets, Fiesta and selected import shops.

**Mango Salsa**

Blend mango, jalapeño, onion and cilantro in a small bowl. Add lime juice and salt; reserve. Can be made ahead 12 hours; cover and refrigerate. Makes about 1 cup.

**Avocado Cream**

Peel and seed avocados; place in blender. Add lime juice and stock; puree to creamy consistency. Makes about 1 cup.

Mangoes are high in fiber, beta carotene and vitamin C. Mango Salsa is a great fat-free addition for fish and chicken. The crab cakes are a very high-fat and high-calorie recipe. Use moderation.

Monterey Peninsula Pinot Blanc (white) or Faiveley Pinot Noir (red – France); any Australian Riesling Vendange Tardive (white – France) or German Riesling Spätlese (white – Germany).

# Orange Scented Chicken

Salt to taste
2 pounds chicken tenders
1 cup all-purpose flour
1/4 cup clarified butter
1/2 cup dry vermouth
Juice of 2 oranges
1/2 pound shiitake mushrooms, sliced
1 pound asparagus, cleaned and bottoms trimmed, stalks cut in half
3 tablespoons butter

Salt chicken tenders; dredge tenders in flour, shaking off excess. Heat large skillet; add clarified butter and chicken. Cook until almost done; pour off excess butter. Add vermouth and orange juice with mushrooms and asparagus. When asparagus is tender, add remaining 3 tablespoons butter and salt. Serves 4.

Asparagus is a good low-calorie choice full of folate and vitamins A and C. To reduce fat, limit butter for sautéing to 2 tablespoons. Eliminate 3 tablespoons added butter.

Zaca Mesa Chardonnay; Fox Creek or Matanzas Creek Chardonnay.

# Blackened Duck Breast with Gingered Pea Shoots and Frizzled Carrots

6 (8-ounce) duck breasts
1/2 cup balsamic vinegar
1/3 cup maple syrup
Salt and freshly ground black pepper to taste
2 tablespoons extra-virgin olive oil or clarified butter
1 tablespoon minced fresh ginger root
Zest of 1 orange, minced
1 pound pea shoots (available at Asian markets, Fiesta, Whole Foods or Rice Epicurean), washed
Oil for deep frying
1/2 pound carrots, julienned 3-inch length

Score skin of duck breasts. Combine vinegar and maple syrup. Rub each duck breast with 1 tablespoon mixture (reserving remainder); season with salt and pepper. Sear skin side down in a large skillet until fat is rendered and skin is a blackish brown. Turn and cook to an internal temperature of 160 degrees on an instant-read thermometer. Let breasts sit a few minutes. Slice diagonally into 8 pieces; reserve.

In same skillet, add remaining vinegar-syrup mixture; reduce until mixture coats back of a spoon. Set aside. In separate skillet, heat olive oil, ginger and zest; quickly sauté pea shoots and set aside. Heat oil to 350 degrees in deep fryer; fry carrots until they start to turn brown and get crisp; drain and salt lightly.

Place pea shoots in middle of plate and arrange duck breast over them. Top with carrots. Drizzle reserved balsamic reduction around edges. Serves 6.

Limit size of duck breast to 6 ounces and remove skin.

Talus Zinfandel; Hendry Block 7 Zinfandel.

# EGGPLANT SANDWICH

2 (1-pound) medium eggplants
  Salt and freshly ground black
  pepper to taste
2 large hothouse tomatoes
1/2 cup balsamic vinegar
8 ounces smoked mozzarella,
  sliced
2 cups all-purpose flour
4 large eggs, beaten
3 cups Japanese bread crumbs
  (Panko, available at Fiesta or
  Whole Foods)
1 cup vegetable oil, divided
4 ounces mesclun greens (see
  Special Helps section)

Trim ends from each eggplant and discard. Cut each eggplant into 4 equal slices; lightly salt and set aside. Cut each tomato into 4 slices; salt and pepper. Drizzle 1 tablespoon vinegar on each slice of tomato. Place 1 slice of cheese on top of each tomato; set aside.

Preheat oven to 350 degrees. Pat each eggplant slice with a paper towel to remove any moisture. Lightly salt and dredge in flour; shaking off excess. Dip into eggs, shaking off excess. Completely coat each slice with bread crumbs. In a medium-hot nonstick skillet, heat 1/2 cup oil and sauté 4 eggplant slices on each side to a golden brown. Remove and keep warm. Repeat with remaining oil and eggplant. Meanwhile, place cheese-topped tomato slices on a cookie sheet and place in oven until cheese melts, about 5 minutes.

For each sandwich, arrange 2 tomato slices on top of each of 4 eggplant slices. Add greens and top with remaining eggplant slices. Serves 4.

Eggplant is very low in calories but the texture soaks up fat like a sponge. To reduce fat, limit oil for sautéing to 1/2 cup. Substitute 2 eggs and 4 egg whites for 4 whole eggs and reduce Mozzarella to 4 ounces.

San Leonino Chianti Classico (Italy); Silverado Sangiovese or Ferrari Carano Sienna.

OLIVE CRUSTED NEW YORK STRIP STEAK WITH ARUGULA *and Roasted New Potatoes*
GRILLED CHICKEN *with Carrot-Cranberry Chutney*
FRITTATA WITH SWEET ONION, SMOKED BACON & FONTINA
APPLE BREAD PUDDING
RASPBERRY CHICKEN SALAD *with Raspberry Vinaigrette*

**P**eople who dine at Riviera Grill come with appetites whet for the latest creations of owner/chef John Sheely. Will it be pepper-dusted Chilean Sea Bass with Sun-dried Tomato Polenta and exotic mushrooms? Herb Crusted Rack of Colorado Lamb with Caponata, Goat Cheese and Baby Spinach? Mashies (mashed potatoes) done with a Cabernet wine reduction that gives them a purplish blush and intriguing what-is-it flavor?

Many loyal customers can't get past ordering the old favorites that established Sheely as a formidable talent when he opened Riviera Grill in 1995. He is known for shrimp wrapped in a crisp shell of kataifi (finely shredded filo dough that resembles shredded wheat), Crispy Potato and Goat Cheese Tart with field greens, and grilled sushi-quality tuna with balsamic vinegar glaze. Some fans could make a meal just on the focaccia dipped in olive oil and shaved Parmesan that is served complimentary as a starter.

## RIVIERA
## GRILL

Devotees will tell you that Sheely's Warm Bittersweet Chocolate Torte would deserve investiture in the Chocolate Hall of Fame if there were such a place. And there are those who dream about the trio of mini crème brûlées.

Since moving to the Radisson Suite Hotel in 1996, Riviera Grill has shifted focus from southern France to the whole Mediterranean. Sheely continues to experiment with new combinations of ingredients – fresh herbs, organic vegetables, olives, capers, figs, vinegars, chutneys, applewood smoked bacon, sun-dried tomatoes, roasted tomatoes and a worldly assortment of cheeses.

He sees some trends developing. Customers are eating more beef (he uses Certified Angus) but also are showing more interest in fish and fresh vegetables, especially root vegetables such as beets, turnips and carrots. He buys miniature Japanese eggplant, heirloom potatoes, baby cipollini onions and other organic specialty vegetables and herbs from local growers and regularly features vegetarian or vegetable entrées on the menu, such as a best-selling Grilled Vegetable Plate with Polenta.

The self-taught chef's formula for success is based on great beginnings – he dry-ages the beef, dries tomatoes, cures salmon and makes his own stocks and sauces. A native Houstonian, he moved to Vail, Colorado after he graduated from Westchester High School because he loved to ski. He lived there 18 years while refining his kitchen skills and eventually owned a small restaurant, L'Ostello. He married while there, and he and his wife Alicia have two daughters, Delilah and Lisa. They returned to Houston in 1995. Moving Riviera Grill to the Radisson has taken him back to his old west Houston neighborhood, he says. He is responsible for all the food, room service and catering for the 173-room hotel as well as private parties, and Alicia, Delilah and Lisa are part of the operation.

*LITE FARE*

Look for interesting vegetables and grains on the Riviera Grill menu – grilled squash and asparagus, roasted tomatoes, mashies and sun-dried tomato polenta. Almost every entrée features a sample of unique carbohydrates. An off-the-menu special is a Vegetarian Tasting of select items. Special requests for dietary or religious needs are encouraged and will be honored.

*Riviera Grill*
*Radisson Suite Hotel*
*10655 Katy Fwy. at*
*Beltway 8*
*Houston, Tx 77024*
*713-974-4445*

# OLIVE CRUSTED NEW YORK STRIP STEAK WITH ARUGULA

Roasted New Potatoes (recipe follows)
2 cups pitted kalamata olives
4 (12-ounce) New York strip steaks (preferably Certified Angus)
   Kosher salt and freshly ground black pepper to taste
2 tablespoons extra-virgin olive oil
1/4 pound arugula
1/4 cup balsamic vinegar

## ROASTED NEW POTATOES

2 pounds small new potatoes
1 garlic clove, minced
2 tablespoons extra-virgin olive oil
1 tablespoon coarsely chopped rosemary
1 tablespoon coarsely chopped thyme
   Kosher salt and freshly ground black pepper to taste
1 tablespoon unsalted butter (optional)

Preheat oven to 400 degrees. Prepare potatoes. Puree olives in food processor or blender; set aside. Season steaks with salt and pepper. Heat oil in ovenproof skillet over high heat. Sear steaks 2 to 4 minutes on each side for medium rare. Turn steaks over and top with olives, pressing olives down with back of spoon. Place skillet on middle rack in oven and cook 5 to 7 minutes for rare to medium rare. Transfer steaks to cutting board and let rest 4 minutes.

Arrange arugula leaves on platter. Cut steaks diagonally into thin slices and arrange on arugula; drizzle with vinegar. Accompany with roasted potatoes, asparagus, small carrots and spinach. Serves 4.

**Roasted New Potatoes**

Preheat oven to 400 degrees. Combine potatoes with garlic, oil, rosemary and thyme in a large bowl; add salt and pepper. Transfer to a roasting pan; roast 45 minutes, or until golden brown and cooked through. Remove from oven and add butter. Serve immediately. Serves 4.

Because the current recommendation for meat consumption is 6 ounces per day, this recipe is adequate for 8 servings. To reduce fat content, decrease olives to 1 cup and oil to 1 tablespoon to sear the steak and 1 tablespoon for potatoes.

San Felice Chianti Classico (Italy); Stag's Leap Winery Petite Sirah.

# GRILLED CHICKEN *with Carrot-Cranberry Chutney*

Carrot-Cranberry Chutney (recipe follows)
4 (4- to 6-ounce) boneless, skinless chicken breast halves, grilled

## CARROT-CRANBERRY CHUTNEY

1 quart water
3 cups dried cranberries
2 cups peeled, diced carrots
2 cups diced celery
1/2 cup diced white onion
3/4 cup sugar
2 tablespoons sherry vinegar
1/4 teaspoon ground nutmeg
1/4 teaspoon ground cinnamon
1 cup chicken stock
1 tablespoon unsalted butter

Prepare chutney; refrigerate until needed. Heat as directed. Slice chicken diagonally and fan out over plate. Spoon chutney over top. Serves 4.

**Carrot-Cranberry Chutney**

Combine water, cranberries, carrots, celery, onion, sugar, vinegar, nutmeg and cinnamon in stainless steel or other non-reactive medium saucepan over high heat. Bring to a boil; stir. Reduce heat; simmer uncovered 30 minutes, or until vegetables are soft and liquid is reduced by three-fourths. Cover and chill. When ready to use, add stock and butter to chutney in small saucepan; heat through. Makes about 1 quart. *Note:* Chutney also can be used on turkey and Fontina cheese sandwich on herb focaccia or focaccia with herb mayonnaise.

Research confirms that cranberries help prevent bladder infections. Combined with the high vitamin A content of carrots, this recipe is tasty and healthful. Enjoy!

Joseph Phelps or Alderbrook Gewürztraminer (white); Kings Estate or Panther Creek Pinot Noir (red – Oregon).

# Frittata with Sweet Onion, Smoked Bacon & Fontina

| | |
|---|---|
| 4 | slices apple-smoked bacon, diced |
| 1 | large sweet onion, sliced |
| 1 | teaspoon minced garlic |
| 2 | teaspoons basil chiffonade (see Special Helps section) |
| | Kosher salt and freshly ground black pepper to taste |
| 2 | Roma tomatoes, peeled, seeded and coarsely chopped |
| 2 | tablespoons balsamic vinegar |
| 10 | eggs |
| 3 | tablespoons shredded Fontina cheese |
| 2 | tablespoons minced fresh parsley |
| 1 | teaspoon extra-virgin olive oil |

Cook bacon in a large skillet until fat is rendered; reserve bacon. Over medium heat, add onion to 3 tablespoons of bacon fat. Add garlic, basil, salt and pepper. Cook over medium heat 15 minutes, or until onion is tender and brown. Add tomatoes and vinegar; remove from heat.

In a large bowl, beat eggs until frothy. Add bacon, onion mixture, Fontina and parsley. Heat oil in nonstick skillet over high heat. While stirring, pour egg mixture into skillet. Stir with a wooden spoon until eggs begin to form small curds. Continue stirring until eggs are firm and set. If desired, flip frittata over and cook 2 minutes or put into preheated 350-degree oven to finish, about 2 minutes. Transfer frittata to large dinner plate and cut into wedges. Serve hot or at room temperature. Serves 4 to 6.

To lower cholesterol and reduce fat, substitute lean turkey bacon for regular and fat-free egg substitute for eggs.

Tavel Rose (France); Caymus Conundrum.

# Apple Bread Pudding

| | |
|---|---|
| 6 | medium-size Granny Smith apples |
| 4 | tablespoons unsalted butter, divided |
| 1 | tablespoon sugar |
| 2 | vanilla beans, split lengthwise, divided |
| 1 | loaf Texas Toast, crust removed |
| 2 1/2 | cups whipping cream |
| 2 | cinnamon sticks |
| 1 | scant teaspoon ground nutmeg |
| 5 | egg yolks |
| 2 | eggs |
| 3/4 | cup sugar |
| | Fresh berries and mint sprigs for garnish (optional) |
| | Caramel sauce (optional) |

Peel, core and julienne apples. Melt 2 tablespoons butter in a large skillet. Add apples, 1 tablespoon sugar and 1 vanilla bean. Sauté over medium heat until apples are caramelized; remove vanilla bean. Cool. Preheat oven to 350 degrees. Cut bread into 1-inch squares; place on cookie sheet and toast 4 to 5 minutes.

For custard: Scald cream with remaining vanilla bean, cinnamon sticks and nutmeg in a medium saucepan. Let steep 20 minutes; strain and discard vanilla bean and cinnamon sticks. In large bowl, whisk together egg yolks, eggs and 3/4 cup sugar until dissolved. Blend a small amount of egg mixture into scalded cream; slowly add cream to egg mixture. Add apples and toast to custard mixture; soak 30 minutes.

Coat a 10-inch springform pan with remaining 2 tablespoons butter; cover outside of pan (but not top) with aluminum foil to prevent leaking. Spoon mixture into prepared pan and place in larger pan. Pour very hot water in larger pan, halfway up the side of the springform pan. Bake 35 to 45 minutes, or until golden brown. Remove from water bath and let cool to room temperature, about 30 minutes. Remove springform ring and slice. Serve warm with vanilla ice cream. Refrigerate leftovers and rewarm in the microwave about 1 1/2 minutes per serving or in a 350-degree oven 10 minutes. Serves 8 to 12.

Serving suggestion: Arrange berries to the side of bread pudding; garnish with mint and drizzle prepared caramel sauce over top.

Divide this dessert into 12 servings before indulging.

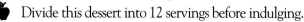 Cinzano Asti Spumanti (Italy); Blandy's Boal Madeira (Portugal).

# RASPBERRY CHICKEN SALAD *with Raspberry Vinaigrette*

Raspberry Vinaigrette (recipe follows)
6 to 8    cups mesclun mix greens
2    cups blanched, thin French green beans (haricots vert)
1    cup finely diced tomatoes, divided
   Salt and freshly ground black pepper to taste
2    slices crisp-cooked, julienned smoked bacon
3    tablespoons shredded Parmigiano-Reggiano cheese
12    leaves Belgian endive (optional)
2    cups fresh raspberries
6    (4-ounce) boneless, skinless chicken breast halves, seasoned and grilled
6    radicchio leaves, cup shaped (optional)

## RASPBERRY VINAIGRETTE

3    tablespoons raspberry vinegar
1    tablespoon Dijon mustard
1    teaspoon minced garlic
1    teaspoon minced shallot
1    teaspoon sugar
1    teaspoon pureed raspberries
1/3    cup extra-virgin olive oil
   Kosher salt and freshly ground black pepper to taste

**P**repare Raspberry Vinaigrette. Combine mesclun, green beans and 1/2 cup tomatoes in a medium bowl; drizzle vinaigrette over top and toss until well coated. Add salt, pepper, bacon and Parmesan; mix well. Divide among 6 plates and garnish with endive, remaining 1/2 cup tomatoes and raspberries. Slice each chicken breast into 3 pieces diagonally and arrange to the side of salad. If desired, mound salad in radicchio cup. Serve immediately. Serves 6.

*Note:* At Riviera Grill, uncooked chicken breast halves are covered with a mixture of extra-virgin olive oil, whole garlic cloves, chopped shallots, basil, oregano and thyme and stored in a covered container in the refrigerator until ready to use.

**Raspberry Vinaigrette**
Combine vinegar, mustard, garlic, shallot, sugar and raspberry puree in a medium bowl. Gradually whisk in oil; add salt and pepper. Makes about 1/2 cup.

 This recipe is loaded with vitamins A and C. To reduce fat, eliminate bacon and prepare vinaigrette with 1/3 cup vinegar and 3 tablespoons oil.

 Adler Fels Gewürztraminer (white); Sanford or Saintsbury Pinot Noir (red).

FACING PAGE, FROM LEFT: *Alicia and John Sheely, Riviera Grill at Radisson Suite; Kathi and Tony Ruppe, Tony Ruppe's.*

FOLLOWING PAGE, FROM LEFT: *Rosalinda Soto, Pierre Gutknecht, Rivoli.*

CHICKEN SALAD MONTE CRISTO
VEAL CUTLET VIENNA STYLE (WIENERSCHNITZEL)
SOUTHERN CORN CHOWDER
CRABMEAT FLORENTINE *with Cream Sauce*
GULF RED SNAPPER FILLET MEUNIÈRE
RASPBERRY SOUFFLÉ *with Raspberry Sauce*

If the Rivoli customers have anything to do with it – and they will – the millennium will bring no startling changes. They will still demand Dover Sole – the real thing from the English Channel – Calf Liver Veronique, Wienerschnitzel, lobster and a full spectrum of dessert soufflés.

The Rivoli is one of Houston's favorite champagne occasion restaurants. For more than 23 years, Houstonians and their guests have come to celebrate birthdays, engagements, anniversaries, graduations, retirements and life's successes under the crystal chandeliers or the striped canopy of the Garden Room. If there is room in the elegant Piano Bar, which has live music nightly, so much the better. The restaurant is now open for many holidays, too. With a foundation of Continental cuisine, the Rivoli menu includes French, German and Italian classics with a smattering of international specialties, such as gravlax, and Cajun as well as an excellent wine list. A collection of fine Cognacs is displayed with Baccarat crystal decanters. Executive chef Pierre Gutknecht, who grew up in Switzerland and is well grounded in French cooking, specializes in the classics, but keeps an open mind on new styles. He has updated the menu with grilled fresh tuna and swordfish, risottos and seasonal specialties such as softshell crab.

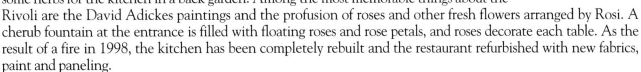

In anticipation of the new millennium, the Rivoli has become more casual, especially at lunch: White linens have given way to colors and waiters have replaced their tuxedo jackets with vests. A fixed-price daily lunch pairs soup and an entrée of the day. Gutknecht is happy to honor special requests, provide vegetarian entrées or prepare cherished dishes that are no longer on the menu, such as Snapper Zielinsky. "We can cook anything here," he says. Co-owners, sisters Rosalinda Soto and Rosi Cantu, say the emphasis is on freshness and quality, polished service and appealing ambiance. Their mother, Emma Ocanas, grows some herbs for the kitchen in a back garden. Among the most memorable things about the Rivoli are the David Adickes paintings and the profusion of roses and other fresh flowers arranged by Rosi. A cherub fountain at the entrance is filled with floating roses and rose petals, and roses decorate each table. As the result of a fire in 1998, the kitchen has been completely rebuilt and the restaurant refurbished with new fabrics, paint and paneling.

Even though customers are devoted to the Continental classics, they are more adventurous now, says Gutknecht. And he's a bit adventurous, too. He used to spend hours in the library every Sunday reading cookbooks and the latest cuisine magazines. Now he just enters the culinary wonderland of the Internet. The Rivoli even has its own web site: http://www.therivoli.com.

---

### LITE FARE

The Rivoli menu provides the basics for healthful dining – lean meats, fish and poultry accompanied with fresh vegetables. For vegetarians a steamed vegetable platter is an off-the-menu option. Chef Pierre personalizes food preparation to the tastes and dietary needs of his customers. Special requests are expected and honored. Just ask and your special dietary need will be filled.

*Rivoli*
*5636 Richmond Ave.*
*Houston, Tx 77057*
*713-789-1900*

# CHICKEN SALAD MONTE CRISTO

| | |
|---|---|
| 1 | (3-pound) fryer |
| | Water |
| 1 | onion, cut in chunks |
| 1/2 | cup celery leaves |
| 1 to 2 | bay leaves |
| | Salt and freshly ground black pepper to taste |
| 2 | slices pineapple, diced |
| 1 | golden Delicious apple, peeled, cored and diced |
| 1 | rib celery, finely diced |
| 1 | cup mayonnaise |
| 1/2 | cup whipping cream, whipped |
| | Juice of 1 lemon |
| | Lettuce leaves |
| | Assorted fruit slices such as cantaloupe, kiwi, strawberries, grapes, orange and papaya |

Cook chicken in water to cover in large stockpot with onion, celery leaves, bay leaves, salt and pepper (see Special Helps section – making stock). Let chicken cool; remove skin, debone and dice.

Toss chicken with pineapple, apple and celery. In a small bowl, combine mayonnaise, whipped cream, lemon juice, salt and pepper. Stir into chicken mixture and adjust seasoning. Chill at least 1 hour before serving. Serve on a bed of lettuce and garnish with fruit slices. Makes 4 to 6 servings.

🍎 Pineapple adds a burst of vitamin C to this delicious chicken salad. For low-fat preparation, substitute fat-free mayonnaise for regular and half-and-half for cream.

🍇 Pine Ridge Chenin Blanc Viognier; Graacher Himmelreich Kabinett or Spätlese (Germany).

# VEAL CUTLET VIENNA STYLE (WIENERSCHNITZEL)

| | |
|---|---|
| 4 | veal cutlets (about 2 pounds) |
| | Salt and freshly ground black pepper to taste |
| 1 | cup all-purpose flour |
| 2 | eggs, beaten |
| 2 | cups dry white bread crumbs |
| 1/2 | cup vegetable oil |
| 1/4 | cup unsalted butter, browned |
| | Capers for garnish |
| 4 | anchovy fillets for garnish |
| 4 | slices lemon for garnish |

Pound veal thin between two pieces of heavy plastic wrap with a meat hammer. Season veal with salt and pepper, dip in flour and shake off excess. Dip floured cutlets into egg, coating both sides. Press veal pieces into a bowl of bread crumbs; coat both sides.

Heat oil in a large skillet; sauté veal until golden brown on both sides. Transfer to a large platter and drizzle with brown butter. Place capers in anchovy fillet, roll and place on top of lemon slices for garnish. Wienerschnitzel is usually accompanied with German fries and a vegetable. Serves 4.

🍎 This recipe is adequate for 8 servings. To reduce fat, decrease oil to 1/4 cup for sautéing and eliminate butter for drizzling.

🍇 Kunstler Riesling Halbtrocken (white – Germany); Chateau de Jacques Moulin-a-Vent Jadot (red – France); Newton Special Cuvée Merlot (red).

# SOUTHERN CORN CHOWDER

| | |
|---|---|
| 2 | cups fresh corn kernels (3 ears), divided |
| 2 | cups chicken broth, divided |
| 1/4 | cup unsalted butter |
| 1/2 | onion, chopped |
| 2/3 | cup diced cooked ham |
| 1 | rib celery, diced |
| 1 | tablespoon all-purpose flour |
| 1 | Idaho potato, peeled and diced |
| 1 | small red bell pepper, roasted, peeled and diced |
| 1/2 | cup whipping cream |
| | Salt and freshly ground black pepper to taste |

Puree 1 cup corn with a little broth; set aside. Melt butter in a saucepan over medium heat. Add onion, ham and celery; cook until onions are translucent. Blend in flour. Add remaining broth, whisk well and bring to a simmer. Add pureed corn, remaining 1 cup kernels and potato; simmer 15 minutes, or until potatoes are tender. Add roasted pepper and cream, bring to a boil and season with salt and pepper. Serves 4 to 6.

🍎 Corn is a good source of folate, which is important during pregnancy. For low-fat preparation, limit butter to 2 tablespoons for sautéing and substitute evaporated skim milk for cream.

🍇 Bouchaine Gewürztraminer; Dopff or Josmeyer Gewürztraminer Vendange Tardive (France).

# CRABMEAT FLORENTINE *with Cream Sauce*

| | |
|---|---|
| 1 | cup Cream Sauce (recipe follows) |
| 6 | tablespoons unsalted butter, divided |
| 2 | shallots, chopped and divided |
| 1 | small garlic clove, chopped |
| 2 | (12-ounce) bunches spinach, stemmed and blanched |
| | Salt and freshly ground black pepper to taste |
| 4 | medium mushrooms, sliced |
| 2 | artichoke bottoms, sliced |
| 12 | ounces jumbo lump crabmeat, cleaned and picked over |
| 2 | tablespoons dry white wine |
| 2 | tablespoons whipping cream |
| | Lemon juice to taste |
| 1/4 | cup toasted pine nuts (pignola) |

### CREAM SAUCE

| | |
|---|---|
| 1 | tablespoon softened butter |
| 1 | tablespoon all-purpose flour |
| 1 | cup milk |
| | Salt and freshly ground black pepper to taste |

Prepare Cream Sauce; set aside and keep warm. Melt 2 tablespoons butter in medium skillet. Add 1 shallot and garlic; cover and cook until their moisture is released. Add spinach, salt and pepper; heat until wilted. Place spinach in mound in center of each of 4 warm plates.

Heat remaining 4 tablespoons butter in same skillet; sauté mushrooms and remaining shallot. Add artichokes and crabmeat; deglaze with wine. Add Cream Sauce and cream; warm but do not boil. Season with salt, pepper and lemon juice. Spoon over spinach and garnish with pine nuts. Serves 4.

### Cream Sauce

Mix butter and flour (beurre manié) in a small custard cup. Heat milk to a boil in a small saucepan; whisk beurre manié into milk. Simmer about 5 minutes, whisking as needed, until thickened. Season with salt and pepper. Makes about 1 cup.

🍎 Spinach is a rich source of vitamin A and folate and a good source of vitamin C and potassium. For low-fat preparation, eliminate butter and use nonstick cooking spray. Reduce pine nuts to 2 tablespoons.

🍇 Kunde Sauvignon Blanc; Jolivette Sancerre or Sauvion Pouilly-Fumé (France).

# GULF RED SNAPPER FILLET MEUNIÈRE

| | |
|---|---|
| 4 | (6- to 8-ounce) snapper fillets |
| | Salt and freshly ground black pepper to taste |
| | All-purpose flour |
| 1/4 | cup vegetable oil |
| 1/2 | cup unsalted butter, divided |
| | Juice of 1 lemon |
| 4 | dashes Worcestershire sauce |
| | Chopped fresh parsley for garnish |
| 1 | lemon, sliced and dusted with paprika for garnish |

Season fillets with salt and pepper; dust with flour. Heat oil in medium skillet; sauté fillets until half done. Add 2 tablespoons butter, turn over and fry to a golden brown. Remove to a platter; keep warm. Brown remaining 6 tablespoons butter in same skillet. Add lemon juice and Worcestershire and pour over fillets. Sprinkle with parsley and garnish with lemon slices. Accompany with boiled potatoes and a green vegetable. Serves 4.

Fish is always a Heart Healthy choice. For low-fat preparation, eliminate oil and use 2 tablespoons butter for sautéing. Eliminate butter in the sauce.

Lindeman's Bin 65 Chardonnay (Australia) or Hess Select Chardonnay; Saintsbury or Markham Chardonnay; Robert Mondavi Reserve or Far Niente Chardonnay.

# RASPBERRY SOUFFLÉ *with Raspberry Sauce*

| | |
|---|---|
| | Butter and sugar to prepare soufflé dishes |
| 6 | eggs, separated |
| 3/4 | cup sugar |
| 3/4 | cup all-purpose flour |
| 1 1/4 | cups milk |
| 1/2 | teaspoon vanilla extract |
| 3 | tablespoons raspberry liqueur |
| 1/2 | pint fresh raspberries, crushed |
| | Raspberry Sauce (recipe follows) |
| | Fresh raspberries for garnish |

**RASPBERRY SAUCE**

| | |
|---|---|
| 1 | cup whipping cream (chill cream, bowl and beaters well) |
| 1/4 | cup raspberry liqueur |
| 2 | teaspoons sugar |

Preheat oven to 400 degrees. Butter 4 (5-inch) soufflé dishes; lightly dust with sugar and set aside. Mix egg yolks with sugar and flour in a medium bowl. Bring milk to a boil in a saucepan; reduce heat to medium. Add a small amount of milk to yolk mixture and return all of yolk mixture to milk, whisking until it is as thick as pastry cream. Stir in vanilla, liqueur and crushed berries.

In a clean electric mixing bowl with clean beaters, beat egg whites until stiff. Fold into soufflé mixture. Divide mixture among soufflé dishes; smoothly round off tops with a spatula. Place dishes a few inches apart on a baking sheet; gently transfer to oven. Bake 12 to 15 minutes; watch carefully and do not let tops burn. Prepare Raspberry Sauce.

Remove baking sheet from oven. Garnish each dish with fresh berries. Make an indentation in top of each soufflé and pour sauce into it, then serve quickly. Makes 4 servings.

**Raspberry Sauce**

Whip cream to soft peaks. Stir in liqueur and sugar.

Satisfy your sweet tooth with a spoonful of this delicious dessert.

Lindeman's Botrytis Semillon (Australia); Freemark Abbey Edelwein (1/2 bottle); Berncasteler Doktor Riesling Beerenauslese (Germany).

SMOKED SALMON TARTARE
FETTUCCINE "FAVORITE"
BREAST OF PHEASANT GRANDMERE
BRAISED RED CABBAGE
STEAK AU POIVRE
KEY LIME CHEESECAKE

Joe Mannke, proprietor and power behind the stove at Rotisserie for Beef and Bird, has a flair for the dramatic. He loves to travel. But when he returns, instead of pasting pictures in an album, he re-creates his impressions in culinary productions. Special dinners are venues for his imagination.

With each trip, he brings back elaborate souvenirs, from new recipes to the china they're served on. Mannke will acknowledge the new millennium with a series of theme dinners tracing the route of Marco Polo. They will incorporate Chinese, Middle Eastern and Indian flavors and wines of the world from the Rotisserie's collection of more than 18,000 bottles. In preparation for the special dinners, Mannke has traveled extensively in the Middle East and China.

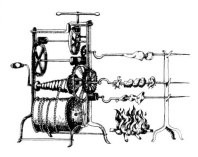

The restaurant, which celebrated its 20th anniversary in 1998, is known for its American cuisine. It has earned accolades from reviewers and the restaurant industry including the Wine Spectator Grand Award for 10 consecutive years, Restaurant and Institutions magazine's Ivy Award and Hall of Fame for Fine Dining. In the past year, the restaurant also received America's Top Table Award from Gourmet magazine and the DiRoNA Award from Distinguished Restaurants of North America.

*Rotisserie for Beef and Bird*

For the millennium, Mannke says they will not forsake recipes that have withstood the test of time. "In fact, we're going back in time for some of our vegetables such as turnips and rutabagas." They have been well received, he says. Mannke flies in lobster and fresh mussels from Maine and fresh salmon from the Northwest and Chile. For a menu original, Cackle Bird, Mannke brings in capons from North Dakota.

A tempting assortment of desserts displayed on a 1930 Majestic cast iron stove near the entry signals diners to save room for home-style desserts – cobblers, bread pudding and fruit tarts, which vary with the seasons. Others can't resist the homemade ice creams, crème brûlée, chocolate mousse or cheesecake.

The Colonial architecture, open-hearth grill and revolving rotisserie in the main dining room underscore the feeling of Colonial tradition that makes the Rotisserie a prime destination for Houstonians at holidays. If it's Thanksgiving, expect an amazing tribute to the season's bounty with the staff costumed as Colonials, Pilgrims and Indians. A commissioned painting by Kenneth Richard Turner, "The First Thanksgiving, 1623 AD" helps set the scene. It depicts some of the Rotisserie's best customers as Pilgrims and Indians. It was joined this summer by another Turner painting portraying the Cherokee Indians' Trail of Tears. The annual Texas Harvest Dinner showcases the state's outstanding foods and wines and other festive vintner dinners present menus and appropriate wines from around the world.

─────────── *LITE FARE* ───────────

Rotisserie for Beef and Bird specializes in fresh, seasonal foods – many of which are native to Texas. Wild game, game birds and fresh seafood are naturally lean and can be grilled with just a touch of olive oil. Grilled vegetables and wild rice make delicious accompaniments to grilled meats. Special requests are welcomed for dietary or religious preferences.

*Rotisserie for Beef
and Bird
2200 Wilcrest
Houston, Tx 77042
713-977-9524*

# SMOKED SALMON TARTARE

| | |
|---|---|
| 6 | crisp Boston lettuce leaves |
| 10 | ounces smoked salmon |
| 3 | tablespoons sour cream |
| 1 | tablespoon fresh lemon juice |
| 3 | tablespoons drained horseradish (fresh preferred) |
| 3 | tablespoons chopped fresh chives |
| 2 | ounces caviar of choice |
| 2 | hard-cooked eggs, cut into wedges |
| 6 | black olives |
| 1 | vine-ripe tomato, cut into 6 wedges |
| 6 | sprigs fresh dill |
| 12 | whole-grain toast wedges or hot Melba toast |

Place lettuce leaves on 6 chilled plates. Grind salmon through a meat grinder and mound on lettuce in equal portions. Combine sour cream, lemon juice, horseradish and chives in a small bowl; spoon over salmon tartare. Top each with a spoonful of caviar. Garnish with egg, olive, tomato and dill. Accompany with toast wedges. Serves 6.

Enjoy the health benefits of this recipe. Salmon is rich in omega-3 oils although high in total fat. Sodium is high because of the smoked salmon. Balance with low-sodium garnishes such as fresh vegetables and fruits.

Gloria Ferrer Sparkling Wine; Jordan "J" Sparkling Wine or Taittinger La Française Brut (France); Pommery Cuvée Louise or Krug Rose (France).

# FETTUCCINE "FAVORITE"

| | |
|---|---|
| 1 | pound dry fettuccine |
| 3 | tablespoons unsalted butter |
| 1/2 | cup minced shallots |
| 1 | cup dry white wine |
| 1/2 | cup chicken broth |
| 3/4 | pound exotic mushrooms (morels or porcini), sliced |
| 3/4 | cup diced red bell pepper |
| 8 | ounces goat cheese (such as Mozzarella Factory) |
| 1 | cup whipping cream |
| 1 | pound fresh asparagus, peeled and trimmed, cut into 1/2-inch pieces |
| | Salt and freshly ground black pepper to taste |
| 1/2 | cup finely cut chives |

Cook pasta in a stockpot of boiling salted water until al dente. Drain and keep warm. Melt butter in a large heavy skillet over low heat and cook shallots until glazed but not brown. Add wine; simmer mixture until wine is reduced by half. Add broth, mushrooms and pepper; cover skillet and simmer until mushrooms are tender. Add cheese and cream; whisk over low heat until cheese is melted. Blanch asparagus in boiling salted water 2 minutes; drain. Stir asparagus into sauce; add salt and pepper. Add pasta; toss. Serve on heated plates and sprinkle with chives. Serves 4.

Decrease fat by using low-fat, low-sodium chicken broth, reducing cheese to 4 ounces and substituting half-and-half for cream.

Benziger Fume Blanc; Duckhorn Sauvignon Blanc (white) or Melini Chianti Classico Selvanella (red – Italy).

# BREAST OF PHEASANT GRANDMERE

2 (3-pound) pheasants
1 teaspoon salt
  Dash of freshly ground black pepper
1 teaspoon chopped fresh rosemary
1/2 cup all-purpose flour
1/2 cup unsalted butter
8 slices lean bacon, coarsely cut
12 large mushrooms, quartered
1/4 cup brandy
1 cup dry white wine
2 medium potatoes, cooked, cooled and diced into 1/8-inch cubes
1/2 cup pearl onions, cooked
1 tablespoon chopped parsley

Remove breasts from pheasants by cutting with a sharp knife along breastbone to wing bone; save remainder for another use. Sprinkle breasts with salt, pepper and rosemary; dust lightly with flour. Melt butter in a heavy skillet; sauté breasts 10 minutes over low heat until golden brown. Remove breasts and place in a heatproof shallow oval baking dish.

Preheat oven to 325 degrees. Add bacon and mushrooms to same skillet and sauté a few minutes longer, until bacon is cooked but not crisp. Add brandy; flambé, lighting carefully with a taper match. Add wine, potatoes and onions; combine well and spoon over pheasants. Bake 10 minutes and sprinkle with parsley. Serves 4.

🍎 Be sure to remove skin from pheasant breast and reduce butter to 1/4 cup for sautéing. Eliminate salt and limit bacon to four slices.

🍇 Saintsbury Garnet Pinot Noir; Cuvaison or Domaine Carneros Pinot Noir.

# BRAISED RED CABBAGE

1/4 cup unsalted butter
1/2 onion, sliced
3 pounds red cabbage, sliced
1 Granny Smith apple, cored, peeled and chopped
2 slices bacon, diced
1 cup cranberry juice
1/4 cup red wine
1/4 cup red wine vinegar
1/4 cup sugar
1 stick cinnamon
4 whole cloves
2 bay leaves
3 juniper berries, crushed
  Salt and freshly ground black pepper to taste
1/2 cup peeled and grated raw potato

Melt butter in a large heavy skillet; add onion and sauté a few minutes. Add cabbage, apple, bacon, cranberry juice, wine, vinegar, sugar, cinnamon, cloves, bay leaves, juniper berries, salt and pepper. Cover and braise mixture over low heat until cabbage is tender, about 30 to 45 minutes. Stir occasionally and check to make sure liquid does not completely evaporate. Remove cinnamon stick, cloves and bay leaves. Adjust seasoning with salt and pepper; add potato. Cook until thickened, about 15 minutes, stirring occasionally. Serves 10.

 Cabbage is a cruciferous vegetable long known to fight cancer. To keep fat content low, reduce butter for sautéing to 2 tablespoons.

# STEAK AU POIVRE

| | |
|---|---|
| 3 | tablespoons black peppercorns |
| 4 | (8- to 10-ounce) sirloin steaks |
| 1 | teaspoon salt |
| 2 | tablespoons vegetable oil |
| 4 | bay leaves |
| 6 | tablespoons brandy |
| 1/4 | cup beef gravy (or canned mushroom soup) |
| 1/2 | teaspoon prepared mustard |
| 1/2 | teaspoon Worcestershire sauce Watercress (optional) |

Crush peppercorns into tiny bits with a rolling pin or a mallet. Sprinkle steaks with salt and press peppercorns into meat on each side until well covered.

Heat oil in a large skillet; sauté steaks 2 minutes each side. Remove steaks to platter and keep warm. Add bay leaves and brandy to pan. Flambé, lighting carefully with a taper match. Add gravy, mustard and Worcestershire; stir and bring to a boil. Place steaks on heated dinner plates, discard bay leaves and ladle sauce over meat. Garnish with watercress; serve immediately. Serves 4.

Follow American Heart Guidelines for meat and limit steak to 6 ounces per person. Sauté steaks in a nonstick skillet covered with nonstick cooking spray. Eliminate added salt.

Concannon Petite Sirah; Ridge York Creek Petite Sirah.

# KEY LIME CHEESECAKE

| | |
|---|---|
| 1 1/2 | cups fine graham cracker crumbs |
| 1/2 | cup packed brown sugar |
| 1/4 | cup unsalted butter, melted |
| 2 1/2 | (8-ounce) packages cream cheese softened |
| 1 | cup granulated sugar |
| 3 | tablespoons all-purpose flour |
| 1 | cup sour cream |
| 3 | large eggs, divided |
| 3/4 | cup fresh lime juice |
| 1 | teaspoon vanilla extract |
| 1 | drop green food coloring (optional) |
| 1 | cup whipped cream |
| 2 | limes, sliced |
| 8 | fresh ripe strawberries, cut in half Fresh mint sprigs |

Preheat oven to 375 degrees. Combine crumbs, brown sugar and butter thoroughly. Pat mixture evenly onto bottom only of a 10-inch springform pan; bake 10 minutes.

In bowl of electric mixer, beat cream cheese with granulated sugar until smooth. Beat in flour and sour cream, then eggs, one at a time. Add lime juice, vanilla and food coloring; combine well. Pour filling over prepared crust. Bake cheesecake on middle rack of oven 20 minutes; reduce temperature to 275 degrees and continue to bake 50 minutes, or until cake tester inserted in center comes out clean. Let cheesecake cool about 30 minutes, cover and refrigerate overnight.

Remove cake from springform pan and transfer to a serving plate. Garnish with whipped cream and lime slices. Cut into wedges, place on individual dessert plates and garnish each with a strawberry half and fresh mint. Serves 16.

Splurge on a sliver.

Penfolds Club Port (Australia); Taylor or Fonseca 10-year-old Tawny Port (Portugal).

FACING PAGE: *Joe Mannke, Rotisserie for Beef and Bird.*

FOLLOWING PAGE: *Susan and Bruce Molzan, Ruggles and Grille 5115.*

MARINATED SEARED OR GRILLED TUNA *with Charred Fruit Salsa*
PLANTAIN CRUSTED PORK LOIN
BLACK BEAN SOUP
ORANGE PAPAYA MOJO
REESE'S PEANUT BUTTER CUP CHEESECAKE *in Chocolate Crust*

The future will move to a Latin beat, says award-winning chef Bruce Molzan, who has a knack for antici-pating trends and designing standing-room-only restaurants. The chef/co-owner of Ruggles Grill and Ruggles Grille 5115 at Saks Fifth Avenue is adding several new eateries to his restaurant family – Ruggles Cafe & Bakery near Rice University; Ruggles at the Ball Park at Enron Field and Ruggles at the nearby Union Station, both to open in 2000, and Ruggles Bistro Latino downtown. If you are going to Ruggles-hop, here's what you can expect:

At the original Ruggles Grill and Ruggles Grille 5115 at Saks Fifth Avenue, you'll find the specialties that made the restaurant famous. They include Snapper Meunière; Grilled Chicken Salad with Apples, Walnuts, Roquefort and Honey-Dijon Vinaigrette; Snapper and Crab Chowder; Spring Rolls of Smoked Chicken and Ginger with Peanut Dipping Sauce; Crab Cakes and grilled steaks. Ruggles Cafe & Bakery offers a light menu of soups, salads and sandwiches plus signature desserts such as White Chocolate Bread Pudding, Chocolate Crème Brûlée Cheesecake and Domino Cake (chocolate cake with alternate layers of white and dark chocolate mousse). A wide selection of coffees and teas help create a convivial coffeehouse atmos-phere for friends to meet for a casual lunch, dinner before an event or late-evening dessert and coffee. The newest facility at the ball park will give Astro fans a full-service restaurant setting with an expanded Ruggles menu.

Molzan says Latin music, food and culture will be a meshing of Caribbean, Latin and Asian, and he has already set the Latin theme in motion at Club Flamingo across the driveway from Ruggles Grill. The club has two personalities – at lunch it's an extension of the restaurant. Late evenings, it fills up with a party-loving crowd who appreciates food, fun and dancing to Latin salsa music in a sophisticated setting.

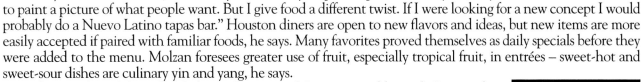

The Ruggles Grill menu has evolved over 13 years. Certain favorites will always remain by customer demand, Molzan says. "I don't try 'to paint a picture' for myself; I try to paint a picture of what people want. But I give food a different twist. If I were looking for a new concept I would probably do a Nuevo Latino tapas bar." Houston diners are open to new flavors and ideas, but new items are more easily accepted if paired with familiar foods, he says. Many favorites proved themselves as daily specials before they were added to the menu. Molzan foresees greater use of fruit, especially tropical fruit, in entrées – sweet-hot and sweet-sour dishes are culinary yin and yang, he says.

Molzan graduated from the Culinary Institute of America, and his wife Susan, who is responsible for Ruggles' desserts, attended C.I.A. Bruce trained briefly with Wolfgang Puck in California. His experiences there inspired Molzan to develop his own regional style and seasonal menus using fresh local ingredients.

*Ruggles Grill*
*903 Westheimer*
*Houston Tx 77006*
*713-524-3839*

*Ruggles Grille 5115*
*at Saks Fifth Avenue*
*5115 Westheimer*
*Houston Tx 77056*
*713-963-8067*

────────── *LITE FARE* ──────────

Both Ruggles and Grille 5115 feature off-the-menu Spa Specials that usually include grilled or steamed fish and vegetables with a fruit salsa. Good choices at Grille 5115 are Tortellini Minestrone, Wild Mushroom Angel Hair Pasta with Grilled Portobello Mushrooms & Vegetables in a Fresh Tomato Basil Sauce or Seasonal Vegetable Pizza. Ruggles offers a Seasonal Vegetable Plate and a 97% Lean Buffalo Burger with Lowfat Cheese. Special requests are encouraged.

# MARINATED SEARED OR GRILLED TUNA *with Charred Fruit Salsa*

2 cups Charred Fruit Salsa
(recipe follows)
1/4 cup extra-virgin olive oil
1/4 cup rum
1/4 cup soy sauce
1/4 cup chopped cilantro leaves
1 teaspoon vanilla extract
1/2 teaspoon ground cinnamon
Salt and freshly ground black
pepper to taste
6 (6- to 8-ounce) tuna steaks

## CHARRED FRUIT SALSA

3 tablespoons extra-virgin olive
oil
1 mango, seeded and peeled
1 small papaya, seeded and peeled
1/2 pineapple, cored and peeled
1 cup cooked black beans
3 tablespoons chopped cilantro
leaves
1/4 cup diced red onion
2 jalapeños, seeded and diced
Juice of 2 lemons
Juice of 2 limes
Juice of 3 oranges

Prepare salsa; reserve. Combine oil, rum, soy sauce, cilantro, vanilla, cinnamon, salt and pepper in a blender or food processor; puree until smooth. Marinate tuna in mixture in large bowl 15 minutes each side. Sear or grill tuna until medium rare, about 1 to 2 minutes each side. Serve immediately topped with fruit salsa. Serves 6.

**Charred Fruit Salsa**

Heat oil in large skillet until very hot. Add mango, papaya and pineapple to skillet; char. Cool fruit on rack; cut into 1/4-inch dice. Place in medium bowl; add beans, cilantro, onion, jalapeños, lemon juice, lime juice and orange juice. Cover and refrigerate at least 1 hour. Makes about 4 cups. Keeps up to 1 week in refrigerator.

What a healthy and delicious combination – tuna and fruit salsa. To decrease fat, reduce oil in salsa and marinade to 2 tablespoons each. Choose 6-ounce tuna steaks and low-sodium soy sauce.

Preston Zinfandel (red); Kent Rasmussen Chardonnay (white).

# PLANTAIN CRUSTED PORK LOIN

1 cup fried plantains
1 cup molasses
1/2 cup Dijon mustard
1/4 cup balsamic vinegar
1 tablespoon ancho chili powder
2 teaspoons ground cumin
1 cup achiote paste (available at
Latin markets)
3 tablespoons chopped fresh
thyme
4 garlic cloves
1 (1-pound) boneless pork loin
1/2 cup extra-virgin olive oil

Preheat oven to 350 degrees. Place plantains in food processor with steel blade; process for 1 minute. Remove and set aside. Place molasses, mustard, vinegar, chili powder, cumin, achiote paste, thyme and garlic in food processor; process until smooth. Rub pork loin with some of molasses mixture; let sit a few minutes to absorb. Repeat procedure twice; then coat with crushed plantains. Heat oil in roasting pan on top of stove; sear pork loin until brown on all sides. Roast uncovered in oven until internal temperature reaches 160 degrees for well done, about 18 to 25 minutes. Slice into 8 medallions. Serves 4.

Pork loin is a lean meat but this crust is high in fat and sodium. Eliminate oil and sauté in a nonstick pan covered with nonstick cooking spray.

Karly Amador Zinfandel (red); Schloss Vollrads Riesling Kabinett or Spätlese (white – Germany).

# BLACK BEAN SOUP

1  cup dried black beans, presoaked (see Note)
9  cups chicken stock, divided
4  slices crisp-cooked bacon, chopped
1  small red onion, diced
1/2  cup chopped cilantro leaves
Salt and freshly ground black pepper to taste
Cilantro sprigs and sour cream for garnish
Tortilla chips (optional)

Combine drained beans and 6 cups stock in a large saucepan. Cover and bring to a boil, reduce heat to low and simmer 45 minutes to 1 hour, or until beans are tender. Add bacon, onion, cilantro, salt and pepper; puree in batches in food processor until smooth. Use extreme care because mixture is hot. To serve: whisk remaining 3 cups stock with soup mixture in saucepan; bring to a boil, reduce heat and simmer 5 minutes. Ladle into bowls and garnish with cilantro sprigs and sour cream. Serve with tortilla chips. Serves 3.

*Note:* To presoak beans, place in saucepan and cover with cold water. Bring to a boil and boil 2 minutes. Remove from heat, cover and soak 1 hour; drain. Or soak overnight in cold water to cover.

Black beans are high in protein and fiber. Accompany soup with fruit high in vitamin C (orange, cantaloupe, strawberries, etc.) to boost iron absorption. For better health benefits, choose a low-sodium, fat-free chicken broth and reduce bacon to 2 slices.

Joseph Phelps Le Mistral; Perrin Châteauneuf-du-Pape (France).

# ORANGE PAPAYA MOJO

2  tablespoons extra-virgin olive oil
1  tablespoon minced garlic
1  small papaya, seeded, peeled and diced
2  oranges, peeled and diced
1  teaspoon sugar
Salt and freshly ground black pepper to taste
1/2  cup chopped fresh mint leaves

Heat oil in medium skillet; sauté garlic and cool. Place garlic, papaya, oranges, sugar, salt, pepper and mint in food processor with steel blade. Puree until smooth. Refrigerate at least 2 hours before serving. Use mojo to top fish, chicken, pork or almost any grilled meat. Makes about 2 cups. Refrigerate covered up to 1 week.

Papaya and oranges are extremely high in vitamin C that builds up your immune system and fights colds. This salsa can accompany meat or fish, dress a salad or be spooned over yogurt or low-fat ice cream. For a better balance of nutrients, reduce oil to 1 tablespoon.

Chateau Reynella Old Cave Port (Australia); Tokaji Aszú 5 Puttonyos Royal Tokaji Wine Company (500 ml – Hungary).

# REESE'S PEANUT BUTTER CUP CHEESECAKE *in Chocolate Crust*

Chocolate Crust (recipe follows)
4 (8-ounce) packages cream cheese, softened
5 eggs, room temperature
1 1/2 cups packed brown sugar
1 cup smooth peanut butter (not natural style)
1/2 cup whipping cream
1 teaspoon vanilla extract
12 Reese's peanut butter cups, broken into small pieces
1/3 cup sour cream
1/2 cup granulated sugar

Preheat oven to 275 degrees. Prepare crust; set aside. Beat cream cheese in bowl of electric mixer until light. Add eggs, one at a time, beating well after each. Add brown sugar, peanut butter and cream; mix until smooth. Blend in vanilla, then fold in peanut butter cup pieces with a rubber spatula. Pour filling into prepared crust. Place springform pan in a larger baking pan. Pour hot water into larger pan to come 1 inch up sides of springform pan. Bake 1 1/2 hours, or until firm and lightly browned.

Combine sour cream and granulated sugar in a small bowl. Spread mixture over cheesecake; return to oven 5 minutes. Remove pan from water bath and let cool on wire rack about 1 hour. Cover and refrigerate about 4 hours. Serves 12.

## CHOCOLATE CRUST
4 1/2 cups broken chocolate sandwich cookies (Ruggles uses Oreos)
1 cup chopped roasted peanuts
1/2 cup unsalted butter, melted

**Chocolate Crust**

Process cookies and peanuts in food processor with steel blade until finely ground. Stir in butter; pat mixture onto bottom and sides of a 10-inch springform pan.

Share a piece with a friend. This recipe is really rich.

Deco Chocolate Port (500 ml); Yalumba Museum Muscat (375 ml – Australia).

AVOCADO FRIES *with Habañero Ketchup*
ROAST RACK OF COLORADO LAMB *on Mushroom-Walnut Bread Pudding with Red Wine Sauce*
UPSIDE DOWN FIG CAKE WITH WHIPPED CREAM

A lot of people are talking about Tony Ruppe's new restaurant. It's that word-of-mouth thing. Have you ever heard of fried avocados with habañero ketchup? Shrimp and crab rellenos with Texas goat cheese? Upside down fig cake? Delicious! The word has spread, and Ruppe's "fine American food and wine" has caught on with Houston's culinary sophisticates. It's no surprise. The food is so ingenious – and pleasing – and Ruppe ("Roop") and his wife Kathi extend genuine hospitality.

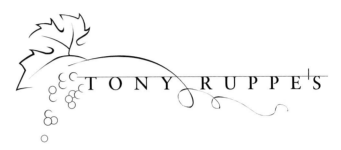

As the former executive chef at the award-winning Four Seasons Hotel, responsible for all the food served there, Ruppe developed a talent for cross-cultural cooking. Travel in Thailand and several Asian cities also has influenced his style. He worked his way up in the profession through Brennan's, the Royal Sonesta and Hyatt Regency in New Orleans. A Cajun or Creole touch often presents itself in some dishes. He has also been a guest chef at the Aspen Food and Wine Festival and at the James Beard House in New York City. Tony Ruppe's opened in December 1998.

Ruppe doesn't foresee big changes in food in the future; no new 'chapter' is being written for the millennium, he says. "Food is a celebration. I think people will still sit down and dine, match foods and wines and share conversations. Multi-ethnic foods seem to be what the public wants now." He sees continued interest in Asian, Caribbean, Indian and vegetarian foods. Latin flavors are getting a lot of attention, but Latin will always be a staple in Houston, he says. Grilling will continue to be popular because of the flavors achieved, and he sees a resurgence of red meats, comfort foods such as slow-braised dishes and mashed potatoes (always mashed potatoes!) and a little more fat for flavor. Ruppe thinks people will continue to eat more fish and seafood, and restaurateurs will have to be creative in finding sources for fresh fish and promoting new and unfamiliar kinds of fish. Fresh herbs will continue to play a big part in his cooking. He likes unusual flavors such as lemon balm and ginger in vinaigrette for a fresh fennel-Granny Smith apple salad, lemongrass in a Thai sauce or epazote in bean soup.

"We will also continue to be concerned about healthful food." Ruppe is apprehensive about the bioengineering of food. "The quality of today's products often suffers because they are grown to withstand shipping and have a long shelf life. There's more flavor in the box than in most tomatoes today," he says.

The carefully selected wine list is organized to pair wines with menu items. With down-to-earth descriptions, such as "lighter reds for grilled, rich fish, poultry and light meats" and "white wines for grilled, light meats and fish with richer sauce," diners can make choices easily even if they are not connoisseurs.

### LITE FARE

Taste is supreme at Tony Ruppe's where this chef/owner blends ethnic flavors and ingredients. Fruits and vegetables enhance the fish, seafood and chicken. Look for the term "broth" rather than "sauce," which signals a low-fat preparation. For example, Soba Noodles and Poached Chicken Breast is served with a Spicy Lemon Grass Broth. Enjoy the 999 Salad Dressing, which has no eggs and uses yogurt rather than mayonnaise.

*Tony Ruppe's*
*3939 Montrose Blvd.*
*Houston Tx 77006*
*713-852-0852*

# AVOCADO FRIES *with Habañero Ketchup*

1/2 cup Habañero Ketchup (recipe
     follows)
1 quart peanut oil for deep frying
2 avocados (just beginning
     to ripen)
1 cup all-purpose flour
1 teaspoon ground cumin
1 teaspoon chili powder
     Kosher salt to taste
     White pepper to taste
2 eggs
1/2 cup milk
1 cup Japanese bread crumbs
     (Panko, available at Fiesta or
     Whole Foods)
     Cilantro sprig for garnish

Prepare ketchup (up to one day in advance); set aside. Heat oil to 350 degrees in deep fryer or deep pan. Cut avocados in half lengthwise; remove seed. Carefully slice each avocado half into 4 wedges. Remove skin from wedges with a paring knife. Combine flour, cumin, chili powder, salt and pepper in a small bowl. Whisk eggs and milk together in a small bowl. Dredge avocado wedges in flour mixture; gently shake off excess flour. Drop wedges into egg mixture to coat. Lift wedges from egg mixture one at a time and coat with bread crumbs.

Deep-fry wedges until golden brown. Remove from oil; drain on paper towels. Place Habañero Ketchup on plate and arrange Avocado Fries around it. Garnish with a sprig of cilantro; serve immediately. Serves 4.

## HABAÑERO KETCHUP

2 tablespoons pure olive oil
1 medium onion, chopped
4 garlic cloves, minced
1 small habañero chili
1 large red bell pepper, stemmed,
     seeded and chopped
4 Roma tomatoes, halved, seeded,
     juiced and chopped
1 bay leaf
1/2 teaspoon ground allspice
1/2 teaspoon ground cinnamon
1/4 teaspoon ground cloves
3/4 cup cider vinegar
1/2 cup packed brown sugar
     Kosher salt to taste

### Habañero Ketchup

Heat oil in a heavy, nonreactive metal saucepan over medium heat; sauté onion and garlic until translucent. Add peppers and tomatoes; sauté until peppers are tender. Add bay leaf, allspice, cinnamon, cloves, vinegar and sugar; simmer until mixture is very soft. Remove bay leaf and puree in a food mill; return to saucepan and simmer 5 minutes. Add salt. Cover and refrigerate; keeps 1 week. Makes about 2 cups.

 Tomatoes are a good source of lycopene, an antioxidant that protects against cancer. The Habañero Ketchup is low fat but the fried avocados are high fat. Use restraint with this recipe.

 Arbor Crest Johannisberg Riesling (Washington); Domaine Zind-Humbrecht Gewürztraminer (France).

# ROAST RACK OF COLORADO LAMB *on Mushroom-Walnut Bread Pudding with Red Wine Sauce*

| | |
|---|---|
| 4 | (4-bone) racks of lamb, Frenched |
| 6 | tablespoons pure olive oil, divided |
| 2 | tablespoons minced garlic |
| 1 | tablespoon minced fresh rosemary |
| 1 | tablespoon coarsely ground black pepper |
| | Kosher salt to taste |
| 4 | servings Mushroom-Walnut Bread Pudding (recipe follows) |
| | Red Wine Sauce (recipe follows) |

## MUSHROOM-WALNUT BREAD PUDDING

| | |
|---|---|
| 6 | cups (1/2-inch) whole-wheat bread cubes |
| 2 | tablespoons pure olive oil |
| 1 | medium onion, diced |
| 3 | ribs celery, diced |
| 1 | tablespoon minced garlic |
| 3 | cups assorted mushrooms, sliced in large pieces |
| 1 | teaspoon minced fresh sage |
| 1 | teaspoon minced fresh thyme |
| 1/2 | teaspoon minced fresh rosemary |
| 3/4 | cup dry white wine |
| 3/4 | cup chicken stock |
| | Kosher salt and freshly ground black pepper to taste |
| 1 | cup lightly toasted walnut pieces |

## RED WINE SAUCE

| | |
|---|---|
| 1 | tablespoon pure olive oil |
| 1 | shallot, minced |
| 3 | garlic cloves, minced |
| 2 | cups red wine |
| 1 | teaspoon minced fresh rosemary |
| 1 1/2 | cups veal or lamb demi-glace (see Special Helps section) |
| | Kosher salt and freshly ground black pepper to taste |

Have butcher clean and French the lamb racks (scrape meat away from ends of bones, leaving bones exposed). Or, substitute leg of lamb or loin. Mix 1/4 cup oil, garlic, rosemary and pepper in a small bowl; rub lamb with marinade. Place lamb in a resealable plastic bag; refrigerate at least 2 hours or overnight.

Prepare bread pudding; reserve. Preheat oven to 500 degrees. Remove lamb from bag and allow any excess oil to drain. Season with salt just before cooking. Place a thick-bottomed skillet over high heat. When hot, add remaining 2 tablespoons oil. Place lamb in skillet and brown on all sides. Place lamb on a rack in a shallow roasting pan and roast to desired doneness, about 18 minutes for rare. Prepare wine sauce; reserve. Let lamb rest at room temperature 10 minutes before carving so juices don't escape. Place bread pudding in center of each plate. Slice racks into chops and arrange on plate with bones leaning against pudding; ladle sauce around meat and bread pudding. Serves 4.

**Mushroom-Walnut Bread Pudding**

Preheat oven to 350 degrees. Lightly toast bread cubes to dry out; set aside. Lightly butter a 2-quart baking dish; set aside. Place a large skillet over medium heat; add oil and sauté onion, celery and garlic until translucent. Add mushrooms, sage, thyme and rosemary; sauté until mushrooms are tender. Add wine and stock; simmer 5 minutes. Add salt and pepper. Add bread cubes and walnuts; gently fold into mushroom mixture. Adjust seasoning if needed. Adjust consistency if needed by adding more bread if too runny or more stock if too dry. Bread should be very moist and almost all liquid absorbed. Spoon mixture into baking dish; bake 30 to 40 minutes until set and nicely browned on top. Serves 6.

**Red Wine Sauce**

Heat oil in a medium saucepan over medium heat. Add shallot and garlic; sauté until translucent. Deglaze pan with wine. Add rosemary and reduce until pan is almost dry. Add demi-glace and simmer until sauce is reduced to the proper consistency, skimming frequently. Add salt and pepper. Makes about 3/4 cup.

🍎 The amount of lamb in this recipe is adequate for 8 servings. To reduce fat content, eliminate oil for rubbing and spray lamb with a nonstick cooking spray then rub in herbs. Also, eliminate oil in bread pudding and sauté vegetables in 2 tablespoons of chicken stock. Reduce nuts to 1/2 cup.

🍇 Wild Horse or Zaca Mesa Pinot Noir; Martin Ray or Robert Mondavi Cabernet Sauvignon.

103

# UPSIDE DOWN FIG CAKE WITH WHIPPED CREAM

| | |
|---|---|
| 1 | cup unsalted butter, divided |
| 1 1/2 | cups packed brown sugar |
| 1 | teaspoon salt, divided |
| 4 | (15-ounce) cans Kadota figs in light syrup |
| 3/4 | cup granulated sugar |
| 2 | eggs |
| 1 1/2 | cups all-purpose flour |
| 1 1/2 | teaspoons baking powder |
| 1 1/2 | teaspoons ground cardamom |
| 1 | teaspoon ground mace |
| 1/2 | teaspoon ground cinnamon |
| 1/2 | cup milk |
| 1 | teaspoon vanilla extract |
| | Whipped cream, lightly sweetened for garnish |

Melt 1/2 cup butter in a small saucepan over low heat with brown sugar and 1/2 teaspoon salt. Stir until well combined. Pour into a 10-inch round cake pan. Discard syrup from figs; remove remaining stems on figs. Slice figs in half lengthwise and arrange in circle, cut side down, on top of sugar mixture. Set aside.

Place oven rack in lowest position; preheat oven to 350 degrees. Cream remaining 1/2 cup butter (cubed and softened) and granulated sugar until light and lemon colored. Mix in 1 egg at a time until well blended. Sift flour, baking powder, cardamom, mace, cinnamon and remaining 1/2 teaspoon salt together. Add one-third of dry ingredients to butter mixture; mix gently until well blended. Add one-third of the milk; mix well. Repeat adding dry ingredients and milk two more times. Stir in vanilla. Pour batter over figs and brown sugar mixture. Place on a baking sheet and bake 40 to 45 minutes until skewer inserted into middle of cake comes out clean. Remove from oven and cool 15 to 20 minutes on a cooling rack. Invert onto a serving platter and gently remove pan. Slice and serve warm with whipped cream. Serves 12.

Figs are high in fiber and are a rich source of magnesium, potassium, calcium and iron. This dessert is low in fat and sodium. Indulge!

Kent Rasmussen Late Harvest Sauvignon Blanc (1/2 bottle); Tenuta Trerose Vin Santo (1/2 bottle).

VENISON BACKSTRAP WITH EAST TEXAS BLACKBERRY REDUCTION
PECAN CRUSTED PORK CHOP
FRESH THYME AND BRIE CHEESE GRITS
ROASTED CORN & LAMB SOUP
SWEET POTATO COBBLER

**G**uests at Sabine can eat their way across Texas and part of Louisiana from a menu that features contemporary adaptations of old favorites. This isn't your grandmother's cooking. Fried catfish is grilled in cornhusks and served with green tomato ketchup; the familiar Cajun maque choux mixture of corn, tomatoes and bell peppers accompanies gazpacho made with green tomatoes; black-eyed peas are mixed with peanut butter in hummus – Texas-style. Grits star in side dishes and even dessert: Imagine, if you can, vanilla or chocolate grits. The food is paired with wines from a well-chosen list.

The restaurant takes its name from the Sabine River, which meanders 555 miles along the Texas-Louisiana border. Co-owners, brothers Bill and Tom Johnson, grew up in southwestern Louisiana and have lived in New Orleans. Bill Johnson is the tastemaker; he managed other Houston restaurants before opening Sabine in 1996. It moved to its present location in 1998. Johnson searches the highways and by-ways of Texas and southwestern Louisiana for the best indigenous specialties. He brings back mayhaws (the fruit of the hawthorn tree), muscadine grapes, elderberries, fresh lady cream peas, greens and hand-made sausages from East Texas. Peaches come from Fredericksburg and apples from Medina in the Texas Hill Country. Louisiana Chicory Farm is the source for several specialty cheeses. Rice comes from Hoppe Farms in Fenton, and tasso and sausages from Iowa ("Ioway") in Louisiana. Johnson also shops farmers' markets.

Sabine's menus change constantly to take advantage of the season's perishables. "If I find something in the afternoon, it could show up on the menu that night or the next day. And we use it all – the apples might go into cobblers, pies, tarts or applesauce." Some things, such as mayhaws, also go into private label jams and jellies that are sold at the restaurant. Johnson and Clay Wilson, a graduate of the School of Culinary Arts at the Art Institute of Houston, who took over as executive chef earlier this year, collaborate on ideas that make the most of the fresh provisions. The juice of Rio Star grapefruit from the Rio Grande Valley goes into sauces, sorbets and other desserts. Cheyenne pecans (which Johnson considers superior to Papershells) are excellent for pies and tarts as well as for breading pork chops or fish. Texas 1015 onions are caramelized for an onion tart, flavor biscuits served atop Roasted Corn & Lamb Soup or star in Sweet Onion Fettuccine with shrimp, crawfish and crab.

For the millennium, Johnson says he will continue to seek out and experiment with indigenous products. He's found the blueberries, but is still searching for equally superior raspberries. He's also looking for smoked meats, sausages and bacon, specially raised chickens, turkey and pork, jerky, unusual salad greens, fresh herbs, fruits and berries. The menu will continue to reflect Texas' and Louisiana's heritage of French, Spanish, English and Native American foods with a strong Southern accent.

─────── LITE FARE ───────

If you are looking for Southern comfort foods, then Sabine is the restaurant for you! Choose healthy accompaniments such as Baby White Lima Bean Salad, Collard Greens and Green Tomato Gazpacho. Many sauces are natural reductions of fruits and vegetables without cream and butter – Texas Blackberry Reduction and Mayhaw Lime Glaze. Requests for special dietary needs will be honored.

*Sabine*
*1915 Westheimer*
*Houston Tx 77098*
*713-529-7190*

# VENISON BACKSTRAP WITH EAST TEXAS BLACKBERRY REDUCTION

| | |
|---|---|
| 1 | tablespoon walnut oil |
| 8 | (3-ounce) venison backstrap medallions |
| | Salt and freshly ground black pepper to taste |
| 1 | tablespoon butter |
| 12 | pearl onions |
| 1 | pint fresh blackberries |
| 2 | tablespoons honey |
| 1 | teaspoon minced fresh rosemary |
| 1 | teaspoon minced fresh thyme |
| 1/4 | cup raspberry vinegar |
| 1 | cup Merlot wine |

Heat oil in a large nonstick skillet over medium-high heat; season medallions with salt and pepper. Sear medallions 30 seconds on each side; remove and keep warm. Add butter and onions to skillet; cook until onions are caramelized (see Special Helps section). Stir in blackberries, honey, rosemary and thyme. Deglaze pan with vinegar and Merlot; reduce until slightly thickened. Toss medallions into sauce and adjust seasoning if necessary. Serve immediately. Serves 4.

Venison is a lean meat with fewer calories and less fat than chicken breast. Enjoy this low-fat preparation.

Reserve St. Martin Merlot (France) or Catena Malbec (Argentina); DeLoach, Rabbit Ridge or Robert Mondavi Merlot.

# PECAN CRUSTED PORK CHOP

| | |
|---|---|
| 2 | cups dry biscuit or bread crumbs |
| 2 | cups very finely chopped pecans |
| 1/4 | cup finely chopped parsley |
| | Salt and freshly ground black pepper to taste |
| 1 | cup buttermilk |
| 6 | eggs |
| 1 | (3- to 4-pound) rack pork loin |
| | Flour for dredging |

Combine crumbs, pecans, parsley, salt and pepper in a medium bowl; set aside. Blend buttermilk and eggs in a medium bowl for egg wash; set aside. Dredge pork loin in flour, then in egg wash. Coat with reserved crumb mixture, place in baking pan and refrigerate 30 minutes so that crumb mixture will adhere.

Preheat oven to 375 degrees. Roast pork about 45 minutes, checking frequently for doneness (meat should be semi-firm to the touch and measure 155 degrees on an instant-read thermometer). Remove and keep warm 15 minutes before carving between bones into single or double chops. Serve immediately. Serves 6 to 8.

Trim fat from pork chops and reduce pecans to 1 cup to decrease fat. There is enough pork for 8 servings. Serve with fresh vegetables and a low-fat rice or pasta.

Rosemount Shiraz (Australia); Hendry Zinfandel; Turley Zinfandel.

# FRESH THYME AND BRIE CHEESE GRITS

|       |                                          |
|-------|------------------------------------------|
| 2     | cups buttermilk                          |
| 2     | cups water                               |
| 1 1/2 | cups quick-cooking stone-ground grits    |
| 1/4   | cup diced Brie cheese, rind removed      |
| 1/2   | tablespoon minced fresh thyme            |
|       | Salt and freshly ground black pepper to taste |

Heat buttermilk and water to a simmer in a large saucepan. Whisk in grits, Brie and thyme; stir until thickened and the consistency of polenta. Add salt and pepper if needed. Serve immediately. Serves 3 to 4.

*Note:* Leftovers may be spread onto a sheet pan and chilled. Cut into shapes, then grill or fry.

🍎 Grits are coarsely ground hulled, dried corn. Stone-ground grits include the germ of the corn and are usually more nutritious. Savor this low-fat and delicious recipe.

# ROASTED CORN & LAMB SOUP

|      |                                          |
|------|------------------------------------------|
| 2    | lamb shanks                              |
| 5    | ears corn, roasted                       |
| 1/4  | cup unsalted butter                      |
| 1    | each, diced: red and green bell peppers  |
| 3    | garlic cloves, minced                    |
| 1    | finely diced red onion                   |
| 1/4  | cup all-purpose flour                    |
| 1/4  | cup red wine                             |
| 2    | quarts chicken stock or water            |
| 1/2  | cup tomato puree                         |
| 1    | large white onion for onion brûlée       |
| 1/4  | cup chopped parsley                      |
|      | Liquid hot red pepper sauce to taste     |
|      | Crème fraîche for garnish                |

Cook lamb shanks, shred meat and reserve meat and bones. Remove kernels from roasted corn; reserve kernels and cobs. Melt butter over low heat in stockpot; add peppers, garlic, red onion and corn kernels. Continue to cook until vegetables are caramelized (see Special Helps section). Add flour, stirring until a medium roux is achieved. Deglaze pan with wine; add stock and tomato puree. Return bones and cobs to soup; cover and simmer on low 1 hour.

For onion brûlée, slice onion in half and place directly on burner until dark brown or brown in a skillet. Add to soup; simmer 30 minutes. Discard onion brûlée, bones and cobs. Add reserved lamb, parsley and hot pepper sauce. Serve in hot bowls; garnish with crème fraîche. Makes 2 quarts. Serves 8.

🍎 To enjoy a lower-fat version of this healthy soup, reduce butter to 2 tablespoons and choose a fat-free, low-sodium chicken broth.

🍇 Guigal Côtes du Rhone (France); Eos or Markham Petite Sirah.

# SWEET POTATO COBBLER

| | |
|---|---|
| 10 | tablespoons unsalted butter, divided |
| 1 | cup all-purpose flour |
| 1 | tablespoon baking powder |
| 2 | cups sugar |
| 1 1/2 | teaspoons ground cinnamon |
| 1/2 | teaspoon ground nutmeg |
| 1/2 | teaspoon ground cloves |
| 1 | cup buttermilk |
| 1 | (29-ounce) can sweet potatoes, drained and diced |
| | Cinnamon ice cream |
| | Molasses, caramel sauce, fresh blueberries or raspberries for garnish |

Preheat oven to 375 degrees. Butter a 13x9x2-inch baking dish with 2 tablespoons butter. Mix remaining 1/2 cup butter, flour, baking powder, sugar, cinnamon, nutmeg and cloves in mixing bowl. Add buttermilk in a slow, steady stream while stirring. Pour batter into prepared dish. Top with sweet potatoes. Bake until set, about 15 to 20 minutes or until knife inserted in center comes out clean (cobbler should still be moist). Remove from oven and let cool to room temperature. Chill at least 1 hour before cutting into squares.

To serve, reheat each serving in the microwave (1 minute on high per square). Top with a scoop of cinnamon ice cream and drizzle with molasses. If desired, also garnish with caramel sauce and fresh berries. Serves 12.

Serve this cobbler with a light ice cream and enjoy.

Banyuls Les Clos de Paulliles (1/2 bottle – France); Lustau Rare Cream Sherry (Spain).

FACING PAGE, FROM LEFT: *Bill Johnson, Aaron Guest, Sabine.*

FOLLOWING PAGE, FROM LEFT: *Charles Dash, Robert Schofield, St. Regis.*

# HOUSTON IS COOKING
## *2000*

BABY SPINACH, BIBB, GRILLED PORTOBELLO MUSHROOM SALAD
*with Warm Apple Smoked Bacon Dressing*
BLACKBERRY DEMI LAMB CHOPS *with Blackberry Demi-Glace*
CRISP POBLANO BLUE LUMP CRAB CAKES *with Smoked Yellow Tomato Coulis*
WHITE CHOCOLATE CRÈME BRÛLÉE

St. Regis Hotel guests number heads of state, heads of corporations and heads of society – patrons who expect the finest in accommodations and cuisine. After a $6.2 Million renovation earlier this year, the former Remington then Ritz-Carlton then Luxury Collection Hotel has gained even more stature as an international destination. It is only one of four hotels to share the name and standards of the St. Regis New York City. Charles Dash, executive chef, finds himself in a worldly kitchen, which may supply Middle Eastern delicacies for a visiting sheik one day and the next serve a wedding reception.

Dash, who is from San Antonio, worked his way up from bus boy and dishwasher at several prestigious hotels, clubs and resorts in Texas. He sees the St. Regis kitchen as a creative venue to expand his repertoire for the millennium. Dash thinks there are several concurrent trends. On one hand "every chef is going to try something new, and many people are adventurous and are interested in trying new things. On the other hand, people want familiar things they're comfortable with – Texans love those big steaks! Many people are going back to family and family values. They want to enjoy being with their loved ones and friends. For them, dining out in the future may be a special occasion; they may use the restaurant as a reward."

Dash believes as the world opens up, hotel kitchens need to be international in scope. In a universal kitchen chefs can learn from a "United Nations of employees," he says. At the St. Regis, the kitchen staff represents

**THE ST. REGIS**

Chinese, Cambodians, Italians, French, Hispanics and Hondurans as well as native Texans. Health- and fitness-conscious guests also influence his menus. Dash searches for the finest regional specialties from fresh herbs and fruit to wild game. He enjoys presenting earthy, wholesome foods in a unique way – he might pair venison and micro-greens or accompany Muscovy duck with couscous, orzo, polenta or risotto. He stuffs handmade spinach ravioli with lobster mousse or tortellini with smoked pheasant mousse. Relishes, chutneys and salsas of tropical fruits and melons compliment poultry, fish and game dishes. Dash also is known for Black Truffle Whipped Potatoes, Roasted Corn Linguine, Chipotle Angel Hair, and tartares and carpaccio of exotic animals such as antelope. He also is an award-winning ice sculptor. He participated in two international competitions earlier this year and won a gold medal in Finland.

As part of the hotel's renovation, guestrooms, The Dining Room, Bar and Grill and the Tea Lounge have been redecorated, butler service has been added and the Sunday brunch reinstated. Personalized butler service is available on the upgraded Astor Floors. The St. Regis is owned and operated by Starwood Hotels & Resorts Worldwide, Inc. As the Luxury Collection, it was named one of the Top Hotels in America by Conde Nast Traveler in 1998.

--- LITE FARE ---

Special requests are encouraged at this restaurant that caters to an international clientele. Customizing dishes to your specific needs, whether health or religious, is a specialty of the house. This menu even has a Fitness Breakfast approved by the American Heart Association. Because almost everything is fresh and prepared when ordered, most requests can be honored. Nutrition information is available from the wait staff.

*St. Regis*
*1919 Briar Oaks Lane*
*Houston, Tx 77027*
*713-840-7600*

# BABY SPINACH, BIBB, GRILLED PORTOBELLO MUSHROOM SALAD *with Warm Apple Smoked Bacon Dressing*

1/2 cup Warm Apple Smoked Bacon Dressing (recipe follows)
8 ounces baby spinach
1 head baby Bibb lettuce
2 medium portobello mushrooms
1/2 cup dry white wine
1/4 cup olive oil

Prepare dressing; reserve. Wash spinach and Bibb lettuce thoroughly; set aside. Remove stems and trim off under side of mushrooms; marinate in mixture of wine and oil 2 hours. Grill mushrooms 10 minutes, cut into fourths and keep warm. Arrange spinach and lettuce on individual plates and top with mushroom quarters. Accompany with dressing. Serves 4.

**WARM APPLE SMOKED BACON DRESSING**

1 medium-size red onion, finely diced
1/2 pound apple smoked bacon, small dice
1 grilled portobello mushroom cap, finely chopped
1 (8-ounce) bottle prepared ranch-style dressing
2 cups whipping cream

**Warm Apple Smoked Bacon Dressing**

Sauté onion and bacon until onion is translucent in a medium skillet. Add mushroom and continue to sauté over low heat. Add ranch dressing to mixture; simmer about 5 minutes. Add cream; whisk well until smooth. Makes about 1 quart. Refrigerate extra.

Spinach is a powerhouse of nutrients with high levels of vitamins A and C, folate and potassium. To balance nutrients, choose a fat-free ranch dressing and substitute half-and-half for cream.

Lagarde Malbec (Argentina) or Saxenburg Pinotage (South Africa); Leasingham Shiraz (Australia).

# BLACKBERRY DEMI LAMB CHOPS *with Blackberry Demi-Glace*

4 lamb chops
1 cup blackberry brandy
3/4 cup Blackberry Demi-Glace (recipe follows)
  Chives for garnish
  Fresh blackberries and raspberries for garnish

Marinate chops in brandy 20 minutes. Prepare Blackberry Demi-Glace; reserve. Grill chops until medium done. Tie 2 chops together with chives; stand in center of plate. Pour half of Blackberry Demi-Glace onto each plate in front of chops. Garnish each plate with 4 to 6 berries. Serves 2.

**BLACKBERRY DEMI-GLACE**

2 cups port wine
1/2 cup chopped shallots
1 bay leaf
2 sprigs of thyme
2 cups demi-glace (see Special Helps section)
1/4 cup blackberry brandy
  Salt and freshly ground black pepper to taste

**Blackberry Demi-Glace**

Combine wine, shallots, bay leaf and thyme in a medium saucepan over medium heat. Reduce by three-fourths and add demi-glace. Simmer 10 minutes, skimming occasionally. Add brandy and season with salt and pepper; strain. If necessary thicken with a mixture of cornstarch and water. Makes about 2 1/2 cups.

Be sure to trim fat from lamb chops. Serve with plenty of fresh vegetables.

Boeger Cabernet Sauvignon; Monticello Estate Pinot Noir; Jordan Cabernet Sauvignon.

# CRISP POBLANO BLUE LUMP CRAB CAKES *with Smoked Yellow Tomato Coulis*

2 cups Smoked Yellow Tomato Coulis (recipe follows)
1 each medium: yellow and red bell peppers, finely diced
1 medium poblano pepper, finely diced
1 teaspoon chopped garlic
2 tablespoons clarified butter
2 pounds fresh blue lump crabmeat, cleaned and picked over
1 tablespoon mayonnaise
1/2 teaspoon Old Bay seasoning
Salt and freshly ground black pepper to taste
1/4 cup half-and-half
2 egg yolks plus 1 egg
1/2 cup Japanese bread crumbs
4 fried basil leaves (optional)

Prepare coulis; reserve. Preheat oven to 350 degrees. Sauté peppers and garlic in butter in a small skillet about 2 to 5 minutes. Let cool then add crabmeat and mayonnaise, Old Bay seasoning, salt and pepper. Use a large biscuit cutter to shape 4 cakes, about 4 to 5 inches in diameter. Make an egg wash with half-and-half, egg yolks and egg. Dip crab cakes in egg wash and lightly bread with crumbs. Sauté crab cakes in same skillet on each side until lightly golden brown. Place on a baking pan and bake about 15 minutes. Serve with pasta. Pour coulis to cover three-fourths of plate; top with cooked angel hair pasta or linguine. Place crab cake on top. Garnish each serving with a fried basil leaf. Serves 4.

## SMOKED YELLOW TOMATO COULIS

5 pounds smoked yellow tomatoes
1/4 cup pure olive oil
1/4 cup canola oil
1 medium-size yellow onion, chopped
2 garlic cloves, chopped
1/2 cup chopped fresh basil
Salt and freshly ground black pepper to taste

### Smoked Yellow Tomato Coulis

To smoke tomatoes: Core tomatoes; cut in half. Using only a wood fire, let fire die down to a smoke in grill. Arrange tomatoes on grill; smoke about 10 to 15 minutes. Remove and let cool.

Heat oils in a large skillet; sauté onion until translucent. Add garlic and continue to cook a few seconds. Add tomatoes and simmer until very soft over medium heat. Add basil and simmer briefly. Puree, strain and check seasoning. Return to blender and blend until smooth. May have to do in batches. Makes about 1 quart. Remainder may be refrigerated as long as 4 days.

🍎 You will find that the coulis is rich in vitamins A and C. To reduce fat content, eliminate canola oil in coulis. Serve with 1 cup of pasta.

🍇 KWV Steen (South Africa) or Folie a Deux Menage a Trois; Zaca Mesa Roussanne or Iron Horse Fume Blanc.

# WHITE CHOCOLATE CRÈME BRÛLÉE

15    egg yolks
1 2/3  cups sugar, divided
2 1/2  teaspoons cornstarch
1     quart whipping cream
2     vanilla beans, split
4     ounces white chocolate, finely
      chopped
1     (17-ounce) package frozen
      puff pastry
      Fresh raspberries

Place yolks, 2/3 cup sugar and cornstarch in a medium bowl. Whip by hand until combined and heat over a water bath to 100 degrees on thermometer. Meanwhile, bring cream and vanilla beans to a boil in a medium saucepan. Blend a small amount of egg mixture into cream; then whisk all of cream into egg mixture. Add chocolate, stirring until chocolate is dissolved. Set bowl in an ice bath and cool completely, stirring every minute until mixture stops steaming. Strain mixture through a fine sieve; cover and refrigerate 2 hours.

Preheat oven to 375 degrees. Cut circles from puff pastry that will fit into a muffin pan or egg poaching ring; cut off excess. Use baking beads or dried beans to fill rings to prevent sides from collapsing during baking. Bake until shells are golden brown and dry, about 35 minutes. Cool. Fill with berries and Crème Brûlée mix. Sprinkle remaining 1 cup sugar on tops of each brulee. Use a propane torch to caramelize tops, to a golden brown color. Or place under oven broiler until tops caramelize. Be careful not to burn sugar. Serve while sugar is warm; garnish with berries. Serves 15.

Indulge in a few bites.

KWV Cream Sherry or Tawny Port (South Africa); Schramsberg Crémant.

CHEESE SOUFFLÉ
EGGPLANT PATTIES IN GINGER AND GARLIC SAUCE
SHREDDED PORK WITH SCALLIONS
SESAME FILET MIGNON
CHICKEN TENDERLOIN SAUTÉED WITH BROCCOLI AND BLACK PEPPER

**T**he ingredients for the delicacies that fill your plate today at Scott Chen's may have been in Japan two days ago or California yesterday. Scott Chen views the millennium as a shrinking world thanks to technology, improved communications and speedy transportation on an international scale. Whether you are in your own home or a fine restaurant you can now dine globally. As a restaurateur, Chen has another view of the millennium – formality and elegance – which may make him stand alone. As owner of the award-winning Empress restaurant on FM 1960 West, Chen set a precedent for French and Asian Fusion Cuisine, in which foods and fine wines are superbly matched. His new namesake restaurant, opened in March 1999, carries Fusion to a higher level. Two of many examples: cold lobster served over a mixture of tropical fruit with Japanese cucumbers; Grilled Softshell Crawfish with the cross-cultural flavor boost of Lemon Butter and Pico de Gallo.

To bear out Chen's prediction of the shrinking world, fresh foie gras, duck breast and baby lamb chops are flown in from New York, and yellowtail tuna arrives from Japan within 48 hours of being caught. Tropical fruit comes in from Hawaii and edible flowers and baby vegetables from California within a day of being picked. Dried mushrooms, dried scallops and vacuum-packed frozen softshell crab come in from various Asian sources every 24 hours.

Chen changes the menu frequently because customers like a new-style cuisine. "Two years is old for a menu now," he says. However, he does retain signature favorites such as Grilled Foie Gras with apple, lychees and Port applesauce; Empress Lump Crab Croquettes; and Lamb Chops with Dill Sour Cream Sauce. "In the future, the healthy concept is due first priority along with quality," he says. "We use very little butter and no coconut oil; everything is first class and prepared fresh."

**EMPRESS**

Tuxedoed waiters provide white glove service in a serenely elegant setting of dark jade green walls, mahogany chairs and moldings, fine paintings and table appointments such as Christofle hotel silver and Riedel wine glasses. A pianist at a black lacquer baby grand piano in the foyer welcomes guests with live music nightly. A fireplace beckons in the cozy bar. The award-winning wine collection at Scott Chen's numbers more than 15,000 bottles, and Empress offers more than 12,000. The glass-enclosed wine room at Scott Chen's is lined with wine racks. It seats 60, and a private room is available for tastings and parties for as many as 20.

Chen has been honored by being invited to cook at the James Beard House in New York several times. Scott Chen's seems destined to follow in the footsteps of Empress, which has won many prestigious awards including the DiRoNA from Distinguished Restaurants of North America, Best of the Best designation from the American Academy of Restaurant and Hospitality Sciences and several from the Wine Spectator.

*Scott Chen's*
*6540 San Felipe at Voss*
*Houston, Tx 77057*
*713-789-4484*

—————————— LITE FARE ——————————

Scott Chen's distinctive cuisine combines continental favorites with oriental flavors for a delightful experience. His East-meets-West specialties blend savory sauces with low-fat food preparation – quick pre-boiling and flash sautéing. Sauces are usually light and can be served on the side. Unique vegetarian dishes feature interesting starches, vegetables and fruits. Special requests are honored and encouraged.

*Empress*
*5419-A FM 1960 West*
*Houston, Tx 77069*
*281-583-8021*

# CHEESE SOUFFLÉ

| | |
|---|---|
| 4 | tablespoons unsalted butter |
| 6 | tablespoons all-purpose flour |
| 2 | cups boiling milk |
| 2 | tablespoons freshly grated Parmesan cheese |
| 6 | tablespoons freshly grated Gruyere cheese |
| | Salt to taste |
| 4 | eggs, separated |
| | Sugar |

Preheat oven to 350 degrees. Melt butter in a medium saucepan; whisk in flour and cook a few minutes. Add milk and cook, whisking constantly until thickened, about 5 minutes. Remove from heat and add cheeses and salt; set aside. Beat egg yolks until foamy and add gradually to cheese mixture. Whip egg whites until stiff; fold in gently. Pour into a buttered, sugared and lightly floured 1-quart soufflé dish. Bake 20 minutes, or until puffed and golden. Serve immediately. Serves 2 to 3.

Enjoy this recipe in moderation. Divide into 4 servings.

Marqués de Cáceres Rioja Reserva (Spain); La Cuvée Mythique (France).

# EGGPLANT PATTIES IN GINGER AND GARLIC SAUCE

| | |
|---|---|
| 1/2 | pound ground pork |
| 1/2 | teaspoon salt |
| 1 | tablespoon cornstarch |
| 1 | cup water |
| 1 1/4 | cups all-purpose flour |
| 2 | (1/4-pound) Japanese eggplants |
| 3 | cups vegetable oil |
| 1 | tablespoon minced green onion |
| 1 | tablespoon minced ginger |
| 1 | tablespoon minced garlic |
| 1 | tablespoon hot bean sauce |
| 3 | tablespoons chicken stock |
| 1 | tablespoon soy sauce |
| 1 | teaspoon vinegar |
| 2 | teaspoons sugar |
| 1/2 | teaspoon freshly ground black pepper |
| 1 | tablespoon cornstarch paste (1 tablespoon cornstarch and 1/2 tablespoon water) |

Mix pork, salt and cornstarch in a small bowl; set aside. Whisk water into flour to make batter in a medium bowl; set aside. Cut off stem and ends of eggplants; cut diagonally into 3/4-inch slices. Score top of each slice two times but do not cut through. Stuff pork mixture into each scored eggplant. Heat oil in a wok. Coat eggplant patties one by one with flour batter; fry several at a time until golden brown. Remove and drain on paper towel. Arrange on a plate.

Remove all but 4 tablespoons of oil from wok. Add onion, ginger, garlic, bean sauce, stock, soy sauce, vinegar, sugar, pepper and cornstarch paste; stir-fry over high heat until well mixed. Pour over eggplant patties. Serves 4.

Eggplant is naturally low in calories and has little fat but can absorb fat calories if cooked in oil. To reduce fat, eliminate oil in the sauce and serve with plain rice. To reduce sodium, eliminate added salt and use low-sodium soy sauce.

Hugel Gentil (France); Ostertag Riesling (France); Trimbach Riesling Cuvée Frederic Émile (France).

# SHREDDED PORK WITH SCALLIONS

| | |
|---|---|
| 1 | pound boneless pork tenderloin |
| 1 | tablespoon dry red wine |
| 2 | teaspoons salt, divided |
| 1 | tablespoon cornstarch |
| 5 | green onions, cut into 3-inch lengths |
| 3 | cups oil |
| 3 | tablespoons hoisin sauce |
| 1/2 | teaspoon sugar |
| 1 | tablespoon chicken stock |

Partially freeze pork; slice very thinly into shreds. Marinate with wine, 1 teaspoon salt and cornstarch 20 minutes. Slice onion lengthwise in slivers; heat oil in a wok. Stir-fry onion slivers a few seconds; remove and drain well on paper towel. Arrange evenly on plate. Stir-fry pork slivers until they separate and the color changes to white. Remove and drain well on paper towel. Remove all but 3 tablespoons oil from wok. Add hoisin sauce, remaining 1 teaspoon salt and sugar; stir-fry over high heat until it boils. Add pork slivers and stock; mix well. Pour over onion slivers. Serves 4.

This cut of pork is lean and a good source of iron and thiamin. To control fat and sodium, eliminate added salt and oil in the sauce. Serve with 1 cup plain rice per serving.

Pedroncelli Mother Clone Zinfandel; Chalone Pinot Noir.

# SESAME FILET MIGNON

| | |
|---|---|
| 2 | teaspoons vegetable oil |
| 1 | tablespoon white sesame seeds |
| 4 | teaspoons sesame oil, divided |
| 1 | pound filet mignon, cut in 2-inch squares |
| 1 | tablespoon minced garlic |
| 1 | teaspoon Old Vintage oyster sauce |
| 1 | teaspoon white wine |
| 2 | tablespoons sugar |
| | Red lettuce leaves for garnish |

Heat wok; add vegetable oil and lightly stir-fry sesame seeds 1 minute. Remove and set aside. Reheat wok; add 1 teaspoon sesame oil and when wok is very hot, add filet squares and stir-fry 30 seconds. Remove meat. Repeat process twice, adding 1 teaspoon sesame oil each time. Drain and set aside. Meat should be very crispy.

Reheat wok and add meat, garlic, oyster sauce, wine and sugar. Stir-fry over moderate heat until all the liquid evaporates and meat is quite dry, crispy and glazed with seasonings. Add sesame seeds; sprinkle on remaining 1 teaspoon sesame oil and stir. Transfer to a serving plate garnished with lettuce leaves. Serves 4.

Use beef tenderloin and trim off all visible fat. Eliminate vegetable oil by using nonstick cooking spray on wok before stir-frying sesame seeds. Serve with plain boiled rice.

Parducci Petite Sirah; Coudoulet de Beaucastel (France); Domaine du Vieux Telegraphe or Chateau de Beaucastel Châteauneuf-du-Pape (France).

# CHICKEN TENDERLOIN SAUTÉED WITH BROCCOLI AND BLACK PEPPER

| | |
|---|---|
| 1 | pound chicken tenderloin or boneless, skinless breasts |
| 1/2 | tablespoon rice wine or dry white wine |
| 1/2 | teaspoon salt |
| 1 | egg white |
| 1 | tablespoon cornstarch |
| 1/2 | cup vegetable oil, divided |
| 2 | cups broccoli florets |
| 1 | green onion, cut into 6 pieces |
| 2 | tablespoons chopped ginger root |
| 3/4 | teaspoon salt |
| 3/4 | teaspoon sugar |
| 1/2 | teaspoon freshly ground black pepper |
| 1/2 | teaspoon sesame oil |
| 3 | tablespoons water combined with 1 teaspoon cornstarch |

Lightly score chicken in a criss-cross pattern. Cut into bite-size pieces. Coat chicken with wine, salt, egg white and 1 tablespoon cornstarch, mixing after each addition. Add 2 tablespoons oil to mixture. Blanch broccoli in boiling water; remove, drain and rinse in cold water, draining on paper towel. Heat remaining 6 tablespoons oil in wok. Stir-fry chicken until it turns white; remove and set aside. Remove all but 2 tablespoons oil from wok. Add onion, ginger root and broccoli; stir-fry until mixture bubbles. Add chicken, salt, sugar, pepper, sesame oil and cornstarch mixture; turn heat to high and stir quickly to mix. Transfer to serving plate. Serves 4.

Broccoli is an excellent source of vitamin C, a good source of vitamin A and folate and is rich in bioflavonoids that protect against cancer. To enhance healthful benefits of this recipe, eliminate salt and reduce oil to 3 tablespoons (1 tablespoon in chicken mixture and 2 tablespoons for stir-frying). Serve with 1 cup plain rice per serving.

Fournier Pouilly-Fumé (white – France);
Guigal Côte-Rôtie (red – France).

FACING PAGE: *Scott Chen, Scott Chen's / Empress.*

FOLLOWING PAGE: *Nicholas, Leslie and Alberto Baffoni, Simposio.*

ASPARAGUS AND SNOW PEAS IN BUTTER SAUCE
OVEN ROASTED SALMON
POTATO GNOCCHI WITH SPINACH AND GORGONZOLA (GNOCCHI DI PATATE E SPINACI GORGONZOLA)
NEW YORK STRIP ALLA ROBESPIERRE *with Herbed Oil*
FLOURLESS CHOCOLATE CAKE

**S**imposio gives diners a chance to savor the flavors of Emilia-Romagna, a gastronomic area in northern Italy relatively unknown to Houstonians until owner Alberto Baffoni opened the restaurant in October 1997. Homemade fettuccine in a Bolognese-style meat sauce, seafood soup, Venetian-style risotto and distinctive game, beef, veal and fish dishes quickly captured the attention of sophisticated food lovers. They recognized a master hand in the kitchen, and it was no surprise that in its first year Simposio was named one of Esquire magazine's Best New Restaurants in America.

"I believe that in the new millennium, many Americans will grow to love and appreciate the same simplicity, excellence and wholesomeness that Italians are so passionate about and respectful of in their cuisine," says Baffoni. The regional food of Italy is healthful, nutritious food unadulterated with heavy sauces, says Baffoni, who comes from Fano on the Adriatic Coast, which borders Emilia-Romagna and Marches. Standardized cooking and recipes may be fine for big corporations in America, but he strives to make the food as authentic as he can using fine-quality fresh ingredients and simple cooking techniques.

Skillful seasoning with fresh herbs and interesting combinations of ingredients takes the place of heavy sauces that mask natural flavors. Hand-made pastas are central to Simposio's menu. Baffoni is known for well-balanced pasta dishes such as Strozzapreti all' Emiliana, tiny hand-rolled tube-shaped noodles known as "strangled priests" in Italy. Another favorite is his Vegetable Lasagna that is lightly sauced with Béchamel.

Simposio is especially popular with well-traveled customers who know authentic Italian food. Customers who have enjoyed some dish at a trattoria in Tuscany or a little restaurant in Milan often ask him to re-create it. Baffoni is constantly experimenting because his customers "have an open palate; they're always ready for new tastes," he says. He keeps a watchful eye for authentic ingredients such as veal-stuffed tortellini and agnolotti (half moon-shaped ravioli), tricolor tagliolini, new vegetables such as broccolini, cheeses, Italian sausage and pancetta, fine olive oils, vinegars and Italian greens. One salad provocatively blends beets, Belgian endive and goat cheese with delicate white wine vinaigrette.

Baffoni graduated from culinary school in Italy, then entered the Italian military as a chef for the officers mess. He has worked in London and the Bahamas. He followed his future wife, Leslie Johnson, to this country and settled in Washington, D.C. where he worked for Bice Restaurant. He decided to open a restaurant here after visiting Houston six years ago. The name Simposio comes from Symposium, a restaurant in Italy owned by Baffoni's teacher and mentor, Lucio Pompili, and from Plato's "Symposium," which featured philosophic discussions and great food. Simposio also means gathering place, which fits in with Baffoni's idea of creating a fashionably casual restaurant with a relaxed European dining ambience. The restaurant in a strip shopping center is tastefully appointed with tapestries and with Giacometti-style metal sculptures by Louisiana artist Ralph Goodyear.

RISTORANTE **S** ITALIANO
SIMPOSIO

─── *LITE FARE* ───

Chef/owner Alberto Baffoni challenges himself to develop alternatives to cream that produce superb sauces without the fat. Soups are thickened with potato purees and risottos are light on butter and contain no cream. Notice many interesting vegetables on this menu such as broccolini that resembles a cross between broccoli and asparagus but is actually a hybrid of broccoli and Chinese kale.

*Simposio*
*5591 Richmond Ave.*
*Houston, Tx 77056*
*713-532-0550*

# ASPARAGUS AND SNOW PEAS IN BUTTER SAUCE

| | |
|---|---|
| 1 | pound asparagus |
| 1/2 | pound snow peas |
| 4 | tablespoons unsalted butter |
| 1 | teaspoon finely chopped shallot |
| 1/4 | cup chicken stock |
| | Salt and freshly ground black pepper to taste |

Wash and peel asparagus; wash and snap ends from peas, discarding fibrous vein. Blanch asparagus in boiling water and plunge into ice water to stop the cooking process. Melt butter in a large skillet; sauté shallots until they release their moisture. Add asparagus, peas and stock; cook over medium heat until liquid is reduced to a light velvety sauce, about 2 minutes. Add salt and pepper. Serves 4.

Asparagus is an excellent source of blood-building folate and infection-fighting vitamin C, and snow peas are an excellent source of vitamins A and C. For low-fat preparation, reduce butter to 1 tablespoon and use fat-free, low-sodium chicken stock (see Healthy Recipe Modifications).

# OVEN ROASTED SALMON

| | |
|---|---|
| 4 | (6-ounce) salmon fillets |
| 2 | tablespoons mixed fresh herbs (parsley, sage, rosemary and thyme) |
| | Salt and freshly ground black pepper to taste |
| 1 | zucchini, sliced 1/4-inch thick |
| 2 | red bell peppers, roasted, peeled, seeded and sliced |
| 2 | green bell peppers, roasted, peeled, seeded and sliced |
| 3 to 4 | tablespoons Herbed Oil, divided (see recipe page 123) |
| 2 | garlic cloves, chopped |
| 1 | teaspoon chopped parsley |

Season salmon well on both sides with mixed herbs, salt and pepper. Cover and refrigerate 30 minutes or as long as overnight. Sear zucchini in a very hot nonstick skillet until golden. Arrange zucchini in 4 fans on a baking sheet. Preheat oven to 400 degrees.

Place each fillet on one of the zucchini fans and bake 10 to 15 minutes, depending on how well done you want the fish. When "milk" appears on surface, fish is done. While fish is baking, slice peppers and sauté in 1 tablespoon of the herbed oil with salt, pepper, garlic and parsley. When fish is done, carefully lift fish and zucchini fans from baking sheet and arrange on four plates. Garnish each with sautéed peppers. Brush salmon lightly with remaining herbed oil for extra flavor. Serves 4.

Salmon is a super source of heart-healthy omega 3's and vitamin B12 and peppers are an excellent source of vitamin A. To reduce fat, decrease oil to 1 tablespoon.

Rex Hill Pinot Gris (white – Oregon); Erath or Willamette Valley Pinot Noir (red – Oregon).

# POTATO GNOCCHI WITH SPINACH AND GORGONZOLA (GNOCCHI DI PATATE E SPINACI GORGONZOLA)

| | |
|---|---|
| 1 1/4 | pounds Idaho potatoes |
| 1/4 | pound chopped fresh spinach, squeezed dry and pureed |
| 1 | egg |
| 1 | tablespoon salt |
| | Pinch of ground nutmeg |
| 1/2 | cup all-purpose flour |
| 4 | ounces Gorgonzola cheese |
| 4 | tablespoons unsalted butter, divided |
| 3/4 | cup whipping cream |
| | Salt and freshly ground black pepper to taste |

Wash and peel potatoes; boil whole until done, when knife inserted in middle comes out easily. Drain and mash while still hot. Place potatoes and spinach in a medium bowl; add egg, salt and nutmeg. Combine in mixer and slowly add flour, mixing lightly to a smooth dough. Dust with flour. Roll portions of dough into long ropes about 1-inch in diameter. Cut each rope into bite-size pieces. Drop individually into a large saucepan of salted boiling water until they float; remove. In a medium skillet, melt cheese with 2 tablespoons butter over low heat. Add cream and simmer 2 minutes until thickened, adding remaining butter if necessary. Toss with gnocchi; season with salt and pepper. Serves 4.

🍎 To reduce fat and sodium, reduce butter to 1 tablespoon, substitute evaporated skim milk for cream and eliminate added salt.

🍇 Mezzacorona Pinot Grigio (Italy); La Lastra Vernaccia Riserva (Italy).

# NEW YORK STRIP ALLA ROBESPIERRE *with Herbed Oil*

| | |
|---|---|
| 1 1/2 | pounds New York boneless strip steak |
| | Salt and freshly ground black pepper to taste |
| | Finely minced mixed fresh herbs (parsley, sage rosemary, and thyme) |
| 1 | tablespoon extra-virgin olive oil |
| 8 | teaspoons Herbed Oil (recipe follows) |
| | Mixed baby lettuce salad for 4 |

**HERBED OIL**

| | |
|---|---|
| 1 | cup extra-virgin oil |
| 6 | tablespoons chopped parsley |
| 1/4 | cup finely minced mixed fresh herbs |
| 1 to 2 | garlic cloves |
| 1 | teaspoon salt |

Cut meat into 4 portions; season well on both sides with salt, pepper and herbs. Rub olive oil on meat; cover. Marinate in refrigerator overnight.

Prepare herbed oil; allow to sit 2 to 4 hours for flavors to marry. Grill steaks to desired doneness, 10 minutes per side for medium rare. Brush each with 2 teaspoons Herbed Oil. Serve with salad. Serves 4.

### Herbed Oil

Combine oil, parsley, mixed herbs, garlic and salt in a small container. Cover and let stand 2 to 4 hours for flavors to marry. Makes about 1 1/3 cups. Also use with Oven Roasted Salmon, page 122.

🍎 Beef is an excellent source of iron and vitamin B12 and sirloin is a relatively lean cut. For low-fat preparation, eliminate added oil and limit Herbed Oil for drizzling to 4 teaspoons.

🍇 Chateau Larose Trintaudon (France); Beringer Knight's Valley Cabernet Sauvignon.

123

# FLOURLESS CHOCOLATE CAKE

2   cups sugar, divided
2   cups unsweetened cocoa
    powder, sifted
3   tablespoons baking powder
1   teaspoon salt
6   eggs, separated
1   cup whipping cream
8   ounces baking chocolate,
    chopped
1/2 cup filling of your choice
    (raspberry or strawberry jam
    with water to thin)
    Whipped cream and fresh
    berries for garnish (if desired)

Sift 1 1/2 cups sugar, cocoa, baking powder and salt together in a large bowl; set aside. In a small bowl, whip yolks with remaining 1/2 cup sugar until thick and pale yellow; set aside. In clean bowl with clean beaters, whip egg whites to stiff peaks; set aside.

Preheat oven to 350 degrees. Gently fold yolks into dry mixture, adding water a tablespoon at a time if necessary. Then gently fold egg whites into chocolate mixture being careful not to deflate them. Spread batter into 2 (8-inch) buttered cake pans. Bake until a toothpick inserted into center comes out clean, about 45 minutes. Remove from oven and cool on a rack. Remove cakes from pans and let sit while making ganache.

Heat cream in a small saucepan until hot. Remove from heat and add chocolate, stirring constantly until smooth and shiny. Keep ganache warm and fluid. Spread filling on top of one of the cakes and place other cake on top. Place filled cake on a cooling rack and pour ganache evenly over cake. Refrigerate until ganache is set, about 30 minutes. To serve, cut into wedges with a warm, dry knife. Garnish with whipped cream and fresh berries. Serves 8.

Gratify your chocolate cravings with this recipe but use restraint – cut into 12 servings and forget the whipped cream. Garnish with plenty of fresh berries.

Banfi Brachetto d'Acqui (Italy); Cline or DeLoach Late Harvest Zinfandel.

POACHED CHICKEN SALAD WITH BRAISED LEEK AND TOMATO CONFIT *and Walnut Vinaigrette*
PASTA WITH FRISÉE, EXOTIC MUSHROOMS, SWEET CORN AND WHITE TRUFFLE OIL
SMOKED THYME MUSHROOM RISOTTO
TASCA'S BEEF RILLET LASAGNA
BANANAS FOSTER BREAD PUDDING

Tasca Kitchen & Wine Bar has introduced many Houston diners to Spanish and multi-cultural specialties since the restaurant opened in July 1998 in an old building downtown. The three partners, Rasheed Rafaey, Grant Cooper and Charles Clark, represent new generation owners who will lead restaurants into the 21st century. Loyal customers have already come to expect the unexpected in Clark's New American Cuisine. He seeks out the unusual such as black truffles and truffle oil from Italy, goose foie gras from Canada and organic and exotic produce – fiddlehead ferns from the East, fresh nettles from Oregon, ramp (a wild green onion) from Virginia and baby root vegetables. They join Spanish classics on a menu of great diversity; it features wild game, Spanish specialty meats and sausages from a vendor in California, Kobe beef from Japan, grass-fed beef from Argentina and fish from many waters. Every other week, Clark does a roast suckling pig stuffed with rosemary branches, which infuse an aromatic smoke.

He brings in little-known Spanish foods that are difficult to find in this country including Blackfoot Serrano ham (a legendary ham that comes only from black-hoofed mountain-raised Spanish pigs), fresh anchovies (bacarones), Bilbao chorizo, different varieties of Spanish olives and salt-cured pork loin. He loves combining these authentic foods with elements of other cuisines – Italian, Moroccan, Asian and even Cajun reflecting his Louisiana background. One of Tasca's best sellers is cornmeal-crusted Sabine River Catfish with Crawfish Mashed Potatoes. The chef predicts that simple, "less is more" plates, natural and organic foods, rustic food, Fusion and Latin cooking, moderation and comfort foods will be strong influences in the early millennium.

Clark spent almost a year in Spain learning the art of making tapas, the famous Spanish appetizer tidbits, and developing a feel for Spanish ingredients and cooking techniques. An ever-changing list of 30 or more tapas sets the theme for Tasca's menu. Among the standouts: Roasted Bone Marrow with Parsley Salad and Sea Salt, Spanish Potato Omelet, Texas Goat Cheese Dumplings with Sambal Chili Oil and Apple & Hickory Smoked Bacon Guacamole with Pasta Chips. Wines are a major focus and the wait staff is well versed in recommending two or three choices for each dish. At least 35 wines are available by the glass. Flights of three wines allow customers to sample a variety. They usually have a theme – "Trip to the Zoo" offers a tasting of Rabbit Ridge, Frog's Leap and Toad Hollow. Order "It's Almost Like Butter" and you get samples of three buttery Chardonnays.

Tasca is an example of Houston's rapidly developing downtown, which blends historic Houston buildings with clean, modern design. This hip, but unpretentious restaurant attracts downtown denizens at lunch and after work and brings suburbanites back to town for before- and after-theater dining and desserts. There is almost always a wait, especially Thursday through Saturday nights when there is live jazz. Reservations are essential on weekends.

*Tasca*
KITCHEN & WINE BAR

--- LITE FARE ---

Tasca's menu is a wonderful combination of lean meats with interesting vegetables and grains accompanied by fruit glazes and chutneys. Look for super grains such as quinoa, risotto and couscous and healthful vegetables such as bok choy, Swiss chard, arugula, beets, leeks and turnips. A vegetarian entrée is usually offered. Enjoy a balance of taste, flavors, textures and nutrients.

*Tasca*
*908 Congress*
*Houston, Tx 77002*
*713-225-9100*

# POACHED CHICKEN SALAD WITH BRAISED LEEK AND TOMATO CONFIT *and Walnut Vinaigrette*

3/4    cup Walnut Vinaigrette (recipe follows)
2    gallons cold water
1/2    pound carrots, coarsely chopped
1/2    pound yellow onion, coarsely chopped
2    pounds boneless, skinless chicken breast halves
2    heads Boston Bibb lettuce
1    head red oak lettuce (baby if possible)
12    arugula leaves
1    (10-ounce) bag fresh spinach
9    Roma tomatoes
2    tablespoons olive oil
   Salt and freshly ground black pepper to taste
2    large leeks
   Fresh chopped herbs, such as mint, flat parsley, curly parsley, cilantro and oregano

Prepare vinaigrette; set aside. Bring water to a simmer in large stockpot; add carrots and onion; simmer 30 minutes. Add chicken and simmer until white throughout, about 7 minutes. Place chicken on sheet pan and set aside until cool; reserve liquid. Carefully slice chicken very thin and set aside.

Preheat oven to 450 degrees. Clean and pat lettuces and spinach dry; store in refrigerator. Cut tomatoes in half and scoop out seeds; remove stem. Brush tomato halves with oil; season with salt and pepper. Place tomatoes on roasting rack over a sheet pan. Roast 10 minutes until edges of tomatoes turn crispy.

Reduce oven temperature to 325 degrees. Cut bright green part off top of leeks; discard. Cut leeks diagonally into 2-inch pieces; wash to make sure all dirt is removed. Place 2 cups reserved poaching liquid in roasting pan and add leeks. Roast in oven 20 minutes, or until leeks start to simmer. Remove leeks from liquid and cool. Mix lettuces and spinach in large bowl. Add vinaigrette; toss until well coated. Divide among 6 plates and garnish with chicken, tomato halves, leeks and herbs. Serves 6.

## WALNUT VINAIGRETTE

3/4    cup vegetable oil
1/2    cup champagne vinegar
1    teaspoon Dijon mustard
1    tablespoon chopped fresh herbs (optional)
1/4    teaspoon sugar (optional)
2    tablespoons finely chopped walnuts
   Salt and freshly ground black pepper to taste

**Walnut Vinaigrette**

Combine oil, vinegar, mustard, herbs, sugar and walnuts in a medium bowl; whisk to blend thoroughly. Add salt and pepper. Makes 1 1/4 cups.

🍎 Packed into this recipe is enough vitamin A for three days, vitamin C for one day and five-and-a-half grams of fiber. For low-fat preparation, eliminate oil by using nonstick cooking spray and reducing vinaigrette to 1 tablespoon per serving.

🍇 San Quirico Vernaccia di San Gimignano (Italy); Ca Del Bosco Pinot Bianco (Italy).

# Pasta with Frisée, Exotic Mushrooms, Sweet Corn and White Truffle Oil

1 1/2  pounds favorite short pasta (penne or ziti)
1  pound frisée or Swiss chard
1  pound portobello, oyster or wood ear mushrooms or a combination
4  ears fresh corn
1  gallon cold water
2  tablespoons olive oil
  Salt and freshly ground black pepper to taste
2  tablespoons white truffle oil

Cook pasta in large pot of boiling water until al dente. Drain; set aside. Clean and stem frisée. Clean and julienne mushrooms. Remove corn kernels from ears and combine with mushrooms.

Add water and corn cobs to a small stockpot, bring to a boil, reduce heat and simmer until reduced by two-thirds. Strain and set aside.

Heat large skillet about 2 minutes and add olive oil. When hot, add pasta and sear until brown, about 2 minutes. Add 10 ounces of corn stock, frisée, mushrooms and corn; sauté until simmering. Add salt and pepper. Divide among plates and drizzle each with about 1 teaspoon truffle oil. Serves 6.

Mushrooms contain glutamic acid, an amino acid that seems to be instrumental in fighting infections. This is a great low-fat recipe. Indulge!

Prunotto Dolcetto d'Alba (Italy); Trerose Vino Nobile di Montepulciano (Italy).

# Smoked Thyme Mushroom Risotto

10  ounces chanterelle mushrooms
6  tablespoons pure olive oil, divided
  Sea salt and freshly ground roasted black peppercorns to taste
1  cup Arborio rice
5  cups hot chicken or vegetable stock, divided
2  tablespoons chopped fresh herbs (thyme, parsley and tarragon)
6  tablespoons unsalted butter
1/4  cup aged Parmesan (Grana Padano)
4  dried whole thyme sprigs for garnish

Preheat oven to 450 degrees. Toss mushrooms in 3 tablespoons oil, salt and pepper. Place on cookie sheet and roast 4 minutes or until golden brown.

Heat remaining 3 tablespoons oil in large skillet 1 minute. Add rice and sauté until light brown, about 3 minutes. Add one-third of the stock and stir slowly with a spoon until almost absorbed. Add another third of the stock, mushrooms and herbs; season with salt and pepper. Fold in butter. Add more of the remaining third of stock if necessary. Cook, stirring constantly, until rice is tender, 20 to 25 minutes. Stir in Parmesan and garnish each serving with a dried thyme sprig. Light with a match so thyme will perfume the risotto. Serves 4.

Mushrooms supply respectable amounts of fiber and complex carbohydrates and are great meat substitutes. Make this recipe low fat by reducing oil and butter to 1 tablespoon each. Use low-fat, low-sodium chicken broth or make your own (see Healthy Recipe Modifications).

Napa Ridge Pinot Noir; Wild Horse Pinot Noir; Gevrey Chambertin Clos St. Jacques Jadot (France).

# TASCA'S BEEF RILLET LASAGNA

3    tablespoons extra-virgin olive oil, divided
2    pounds beef tenderloin tips, cut into 1/4-inch cubes
8    ounces Maytag blue cheese
8    ounces ricotta cheese
1/4  cup chopped fresh herbs (parsley, basil, thyme and oregano), divided
     Salt and freshly ground black pepper to taste
1    pound dried lasagna noodles

Preheat oven to 350 degrees. Heat 2 tablespoons oil in large skillet. Thoroughly brown meat on all sides to medium rare; set aside. In a bowl, blend the two cheeses, 2 tablespoons chopped herbs, salt and pepper; set aside.

Bring a large pot of water to a rolling boil and blanch noodles until pliable. Drain and rinse in cold water. Line bottom of a lasagna pan or an 13x9x2-inch pan with noodles; place half the beef on top, then cover with half the cheese mixture. Repeat layers and finish with a third layer of noodles on top (may come above top of pan). Brush noodles with remaining 1 tablespoon oil and sprinkle with remaining 2 tablespoons herbs. Cover pan with foil. Bake 40 to 50 minutes, until center is hot. Cut into 8 or 9 squares; serve immediately. Serves 8 to 9.

To reduce fat, cut oil to 1 tablespoon on top layer of noodles, use nonstick skillet covered with nonstick cooking spray to sauté and limit blue cheese to 4 ounces.

Cornacchia Montepulciano D'Abruzzo (Italy); Allegrini Valpolicella Palazzo Della Torre (Italy).

# BANANAS FOSTER BREAD PUDDING

3    (2-day old) French bread baguettes, about 15 to 18 inches long
1 1/2  cups unsalted butter
2    tablespoons ground cinnamon
1    cup chopped pecans
1    cup granulated sugar
1    cup brown sugar
2 1/2  cups whipping cream
5    eggs
4    medium bananas, sliced
     Favorite ice cream

Cut bread into 1/2-inch cubes; set aside. Bring butter, cinnamon, pecans and sugars to a simmer in a medium saucepan. Add bread cubes to sugar mixture; stir until bread is well coated. In a large bowl, mix cream and eggs; add bananas. Fold sugar and custard mixtures together, distributing bananas evenly. Pour into a buttered 11x7x2-inch pan. Let stand 30 minutes to 1 hour until bread has absorbed liquid. Preheat oven to 325 degrees.

Bake 1 hour or until mixture is set. Let cool 3 hours; refrigerate covered overnight. Cut into squares. Warm in microwave oven 1 minute on high per square before serving. Accompany with favorite ice cream, such as vanilla or cinnamon. Serves 8.

Enjoy this wonderful dessert but in small pieces – cut into 15 squares. Top with fat-free or low-fat ice cream or yogurt.

Cella Asti Spumante (Italy); Ferrari-Carano El Dorado Gold; Far Niente Dolce.

FACING PAGE, FROM LEFT: *Grant Cooper, Charles Clark, Rasheed Rafaey, Tasca.*

FOLLOWING PAGE, FROM LEFT: *Jeff Vallone, Grotto; Jon Paul, Tony's; Bruce McMillian, Tony's; Joey Vallone, Vallone's.*

WILD MUSHROOM RISOTTO, ASPARAGUS, CHIVES AND PARMIGIANO-REGGIANO *with Asparagus Sauce*
VALLONE'S QUICK MARINATED GRILLED SWORDFISH (PESCESPADA "IN FRETTA")
TONY'S CAPON WITH INTENSE GARLIC AND SAGE SAUCE
(CAPON ALLA SALVIA ED AGLIO)
LA GRIGLIA PASTA WITH CHICKEN, TOMATOES, SWEET PEPPERS
AND ARUGULA (PENNE DAL DIO)

Tony Vallone's restaurant dynasty in Houston began with the original Tony's in 1964, which featured Italian food "when you couldn't give it away," he says. Back then, when Houston thought that the only companion to spaghetti was meatballs, Tony's introduced finer Italian food to the city. Vallone says he was the first to serve marinara sauce in Texas and popularized pasta and seafood dishes in the mid '60s. In only a few years, especially after the restaurant moved to the Galleria area in 1971, Tony's gained a reputation as the destination restaurant for the movers, shakers, trendsetters and celebrities.

Vallone says a fine restaurant is a combination of the kitchen for quality, the front for service, plus the ambiance and timing. Tony's has all of that and one more attraction – Tony Vallone himself. Knowing his faithful clientele and their culinary whims, he is a perfectionist, obsessive about every detail. Even the Italian government has noticed. Earlier this year, Tony's was recognized as one of 18 restaurants outside of Italy certified for their authenticity. Another reason he gains customers' respect is his knowledge of wines, which he collects with a passion.

Menus have evolved along with lifestyles. In the past 28 years, Italian gave way to classic French-style with butter, cream and flour-thickened sauces, then to updated Italian with lighter, more healthful fare. Each Vallone restaurant attracts a different clientele – Anthony's appeals to the expense account-lunch crowd, the ladies who lunch, couples seeking a romantic dinner or celebrating an occasion. The two Grottos, run by Vallone's son Jeff, satisfy diners in the mood for casual dress and Neapolitan food (Vallone's family came from Naples.) La Griglia is a high-energy casual restaurant where traditional Italian and contemporary cooking merge. Vallone's Steak House, managed by son Joey Vallone, caters to smart, casual diners of any age who enjoy fine steaks and seafood in pleasant surroundings.

Vallone's basic philosophy – use only the best – will carry over to the 21st century. The restaurants will continue to use the freshest and finest specialties from around the world – fish, cheese, game, porcini and portobello mushrooms and white truffles flown in from Italy (Vallone says in recent years he has paid as much as $1400 a pound for truffles in season), caviar and locally grown fresh herbs. Each Vallone restaurant has its own butcher and baker. Fish and meats are still cut by hand; soufflés are made by hand to order. The demi-glace is still patiently made with bones, stock, red wine, tomatoes and vegetables. Pastas for all the restaurants are hand-made.

Vallone predicts that as we move into the millennium menus will continue to change with the seasons and customers will still be eating a lot of beef, game and fish; pasta will continue in popularity and there will be even more emphasis on fresh vegetables. Admirers of the lush desserts need not fret – butter and cream will remain to delight fans of Tony's crème brûlée, Elizabeth's Praline Cheesecake, soufflés and vacherin.

―――――――――――――――― *LITE FARE* ――――――――――――――――

Tony's restaurants embrace the Mediterranean style of cooking that features grilling and roasting rather than frying and sautéing, olive oil rather than butter and flavoring with fresh herbs and spices rather than heavy sauces. Look for Spa Selections and Light items that feature smaller portions of lean meats and fish accompanied by fresh vegetables and hearty grains. Special requests are encouraged and taken seriously.

*Tony's*
*1801 Post Oak*
*Houston, Tx 77056*
*713-622-6778*

# ANTHONY'S WILD MUSHROOM RISOTTO, ASPARAGUS, CHIVES AND PARMIGIANO-REGGIANO *with Asparagus Sauce*

Asparagus Sauce
(recipe follows)
1 tablespoon olive oil
1/2 white onion, chopped
2 garlic cloves, minced
5 cups mixed exotic mushrooms, sliced: cremini, oyster, shiitake and portobello
2 tablespoons dried porcini mushrooms (soaked in warm water; reserve soaking liquid)
2 cups arborio rice
4 to 5 cups chicken stock or water, divided
1/2 teaspoon kosher salt
Freshly ground black pepper to taste
1/4 cup freshly grated Parmigiano-Reggiano cheese
2 tablespoons chopped chives
8 to 10 chive blossoms (optional)
1/4 cup cooked, sliced asparagus from Asparagus Sauce

## ASPARAGUS SAUCE
1 1/2 pounds asparagus
1 teaspoon cornstarch
1 tablespoon water
Salt and freshly ground black pepper to taste

Prepare Asparagus Sauce; set aside. Heat oil over medium-high heat in large saucepan. Add onion; sauté until golden, about 5 minutes. Add garlic and cook 1 minute. Add mushrooms; sauté until well cooked and mixture is dry. Add rice and stir to blend. Add porcini liquid and 1 cup stock; cook, stirring until liquid is absorbed. Continue adding stock 1 cup at a time, stirring well after each addition until all liquid is absorbed, about 18 to 20 minutes. Add salt and pepper just before done. Stir in Parmesan, chives, blossoms and reserved sliced asparagus. Place risotto in bowl; arrange reserved asparagus tips around risotto and ladle sauce around edge of bowl. Serves 6.

### Asparagus Sauce
Trim woody ends and peel asparagus. Bring a large saucepan of water to a boil over high heat. Add asparagus and cook until it turns bright green, about 3 minutes. Immediately plunge asparagus into ice water; drain. Cut off top 2 inches of asparagus; reserve for garnish. Slice off 1-inch from bottom; set aside to add to risotto as directed. Place stalks in juicer and extract juice; discard pulp. (Or, place stalks in a blender with 1 cup chicken stock and process until smooth.) Place juice in a small saucepan and bring to a boil over high heat. Combine cornstarch and water in a small custard cup. Reduce heat and gradually stir in cornstarch mixture. Add salt and pepper and cook until thickened, about 2 to 3 minutes. Makes about 1 cup.

The high glutamic acid content of mushrooms may boost your immune function. This recipe is low in fat but high in sodium. To reduce sodium, use low-sodium chicken broth or prepare your own low-sodium, low-fat chicken stock.

Perdera Rosso Argiolas (Italy); Bruno Giacosa Barbera d'Alba (Italy); Giacomo Conterno or Aldo Conterno Barolo (Italy).

# ANTHONY'S

# VALLONE'S QUICK MARINATED GRILLED SWORDFISH (PESCESPADA "IN FRETTA")

| | |
|---|---|
| 1 | cup extra-virgin olive oil |
| 1 | cup dry white wine |
| 1/2 | cup balsamic vinegar |
| | Juice of 2 limes |
| 1 | tablespoon Worcestershire sauce |
| 3 | large garlic cloves, crushed |
| 2 | shallots, minced |
| 2 | bay leaves |
| 3 | sprigs fresh rosemary, crushed |
| 2 | tablespoons finely chopped fresh mint |
| 20 | black peppercorns, crushed |
| | Pinch of crushed red pepper flakes |
| 1 | teaspoon crushed dried oregano |
| | Seasoned salt to taste |
| 4 | (8- to 10-ounce) swordfish fillets, cut at least 1-inch thick |

Combine oil, wine, vinegar, lime juice, Worcestershire, garlic, shallots, bay leaves, rosemary, mint, peppercorns, red pepper flakes, oregano and salt in large container; mix well. Let stand at room temperature 15 minutes, stirring often. Add fish; cover and marinate no more than 30 minutes, turning at least twice.

Char grill or broil fish 3 to 4 minutes on each side, basting frequently. Heat half the marinade, whip with a fork and put a teaspoon or so over each piece of fish. Discard remaining marinade. Serve immediately and accompany with green beans and lemon. Top beans with crossed pimiento strips. Serves 4.

*Note:* This same preparation is excellent with tuna, chicken or pork.

🍎 Swordfish is a rich source of blood-building vitamin B12 and niacin while its omega-3's also help keep your arteries healthy. Even with oil in the marinade, this recipe is fairly low fat, but the portions are large. Use 6-ounce fillets and enjoy.

🍇 Gavi la Scolca (Italy); Cabreo La Pietra Ruffino (Italy).

# TONY'S CAPON WITH INTENSE GARLIC AND SAGE SAUCE (CAPON ALLA SALVIA ED AGLIO)

| | |
|---|---|
| 1 | (4 1/2- to 5 1/2-pound) capon or large chicken, cut into 8 pieces |
| 3 | cups Chianti or other dry red wine |
| 16 | fresh sage leaves, divided |
| 18 | garlic cloves, divided |
| 1 | whole clove |
| 6 | tablespoons extra-virgin olive oil |
| 2 | tablespoons unsalted butter |
| | Seasoned salt and freshly ground black pepper to taste |
| 5 | tablespoons tomato paste |
| 1 | cup chicken broth |
| | Sage leaves for garnish |
| 2 | tablespoons chopped parsley for garnish |

Place chicken in a large container. Add wine, 6 sage leaves and 5 crushed, but whole garlic cloves. Marinate chicken covered in refrigerator at least 1 hour. Add whole clove to marinade no more than 15 minutes before removing chicken.

Finely chop remaining 10 sage leaves and 13 garlic cloves together; set aside. Heat oil and butter in a large skillet over medium heat. Add chicken and sauté 4 to 5 minutes, or until chicken is golden all over. Add chopped sage and garlic; sauté 2 minutes. Discard whole clove from marinade and add 1 cup marinade to skillet, cook 10 minutes. Cooking time will depend on size and firmness of chicken. A capon will take longer than a chicken; poultry should be half cooked at this point. Season with salt and generously with pepper. Dissolve tomato paste in broth; add to skillet and complete cooking, about 20 minutes. When done, transfer chicken and sauce to a large serving platter; garnish with a lot of sage leaves all around; sprinkle parsley over top. Serves 4 to 6.

🍎 Leave skin on capon during sautéing but remove before eating. Reduce oil and butter to 1 tablespoon each for sautéing. This recipe can serve 6 adequately.

🍇 Cecchi Sangiovese or Antinori Santa Cristina (Italy); Querceto Ilpico (Italy).

# LA GRIGLIA PASTA WITH CHICKEN, TOMATOES, SWEET PEPPERS AND ARUGULA (PENNE DAL DIO)

| | |
|---|---|
| 1 | pound penne or ziti pasta |
| 6 | tablespoons extra-virgin olive oil |
| 1 | cup chopped shallots or red onion |
| 3 | medium-size red bell peppers, roasted, peeled, seeded and chopped |
| 3 | heaping tablespoons chopped very ripe tomato |
| 1 | scant teaspoon sugar |
| 4 to 5 | large garlic cloves, minced |
| 5 to 6 | boneless, skinless chicken breast halves, diced into 1/2-inch pieces |
| | Seasoned salt and freshly ground black pepper to taste |
| | Crushed red pepper flakes to taste |
| 1 | teaspoon crushed dried oregano |
| 2 | teaspoons dried thyme |
| 2 | cups arugula leaves, chopped in 1-inch pieces |
| 8 | large leaves fresh sweet basil, torn into pieces |
| 4 | tablespoons freshly grated Parmigiano-Reggiano cheese |

Cook pasta in a large stockpot of boiling water until al dente; drain. Set aside and keep warm. Heat oil in a large skillet; sauté shallots, stirring over medium heat 3 minutes until lightly browned. Add peppers, tomato, sugar, garlic and chicken; sauté, stirring about 4 minutes. Add a pinch of salt, pepper, pepper flakes, oregano, thyme and arugula. Cook 3 to 4 minutes, stirring to blend well. Toss pasta with sauce. Garnish with basil and serve at once with cheese. Serves 5 to 6.

*Note:* Swordfish may be substituted for chicken.

Red peppers are a good source and even higher in vitamin C than green. To keep fat calories under control, reduce oil for sautéing vegetables to 2 tablespoons. This recipe is plenty for 6 servings.

Ruffino Fonte al Sole (Italy); Brolio Casalferro (Italy).

*la griglia*

# THE END HUNGER NETWORK

The eating is good in Houston. Our city has been blessed with a wealth of talented and innovative chefs. Even as they collect guidebook stars and places on "Best of" lists, Houston's outstanding chefs are dedicated to feeding folks whose names won't appear on tonight's reservation list. In a delicious display of caring, Houston chefs save some of their best for families who otherwise couldn't put food on the table, working under the auspices of the End Hunger Network and Taste of the Nation.

From its very beginning, the End Hunger Network has had a special relationship with the hospitality industry. In fact, it was a restaurateur who conceived the hunger-relief organization's very first program. One April day in 1985, Walter Aymen of Boca del Rio joined the End Hunger Network's founder, Mary Barden Keegan, on a tour of a women and children's shelter. The homeless shelter was packed with clients but when Aymen opened the refrigerator, all he found inside was a lone bottle of ketchup. His first thought was of all the food sitting in his restaurant kitchen – and Aymen hauled carload after carload of that food to the shelter in time for dinner.

Working with Mary Keegan, Aymen recruited nine chefs to donate the surplus from their kitchens – and thus was the End Hunger Food Loop born. Today, chefs at some 90 restaurants, hotels, hospitals and corporate cafeterias share prepared food with 23 shelters and soup kitchens. Whether their métier is Continental cuisine or down-home barbecue, the men and women in toques stand solidly behind Food Loop's efforts to insure that no wholesome, nutritious food goes to waste while 580,000 of our neighbors go hungry. In 1999, the unused bounty from their kitchens is providing 300,000+ meals for Houston's hungry – and the Food Loop is still adding to its roster. Next time you're at your favorite eatery, ask the chef if his/her establishment is a Food Loop donor – and note your appreciation.

**RED BARREL**

You, too, can taste the fruits of local chefs' passion for feeding all Houstonians. Each spring for eleven years now, some 50 of the city's finest cook for the cause at Share Our Strength's Taste of the Nation. Join us on April 9, 2000, for Houston's premier tasting event, hosted by Chef Jim Mills of Olivette at The Houstonian. (Tickets are $60; call 713-532-3663 for details.) Last year, Taste of the Nation netted $96,500 to support the work of the End Hunger Network and other local and national hunger-relief charities.

Cooking professionally isn't a prerequisite for pitching in. When grocery shopping for you family, buy an extra canned good or a prepackaged "Buy, Bye Hunger!" bag and deposit it in the Red Barrel. Red Barrels are located near the entrances of all Fiesta, Gerland's, H-E-B, Kroger, Randalls and Rice supermarkets. Each Barrel supports the work of the food pantry serving the surrounding neighborhood.

*Every entrée, every can donated brings nourishment and hope to families in sore need of both. On their behalf, heartfelt thanks to all the passionate chefs, to Ann and Fran for their legacy of love and to all who lend their energy, financial support and food. Together, we are ending hunger in Houston!*

FOOD LOOP

# ANN STEINER

Ann Steiner is a syndicated microwave columnist who with her co-author, CiCi Williamson, created and published two microwave cookbooks – "Microwave Know-How" and "Micro Quick!". The duo also developed and appeared in a microwave cooking video and have written articles for several professional and popular publications.

Her varied interests in the culinary arena include: cookbook editing (this is her fourth "Houston Is Cooking" publication), recipe development and testing for major food companies, cooking seminars and teacher training. Ann also has served as a judge for the national Beef Cook-Off and Celebrity Microwave Cooking Contest.

She received a Master's Degree from Ohio State University and a Bachelor's Degree from Miami University (Ohio). In 1992, the Federation of Houston Professional Women selected Ann as one of their "Woman of Excellence" honorees. She is a member of the Houston Culinary Guild, Les Dames d'Escoffier and the International Association of Culinary Professionals.

Married to high-school sweetheart Bill, Ann is also mother to Cindy, Cathy and Jeff, sons-in-law, Steve and Mike and Nanna to Christa, Madelyn, Adam, Katie and Kyle.

# SPECIAL HELPS

Some terms and recipes from professional chefs may be unfamiliar to home cooks. Here are several terms that you may see frequently.

**Achiote**—A yellow seasoning and color from the seeds of the annatto tree. Used in Central and South American, Indian, Mexican and Southwestern cooking.

**Ancho chilies**—Dried poblano peppers; dark reddish brown, about 4 inches long.

**Brown Sauce**—(Sauce Espagnole). One of the foundation or "mother" sauces of French cooking; the base for many other sauces. Here is an easy recipe.

    2   tablespoons oil
    1   small onion, finely chopped
  1/2   carrot, grated
    1   tablespoon finely chopped
        fresh parsley
        Pinch of dried thyme
    1   bay leaf
  1 1/2 tablespoons all-purpose flour
  1 1/2 cups beef stock or bouillon (see
        Beef Stock recipe that follows,
        use canned or dissolve 1
        teaspoon instant bouillon
        granules in 1 1/2 cups boiling
        water)
        Salt and freshly ground black
        pepper to taste

Heat oil in large skillet. Add onion, carrot, parsley, thyme and bay leaf. Stir in flour and simmer slowly until browned, about 10 minutes. Whisk in stock, season to taste (don't over-salt) and simmer about 2 minutes. Strain. Makes about 1 1/2 cups.

**Capers**—The small green berry-like buds of the caper bush used as a condiment or to give piquant flavor to sauces. Usually available bottled or pickled in vinegar.

**Caramelize**—(particularly onions). Toss sliced onions with a little olive oil and sugar, and heat slowly over medium-low heat until soft and dark brown. Do not let burn. Use with beef and grilled meats, fajitas, burgers or as a garnish.

**Chiffonade**—Thinly shredded lettuce or other vegetables used raw or in sautés. In French, the term means made of rags.

**Chipotle**—Dried, dark red smoked jalapeños.

**Chocolate**—To melt in the microwave: Place chocolate in a glass dish and melt on medium (50-percent) power, about 1 1/2 to 2 minutes per square, stirring midway through. Chocolate may not look melted; test by stirring to smooth.

**Clarified butter**—Often used in delicate, fine dishes because it doesn't burn as easily as whole butter. Melt butter (preferably unsalted) over low heat until foam disappears from top and sediment and milk solids collect in bottom of pan. Pour off clear butter; discard sediment.

**Concassé**—Crushed, seeded fruit or vegetables, especially tomatoes.

**Confit**— (confee) — Cooked meat (usually duck or goose) preserved under a layer of fat.

**Coulis**—(coulee) — Pureed mixtures of fruits or vegetables.

**Cream**—When chefs list cream as an ingredient, they usually mean heavy cream of at least 36 percent butterfat. Whipping cream doubles its volume when whipped. Most whipping cream now is ultra-pasteurized for longer shelf life. Better texture and optimum volume are achieved if the cream, bowl and beaters are thoroughly chilled before the cream is beaten. Heavy cream is usually labeled whipping cream, although some supermarkets stock heavy whipping cream. If light cream is specified, look for cream labeled coffee cream or table cream.

**Deglaze**—Pour off all but a tablespoon or two of accumulated fat from sautéed food; add stock, water, wine or liquid called for in the recipe and simmer, scraping up browned bits from bottom of pan with a wooden spoon.

**Demi-glace (DIM-ee-glahs)**—A rich, brown sauce based on basic espagnole (see Brown Sauce listing above). It is mixed with beef stock and sherry or Madeira and simmered slowly until reduced by half to a thick glaze. Often used as the base for other sauces and as a glaze added to the pan at the last minute.

**Flambé**—To flame a dish by adding high-alcohol content liquor or liqueurs and, when warm, igniting with a match or by tilting the pan close to the flame and lighting it from the burner just before serving. If inexperienced, it's easier to light it with a taper match.

**Herbs**—Fresh are preferred if of good quality. The rule of thumb in substituting dried herbs is one teaspoon dried for three teaspoons fresh.

**Japanese bread crumbs**—Fine dry bread crumbs that make a light, delicate coating for frying. Frequently used with crab cakes. Available at Fiesta, Japanese and selected Asian markets.

**Nopales**—(no-PAH-les) — Fleshy pads of the cactus (nopal) that also produces prickly pears (cactus pears).

**Olive oil**—Extra-virgin olive oil is preferred by most chefs because it is the finest quality and has distinctive flavor. Generally it is used for salad dressings and uncooked dishes because it has a low smoking point. Some chefs use it for frying but most prefer a less expensive grade of olive such as superfine virgin, virgin or "pure" for everyday use. Store olive oil in a cool, dark place.

**Pasta**—Make your own or purchase from supermarkets or pasta shops. Fresh pasta is best with light, fresh tomato sauces or delicate cream sauces; dried pasta, with heartier, long-simmered meat and red sauces.

Fresh pasta takes only 3 to 5 minutes to cook; dried may take as long as 15 minutes. Pasta should always be cooked "al dente," which means firm to the tooth. It should lose its floury taste, but not be hard or mushy. Never rinse cooked pasta with cold water unless using it for salads or holding it to serve later. Rinse in cold water or hold in ice water until needed. Plunge strainer of pasta into hot water to revive it, then drain and serve. For best quality, hold pasta in cold water no longer than 30 minutes.

**Roasted Garlic**—Remove the papery outer skin, but leave heads of garlic whole. Slice off about 1/4-inch of top. Place in one layer in baking dish that has a cover; drizzle with olive oil or dot with butter. Cover pan and roast at 350 degrees until cloves are soft, about 45 minutes. Use in recipes or separate cloves and squeeze to extract garlic pulp. Discard skins. Spread garlic on bread rounds or toasted French bread or use in dressings. Four heads of garlic yield about 1/4 cup. Alternatively, wrap each head of garlic in aluminum foil and bake at 350 degrees 1 hour. Let cool 10 minutes.

To roast garlic in the microwave, prepare heads in same way as above.

Method I: If using a terra cotta garlic baker (available in cookware stores and housewares section of department stores), soak baker in cool water for 5 minutes. Place prepared head of garlic in baker and microwave on high 3 to 4 minutes. Let stand 5 minutes before squeezing garlic from skin.

Method II: Place prepared head of garlic in a glass custard cup. Cover with vented plastic wrap. Position a 1-cup glass measure filled with tap water alongside covered cup. Microwave on high 4 to 5 minutes. Let stand 5 minutes before squeezing garlic from skin.

**Roasted Peppers**—To roast fresh peppers, rinse and dry, place on a baking sheet in a 350-degree oven 7 to 10 minutes (or broil 4 to 5 inches from heat 5 minutes on each side, until surface of peppers is blistered and somewhat blackened). Drop into ice water and let sit a few minutes until skins rub off easily. You also can place roasted peppers in a paper bag or plastic bag and let sit until skins rub off easily.

Handle jalapeños and other hot chilies with care as peppers and fumes can irritate skin and eyes. Wearing rubber gloves is recommended. Removing walls and seeds of peppers cuts the heat.

**Roasted Tomatoes**—Rub tomatoes with olive oil; place on a baking sheet. Roast in 450-degree oven until charred. Remove from oven; let cool, then peel. Or heat a heavy cast-iron skillet until very hot. Add tomatoes and cook, turning occasionally, until skins begin to blacken and blister, about 10 minutes. Let cool until they can be handled, then peel.

**Reduce**—Cook a mixture down slowly until reduced by half or the amount specified. In contemporary cooking, reductions are frequently used to concentrate flavors or thicken sauces instead of thickening with flour or other starches.

**Roux**—A mixture of flour and fat that is the thickening base for many sauces and soups, particularly gumbo. The usual method is to heat oil until it is at the smoking point, then to whisk in flour and stir constantly until mixture is a dark mahogany brown, almost black. Roux requires close attention; it must be stirred or whisked almost constantly for 45 minutes to an hour or it will burn. Roux is much easier to make in the microwave. The following method is from newspaper microwave columnists Ann Steiner and CiCi Williamson in their first book, "Microwave Know-How:" Heat 1/2 cup each oil and flour in a 4-cup glass measure. Microwave on high (100-percent) power 6 to 7 minutes, stirring every minute after 4 minutes, until a deep brown roux is formed.

**Salad Greens**—Salad greens include a mixture of gourmet baby lettuces, which are sometimes called field salad, corn salad, field greens, lamb's lettuce, field lettuce and mâche, mesclun or spring mix. Mixes sold in markets often are made up of arugula, radicchio, baby oak leaf and red tip lettuces, frisée, watercress and two popular Japanese greens, mizuna and tat soi. Tat soi is slightly peppery like watercress.

**Scald**—Heat (usually milk) until bubbles form at edge of pan.

**Stock**—Stocks made on the premises are the rule in professional kitchens.

If you use canned broth, buy a good quality product. Avoid salty broth; purchase low-sodium broth or reduce salt in the recipe.

When making stock at home, use a nonaluminum pan. For clear stock, skim foam and scum off top as it accumulates. Stir as little as possible to prevent clouding. Stock should simmer slowly, not boil. Cool quickly (setting the pan of stock in a container or sink of cold water speeds the cooling process). Chill, then remove congealed fat from top. Refrigerate or freeze.

**Beef or veal stock:** Combine 2 to 4 pounds beef bones and meaty soup bones or veal bones and trimmings (brown half the meat) in a saucepot. Add 3 quarts cold water, 8 peppercorns, 1 each: onion, carrot and celery rib, cut in pieces; 3 whole cloves, 1 bay leaf, 5 sprigs parsley and other desired herbs such as dried thyme. Bring to a boil and skim off foam. Simmer covered 3 hours, skimming occasionally. Strain stock, cool quickly and refrigerate or freeze. When cold, remove any solid fat that has risen to the top; remove fat before freezing.

**Chicken stock:** Place 3 pounds bony chicken parts in a stockpot with 3 quarts cold water, a quartered onion stuck with 2 whole cloves, 2 each: celery ribs and carrots; 10 peppercorns, 5 sprigs parsley and 1 bay leaf. Cover pot, bring to a boil over medium heat, then reduce heat and simmer stock partially covered, 2 to 3 hours. For clear stock, skim off foam and scum on the surface. Add

salt to taste after about 1 hour. Strain stock and discard bones and solids. Let cool. Refrigerate or freeze when cool.

**Fish stock:** Place 2 pounds fish bones, trimmings and head in a stockpot. Add 2 quarts cold water, 1 each: thinly sliced onion and peeled carrot; 10 white peppercorns, a large bay leaf, a sprig of thyme, 10 parsley sprigs and 1 teaspoon salt. Bring to a boil, reduce heat and simmer covered about 1 hours. Strain through a fine strainer, cool quickly and refrigerate or freeze. Makes about 1 3/4 quarts.

**Shrimp stock:** Place shells from 1/2 pound of shrimp in saucepan with water to cover. If desired add a little salt, parsley, crumbled dried thyme and a bay leaf (or make a bouquet garni of herbs tied in a cheesecloth bag). Bring to a boil, reduce heat and simmer 10 to 15 minutes. Strain and use or cool quickly and refrigerate or freeze.

**Sweat**—Place chopped vegetables or other ingredients in a partially covered pan over low heat and heat until moisture beads form and vegetables are softened. Some chefs do not cover the pan.

**Vinegar**—Use clear white vinegar unless recipe specifies another type such as cider, fruit-flavored, rice wine or balsamic vinegar (dark, aged Italian vinegar).

**Zest**—The thinnest colored part of the peel only (no pith or white membrane); usually refers to citrus fruit.

# SHOPPING GUIDE

Houston offers an increasing number of sources for ethnic and special ingredients called for in recipes in "Houston Is Cooking *2000*." Specialty supermarkets are stocked with exotic produce and spices, fresh herbs, special sauces, condiments, flavored oils and vinegars, juices, pastas, breads, pastries, frozen patty shells and filo dough, canned imported items as well as a wide variety of coffees and teas.

Ethnic markets run the gamut from Mexican and Latin America to Middle Eastern, Caribbean, Chinese, Japanese, Korean, Vietnamese, Thai, Indian and Pakistani. Visiting these markets makes for interesting weekend excursions.

Bakeries such as **French Gourmet** (two locations) sell ready-made puff pastry dough in addition to specialty breads, cakes and other pastries.

Bread bakeries that offer artisan and specialty breads include **Empire Baking Company**, 1616 Post Oak Blvd.; **French Riviera Bakery & Cafe**, 3032 Chimney Rock; **Great Harvest Bread Company** (two locations); **la Madeleine** (several locations); **La Victoria**, 7138 Lawndale; **Moeller's Bakery**, 4201 Bellaire Blvd.; **Patisserie Descours**, 1330-D Wirt Road; **Stone Mill Bakers** (two locations); **Three Brothers Bakery** (three locations); and **Whole Foods Markets** (three locations). **Schlotzsky's Deli Marketplace**, 2929 Kirby Dr. (713-807-9800), bakes its own sandwich breads and buns in-house as well as **Bread Alone** artisan breads, specialty breads baked in a brick oven on a 6,000-pound baking stone; other pastries and desserts.

## GENERAL

**Auchan**, 8800 W. Sam Houston Parkway, Houston, 77099 (281-530-9855). A hypermarket stocked with a United Nations of imported foods from around the world including hundreds of cheeses, international wines, spices, fresh produce, meats, seafood and fish, a full range of grocery items and baked goods from the in-store bakery.

**Fiesta Marts**, 44 locations in the Houston area. Excellent source for fresh produce and foodstuffs from the world's markets — baked goods, ethnic foods, specialty foods, meats and seafood, cooking utensils, condiments, spices, wide selection of Mexican cheeses, prepared take-out foods and wines. Stores vary in size and character with the neighborhoods they serve. Some have coffee and tea bars, in-store delicatessens and sushi bars. Fiesta at 1005 Blalock Dr. off I-10 (the Katy Freeway) offers regularly scheduled cooking classes. Call 713-869-5060, extension 299.

**Kroger Signature stores** (36 locations throughout the city) are special-concept stores that showcase in-store delicatessens, bakeries and salad bars; gourmet foods and wines; fresh meats, seafood and cheese; prepared take-out items; and floral shops. Some do catering. At the Signature Store, 3665 Highway 6 at Settler's Way in Sugar Land (281-980-8888), a wine steward is in charge of what Kroger boasts is the largest selection of wines in a Texas supermarket. The produce department offers more than 450 varieties including imported, ethnic and organic items, prepared salads, bagged vegetables and a juice bar. Aurora Black Angus Beef is an exclusive at Kroger.

**Randalls Flagship stores** (11 locations). Top-drawer supermarkets known for fresh meats, fish and seafood, produce, domestic and imported specialty foods. Flagship stores have in-store bakeries with a pastry chef; specialty breads; delicatessens; coffee-tea bars; expanded wine departments; fresh salad bars; take-out specialties including an assortment of hand-made pizzas, sandwiches, salads and rotisserie chicken; and floral shops. They offer Busy Chef by Randalls home meal replacements and catering and can do party trays, corporate luncheons and events from 10 to 500. High quality packaged meals featuring good-as or better-than-homemade specialties are a holiday tradition.

**Rice Epicurean Markets** (eight locations). In 1998 Rice closed its other stores to concentrate on the Epicurean Markets, which are combination supermarkets and specialty food and beverage stores. You can always find the newest, trendiest and highest-quality products along with a complete stock of supermarket merchandise, paper goods, accessories and fresh flowers. Home meal replacement options include take-out foods, prepared items, fresh sushi prepared in-store, delicatessen specialties, soup and salad bars and ready-to-cook meats and seafood. Rice Epicurean is the exclusive supermarket source for Mrs. See's Candy, Honey Baked Ham and kolaches from the Bon Ton Bakery in La Grange.

Full-service catering offers food and wines; servers; flowers; linen, china and silver rental; professional chefs; plus many more chefs and support staff. Catering director is Douglas Dick, and catering managers, Luzia Turner and Dorothy Thraen.

Another special feature is the Cooking School at Rice Epicurean Market, 2020 Fountainview. Director Peg Lee conducts regular classes with local and international chefs, food personalities and cookbook authors as frequent guests. Call 713-954-2152 for information.

**Whole Foods Markets** (three locations) showcase natural foods: organically grown fruits and vegetables, imported and domestic sauces, condiments, bulk grains, cereals, herbs, spices and seasonings, cheeses, dairy products including yogurts and ice creams, frozen foods, additive-free meats and chicken, specialty breads and other baked goods, wines, beers, teas, coffees, health foods, local and regional products including preserves, sauces and cookies.

Stores feature Whole Foods' own brand-name breads, jarred sauces, in-house bakeries, juice bars and delis with an international mix of natural pasta and rice dishes, sandwiches, salads, hot entrées and side dishes. Catering available.

**Urban Foods**, 909 Texas Ave. at Main (713-225-3663) This compact, well-stocked grocery store opened in July, 1999 off the lobby of the Rice Lofts downtown, as part of the exciting rejuvenation of downtown. It has the look of a New York neighborhood grocery and serves Rice tenants and other downtown denizens with the basics and more. You can buy bread, peanut butter and jelly or complete gourmet meals – prepared or ready-to-cook meats, fruits and vegetables, milk, ice cream, pasta, rice, sauces, salsas, imported cheese, chips and dips, candy, ready-to-cook entrées, salads, side dishes and excellent made-to-order sandwiches. One tenant has in a regular order for canned chili. Owners Richard and Doreen Kaplan, who own Acute Catering, also offer take-out, lunch and dinner specials. And Urban Foods delivers in its service area.

## SPECIALTY SHOPS

**Bering's**, 6102 Westheimer (713-785-6400) and 3900 Bissonnet (713-665-0500). Bering's has been serving Houston's hardware, housewares and kitchen needs for generations. You'll find distinctive gourmet/gift items here including sauces, salsas and other specialty foods, candies and fine chocolates, ground-to-order coffees, teas,

cookware, china, silver and other table appointments, cookbooks, small appliances and decorative objects.

**EatZi's Market & Bakery**, 1702 Post Oak Blvd. (713-629-6003). EatZi's revolutionized the take-out scene in Houston when it opened here in August 1997. It is part grocery store, part take-out and prepared foods, part cook-to-order restaurant, bakery and salad bar. More than 200 items are offered daily including prepared entrees, salads and vegetables; pizzas; rotisserie meats and vegetables, fresh soups and made-to-order sandwiches. The bakery turns out artisan breads such as white chocolate-apricot-almond, dark pumpernickel, chabatta, whole-grain breads and cranberry-ginger rounds as well as indulgent cakes, cookies, muffins and cinnamon rolls. The deli case dispenses everything from pasta salads, wrap sandwiches, hummus, tabbouleh, stir-fries, grilled salmon and chicken salad to roast garlic and green beans. Prepared foods run the gamut from grilled chicken salad to lasagna, quiche, King Ranch chicken and ravioli to Greek salad and sushi. You can select ready-to-cook meats and chicken to take home or have them cooked to order in the wood-burning oven or grill. Fruits and vegetables, greens and exotic fruit are available fresh or in prepared fruit or vegetable salads. You can select a take-out party from eatZi's wide variety of cheeses, dips, jarred sauces, salsas, condiments, crackers, deli meats, pizzas and beverages or have the whole thing catered. Wines and fresh flowers are the final touch.

**Leibman's Wine & Fine Foods**, 14010-A Memorial Dr. at Kirkwood (281-493-3663). Ettienne Leibman hand-picks an extensive collection of wines, hard-to-find spices, oils, vinegars, mustards and other condiments, imported pastas, candies including Godiva chocolates and sugar-free varieties, specialty meats and one of the city's best selections of cheese. In-store deli provides exceptional Chicken Salad Afrique, sandwiches, pasta and rice salads, scones and incomparable English bread pudding, a house specialty. Catering available for kosher holidays, luncheons and corporate and special events. Excellent source for custom gourmet gift baskets.

**Richard's Liquors and Fine Wines** (several locations). Established in 1949, Richard's has done much to educate Houston's palate for fine wines. Larger stores feature wines from around the world including great vintages and large selections of French Bordeaux and Burgundies, specialty

Cognacs, brandies, fruit brandies and Scotches, imported and domestic cheeses, and imported deli meats including Italian pancetta bacon, prosciutto, Westphalian and Black Forest hams. Custom gift baskets are a specialty.

**Spec's Liquor Warehouse & a Whole Lot More Store,** 2410 Smith St. (713-526-8787). Spec's is a 28,000-square-foot facility packed with one of the city's most impressive collection of wines, liquors, liqueurs and specialty foods. Here you will find pâtés; more than 300 domestic and imported cheeses; spices and seasonings; oils and vinegars; salsas; sauces; pastas (more than 300); coffees (more than 90, most roasted in-house) and teas; preserves; chocolates and other candies; specialty meats and condiments. In-house delicatessen features made-to-order sandwiches, soups and salads.

Family-owned and operated, Spec's is known for wide selections of wine and specialty foods at good-value prices and for custom-designed gourmet gift baskets and party supplies.

**Yapa Kitchen and Fresh Take Away,** 3173 W. Holcombe Blvd. (713-664-9272). High-quality prepared foods include fresh pasta, sauces, imported oils, vinegars, cheese, gourmet foods and desserts from Marilyn Descours' Patisserie Descours. Chef's menu daily. Catering available. Wine tastings and cooking classes offered.

## MISCELLANEOUS

**Cost Plus World Markets** entered the Houston retail scene in 1996 and now has five stores. They offer imported specialty foods – pastas, bread mixes, rice, dried beans, sauces, spices, seasonings, condiments, more than 40 teas and their own private-label coffees, salsas and sauces from all over the world. Beans can be ground to order for more than 60 coffees. Also a resource for housewares; linens, pottery, flatware and crystal; decorative objects; furniture; and clothes.

**Williams-Sonoma** (four locations) features everything to outfit the gourmet kitchen from fine-quality cooking utensils and small appliances, many exclusive, to table linens and specialty food items. Their forte is gourmet oils and vinegars; pasta; grains; salsas and sauces; china, pottery and table accessories; coffee grinders and coffee makers; spices; cookbooks; gadgets and housewares. Cooking demos and classes offered regularly.

## INTERNATIONAL MARKETS

### Asian

*There are several markets in Chinatown east of Main Street around McKinney and St. Emanuel and another cluster outside Loop 610 on and around Bellaire Boulevard and further west on Highway 6.*

**Asiatic Import Company,** 909 Chartres (713-227-7979). Family-owned; offers bottled sauces, canned goods, condiments, spices and seasonings, wine, teas as well as cooking utensils and gift items.

**Daido Market,** 11138 Westheimer (713-785-0815). Japanese market with mostly basic seasonings and sauces, canned goods and limited fresh produce, seafood and tuna.

**Diho Market,** 9280 Bellaire Blvd. (713-988-1881). Extensive stock of Chinese and Asian products, fresh meats, fish, wines, sauces, frozen and prepared items, fresh produce and standard sauces and condiments.

**Dynasty Supermarket** in Dynasty Plaza, 9600 Bellaire Blvd. (713-995-4088). Full-line supermarket of Asian and Chinese staples, condiments and hot deli items, meats, fresh fish and seafood, wines and beers.

**Hong Kong Food Market,** 5708 S. Gessner Dr., (713-995-1393); 10923 Scarsdale (281-484-6100) and 13400 Veterans Memorial Dr. (281-537-5280). Full-service supermarkets with wide range of fresh Asian produce; exotic fruits, juices and vegetables, such as Chinese water spinach; fresh meats, chicken and fish; fresh lobster and other seafood; sauces; baked goods; tofu; noodles and rice; spices, seasonings and condiments; fresh bamboo leaves.

**Kazy's Gourmet,** 11346 Westheimer (281-293-9612), offers Japanese ingredients and specialties.

**Kim Hung Supermarket,** 1005 St. Emanuel (713-224-6026) and 12320 Bellaire Blvd. (281-568-3040). Full-service markets specializing in Chinese and Asian imported foods, fresh produce, fresh seafood, sauces, condiments and noodles.

**Long Sing Supermarket,** 2017 Walker (713-228-2017). Small-scale supermarket with hot deli; fresh produce, meats, fish and seafood; frozen prepared items; condiments, sauces, seasonings, noodles and tofu.

**Viet Hoa Supermarket**, 10828 Beechnut (281-561-8706). Complete supermarket with fish market, produce shop and wide assortment of Asian ingredients including Chinese, Vietnamese and Thai specialties.

**Vientiane Market**, 6929 Long Point (713-681-0751). Small but well-stocked market specializing in Thai and Vietnamese foods, some Chinese. Selection of fresh produce; meats and fish; canned goods, traditional sauces, spices, seasonings such as tamarind and yanang leaves, pickles, pickled limes and mixes; cassia flowers, noodles, spring roll skins, coconut milk, palm sugar, curry pastes, fish powder and chilies.

**Welcome Food Center, Inc.,** 9180 Bellaire Blvd. (713-774-8320).  Supermarket featuring fresh meats, fish and seafood, fresh produce, staples of Asian cooking.

### Middle Eastern, Persian

**Abdallah's**, 3939 Hillcroft (713-952-4747) is a restaurant providing Middle Eastern dishes such as hummus, tabbouleh and vegetables; stocks a boutique assortment of Middle Eastern spices, herbs, breads, canned goods and pre-pared desserts. Take-out available.

**Antone's Import Co.** (several locations). Specializes in spices, sauces, Middle Eastern and other imported foods and wines along with world-class poor boys.

**Droubi's Imports and restaurants** – several locations including Droubi's Bakery & Delicatessen, 7333 Hillcroft (713-988-5897); and 3163 Highway 6 South in Sugar Land (281-494-2800). Middle Eastern, Arabic, Greek, Turkish and Persian specialty foods as well as European imports and kosher foods from Israel.  Known for Middle Eastern breads, hummus, falafel, tabbouleh, shish kebabs and deli classics. Take-out and full catering available.

**Phoenicia Specialty Foods**, 12126 Westheimer (281-558-8225). Middle Eastern and Mediterranean grains, rice, beans, sauces, spices, pastries, meats, cheeses and other gourmet foods at top-value prices. Many available in bulk. Phoenicia Deli, which offers some products and take-out Middle Eastern specialties, such as tabbouleh and falafel, is nearby.

**Super Sahel**, 5627 Hillcroft (713-266-7360). Small shop with necessities for Persian cooking such as basmati rice, couscous, pickled garlic, ghormeh sabji herb mix, barberries, canned okra, sumac and other traditional spices, sesame candy; pomegranate and other exotic syrups and preserves, chutneys.

**Super Vanak International Food Market & Deli**, 5692 Hillcroft (713-952-7676). Stocks all the staples of Persian and other Middle Eastern cuisines – sour cherry and pineapple syrups, mint water, barberries, fig jam, quince preserves, teas and coffee, pickles, sumac and spice mixes, pickled lemons, camomile flowers; curry paste, chutneys, fesenjoon (a mixture of walnuts, tomato paste, mushrooms, pomegranate paste and juice, onion and canola oil); taftoon bread, basmati rice, tahini, dried fruits.

### Indian

**Essence of Asia,** 1730 Williams Trace Blvd. Suite G (281-265-2100). A newer purveyor of necessities for Indian cooking in the Sugar Land area.

**Fyza's Groceries,** 12403 Veteran's Memorial Dr.  (281-537-0055). Serves the Indian community in the FM 1960 area.

**India Grocers**, 6606 Southwest Freeway at Hillcroft (713-266-7717) is stocked with classic spices and foods from India, Pakistan and around the world. Wide variety of rices, dal (lentils), spices, gram flour (besan), pickles, chutneys and other condiments, ghee (clarified, reduced butter), pistachios, peanuts, cashews, almonds and other nuts, tahini and other pastes, mixes, fresh produce including popular Indian vegetables and mangos, breads, desserts, frozen and canned foods at good-value prices.

**Keemat Grocers**, 5621 Hillcroft  (713-781-2892).  Small shop well-stocked with basics of Indian cooking – rice, spices and spice mixes, bulk nuts, coconut, garlic, fresh produce including mangoes and the mangoes used for pickles, curry mixes, canned mango pulp, vegetables, chutneys and relishes.

**Patel Brothers**, 5815 Hillcroft (713-784-8332). Stocks all the accoutrements of Indian cooking from almond oil and fresh curry leaves to exotic ice creams. Good source for saffron and other spices, raisins and figs, cashews, pistachios and other nuts, ginger and garlic pastes, dal (lentils), a wide variety of chutneys, tamarind and fresh fruit, especially mangos in season.

# HEALTHY RECIPE MODIFICATION TIPS *by Linda McDonald, M.S., R.D., L.D.*

The secret to healthy eating is to enjoy foods that not only taste good but are good for you. No food or recipe is "good" or "bad." How an individual food or recipe fits into a total diet determines the health benefits. Understanding food and learning how to use basic principles of balance, variety and moderation is smart eating.

The LiteFare tips, recipe modifications and nutrition information are provided to help you make informed choices. Use the nutrient analysis chart to check the difference between the original recipe and the modified version. Then decide whether to use the suggested modifications based on your particular health needs and your eating plans for the rest of the day. Remember that balance, variety and moderation are the keys to eating healthy.

## RECIPE MODIFICATIONS

Recipes are usually modified to change one or more of the ingredients so that the outcome is more beneficial. The four basic reasons for modifying recipes are:

- To reduce fat and cholesterol.
- To reduce sodium.
- To reduce sugar.
- To add fiber.

A recipe can be modified in four ways:

- Eliminate an ingredient.
- Change the amount of an ingredient.
- Substitute one ingredient for another.
- Change the cooking method.

### TO REDUCE FAT & CHOLESTEROL:

Limit the portion of meat, fish or poultry to 3-4 ounces per serving. The current dietary recommendations are to eat no more than 6 ounces of lean meat, poultry or fish per day.

Choose lean cuts of meat and trim all visible fat before cooking. This includes removing the skin of poultry, which can be done before or after cooking. If you are using a moist cooking method (stewing, boiling or covered casserole), remove the skin before cooking. If using a dry cooking method (baking, broiling or grilling), leave the skin on during cooking to keep the product from drying out, but remove the skin before eating.

Marinate lean cuts of meat to tenderize them by breaking down muscle fiber. This is done by the acid part of the marinade — vinegar, wine, pineapple juice, etc. Oil is not necessary. Prick the meat all over with a fork to allow the marinade to penetrate thoroughly.

Plan a variety of proteins — animal and vegetable. Cycle red meat, poultry and fish with dried beans, peas and lentils.

Use non-fat or 1-percent dairy products. Replace whole milk cheese with cheese made from skim milk, such as part-skim milk mozzarella. Try some of the new low-fat cheeses.

Select sharp Cheddar and other strong tasting cheese. Place cheese on top to have the strongest influence on your taste buds.

Prepared meats and cheeses should have no more than 5 grams of fat per ounce. Check the labels or ask the grocer where you shop.

Use fewer egg yolks and whole eggs in cooking. Substitute two egg whites for each whole egg.

Prepare eggless pasta in place of egg pastas. Most dry pastas are eggless, and most fresh pastas use eggs, but check the ingredient lables.

Sauté with broth, wine or water instead of oils or butter.

Microwave vegetables in a covered dish with just a small amount of water, rather than sautéing in oil or butter.

Make stocks, soups, sauces and stews ahead of time. Chill, then remove all hardened fat from the top. If there is no time to do this, skim off as much fat as possible. Then add several ice cubes. The fat will congeal and cling to the ice cubes, which can be discarded.

If you can't make your own stocks, look for low-fat, low-sodium canned beef or chicken broth. Be sure to defat canned broth by chilling until fat hardens, then skim off.

Use nuts, seeds, olives, cheese, butter, margarine and oils in moderation.

Olive and canola oils are the best choices for cooking. Use olive oil for sautéing and in salad dressings; choose canola for baking. But remember that oils are still fats.

Low-fat cooking methods include broiling, baking, roasting, poaching and stir-frying. Utensils for low-fat cooking are nonstick cookware, nonstick cooking spray and steamers.

*Try the following low-fat substitutions:*

**Cream:** 1/3 cup non-fat dry milk in 1 cup skim milk or canned evaporated skim milk.

**Sour Cream:** Plain non-fat yogurt or a blend of 1 cup fat-free or 1% cottage cheese + 1 tablespoon lemon juice.

**Mayonnaise:** 1 cup plain non-fat yogurt and 1/2 cup light mayonnaise.

### To Reduce Salt and Sodium:

Salt is an acquired taste. Your taste for salt will diminish as you gradually reduce the amount you use. You will begin to enjoy the taste of the food rather than the salt.

Eliminate or reduce salt in all recipes except yeast breads where salt is necessary to control the growth of the yeast. Even in yeast breads, salt can usually be reduced; one teaspoon per tablespoon of dry yeast.

Use salt-free or low-sodium canned products. Rinse canned products, such as beans, with water before using.

Salt is not necessary in the boiling water when cooking pastas, rice or other grains.

Add salt last, after tasting the food. Use just enough salt to correct the food's flavor. Remove salt shaker from the table.

Nothing else tastes exactly like salt, but other seasonings can enhance the flavor of foods and compensate for the salt you eliminate. Use the following seasonings to add zest to foods:

**Lemon or Lime Juice** — Use on salads and cooked vegetables. For more juice, microwave 30-60 seconds before juicing.

**Citrus Zest** — The thin outer layer of an orange, lemon or other citrus peel. Adds flavor to baked goods, sauces and other dishes. Use a zester or grater.

**Flavored Vinegars** — Balsamic, tarragon, raspberry or wine.

**Dried Onion Flakes, Onion or Garlic Powder, Garlic Cloves.**

**Condiments** — Worcestershire sauce, hot pepper sauce, mustard, soy, etc. are relatively high in sodium, but if used sparingly, can enliven foods without overdoing the sodium. Use a low-sodium version when available.

**Herbs** — Fresh herbs have the best flavor, but if not available, substitute 1/2 to 1 teaspoon dried herb per tablespoon of fresh herb. Crush the dried herb to release the flavor.

**Wines & Liqueurs** — If cooked at or above boiling temperature, the alcohol evaporates, eliminating most of the alcohol and many of the calories while the flavor remains.

### To Reduce Sugar:

Sugar can be reduced by one-third to one-half in most recipes. In cookies, bars, and cakes replace the sugar you have eliminated with non-fat dry milk.

Brown sugar or honey is sweeter than sugar and may be substituted for white sugar using considerably less. Nutritionally they are all the same, so there is no advantage to brown sugar or honey.

Flavor can be enhanced with spices (cinnamon, nutmeg or cloves) and extracts (vanilla, almond, orange or lemon). Doubling the amount of vanilla a recipe calls for will increase the sweetness without adding calories. Be careful about increasing spices to boost flavor when sugar is decreased. Cloves and ginger can easily overpower the recipe. Safest spices to increase are cinnamon, nutmeg and allspice.

When reducing sugar in a recipe, substitute fruit juice for the liquid or add fruits such as raisins, dried apricots, dates, prunes or bananas. Frozen orange or apple juice concentrate can be added. One tablespoon concentrate equals 1/4 cup fresh juice.

### To Add Fiber:

Use more whole grains (bulghur, brown rice, corn, barley and oatmeal), vegetables, dried beans, split peas and lentils.

Substitute whole-wheat flour for white flour whenever possible. It is heavier than white flour, so use less; 7/8 cup whole-wheat flour for one cup white flour. Experiment to find out what works best in recipe. Some recipes will turn out well with all whole-wheat flour, others are better when half whole-wheat and half white flour is used.

Add wheat bran, oat bran, oatmeal or farina to baked products, cereals, casseroles and soups. Start with one or two tablespoons and increase gradually. Substitute up to 1/2 cup oatmeal or oat bran for part of the flour in baked goods.

Use unpeeled potatoes whenever possible in soups, stews or for oven fries.

Use whole-grain pastas and brown or wild rice.

# RECIPE NUTRITIONAL ANALYSIS

The information listed below was calculated by computer nutrient analysis of each recipe and the recipe prepared according to the modification tip (*Modified Recipe). Because the nutrient content of food varies depending on growing conditions, season, transit time to market and other factors, the numbers given should be considered estimated values.

The nutrient analysis is for one serving. If a range of servings is given (serves 6 to 8), the first number was used for the analysis. If you serve more or less than the suggested serving, adjust the nutrient numbers accordingly.

The nutritional analysis of each recipe includes all the ingredients that are listed in that recipe, except for ingredients for which no amount is given, for instance "salt to taste" or ingredients labeled as "optional." If an ingredient is presented with an option ("1 cup chicken or vegetable broth" or "2 to 4 tablespoons") the first item or number listed was used in the nutritional analysis.

\* *Recipes modified according to the instructions at the end of the regular recipe designated with an apple. Regular recipes with an asterisk that are considered fairly healthy. Fat and sodium levels may still be higher than recommended.*

| | Portion | Calories | Protein (g) | Carbohydrate (g) | Fat (g) | % Fat Calories | Cholesterol (mg) | Sodium (mg) | Dietary Fiber (g) |
|---|---|---|---|---|---|---|---|---|---|
| Alsatian Onion Tart (Chez Nous) | 1 serving | 768 | 14 | 51 | 57 | 66% | 282 | 660 | 3 |
| Apple Bread Pudding (Riviera) | 1/8 recipe | 697 | 11 | 74 | 41 | 52% | 304 | 470 | 4 |
| *Modified Recipe | 1/12 recipe | 465 | 8 | 50 | 27 | 52% | 203 | 313 | 3 |
| Asparagus & Snow Peas in Butter Sauce (Simposio) | 1 serving | 152 | 4 | 10 | 12 | 66% | 31 | 49 | 4 |
| *Modified Recipe | 1 serving | 76 | 4 | 10 | 3 | 35% | 8 | 48 | 4 |
| Avocado Fries with Habañero Ketchup (Tony Ruppe's) | 1 serving | 580 | 8 | 34 | 48 | 72% | 110 | 69 | 6 |
| Baby Spinach & Mushroom Salad & Dressing (St. Regis) | 1 serving | 162 | 6 | 6 | 13 | 70% | 24 | 159 | 4 |
| *Modified Recipe | 1 serving | 96 | 5 | 8 | 5 | 45% | 9 | 155 | 4 |
| Bananas Foster Bread Pudding (Tasca) | 1/8 recipe | 1122 | 13 | 102 | 77 | 60% | 328 | 429 | 5 |
| *Modified Recipe | 1/15 recipe | 598 | 7 | 54 | 41 | 60% | 175 | 229 | 3 |
| Beef Medallions with Gorgonzola (Aldo's) | 1 serving | 569 | 37 | 4 | 42 | 67% | 173 | 263 | 0 |
| *Modified Recipe | 1 serving | 392 | 34 | 4 | 23 | 53% | 121 | 265 | 0 |
| Beef Rillet Lasagna (Tasca) | 1/8 recipe | 550 | 39 | 40 | 25 | 41% | 101 | 485 | 2 |
| *Modified Recipe | 1/12 recipe | 470 | 36 | 40 | 17 | 34% | 90 | 288 | 2 |
| Black Bean Soup (Ruggles) | 1 serving | 489 | 37 | 44 | 18 | 33% | 22 | 2741 | 10 |
| *Modified Recipe | 1 serving | 391 | 28 | 46 | 12 | 27% | 22 | 534 | 10 |
| *Blackberry Lamb Chops with Blackberry Demi-Glace (St. Regis) | 1 serving | 429 | 42 | 6 | 16 | 35% | 138 | 264 | 1 |
| Blackened Duck Breast with Pea Shoots & Carrots (River Oaks) | 8 oz breast | 660 | 58 | 24 | 36 | 49% | 308 | 213 | 3 |
| *Modified Recipe | 6 oz breast | 440 | 49 | 24 | 15 | 32% | 243 | 202 | 3 |
| Braised Lamb Shanks (Damian's) | 1 serving | 497 | 51 | 15 | 23 | 43% | 127 | 2463 | 2 |
| *Modified Recipe | 1 serving | 313 | 38 | 15 | 9 | 26% | 113 | 267 | 2 |
| Braised Red Cabbage (Rotisserie) | 1 serving | 148 | 3 | 21 | 7 | 38% | 16 | 61 | 3 |
| *Modified Recipe | 1 serving | 128 | 3 | 21 | 4 | 29% | 10 | 61 | 3 |
| Breast of Pheasant Grandmere (Rotisserie) | 1 serving | 816 | 55 | 33 | 47 | 52% | 205 | 1090 | 3 |
| *Modified Recipe | 1 serving | 622 | 52 | 33 | 27 | 39% | 155 | 290 | 3 |
| Capon with Intense Garlic & Sage Sauce (Tony's) | 1/4 recipe | 923 | 82 | 4 | 60 | 59% | 254 | 401 | 1 |
| *Modified Recipe | 1/6 recipe | 336 | 41 | 3 | 15 | 42% | 125 | 296 | 0 |

| | Portion | Calories | Protein (g) | Carbohydrate (g) | Fat (g) | % Fat Calories | Cholesterol (mg) | Sodium (mg) | Dietary Fiber (g) |
|---|---|---|---|---|---|---|---|---|---|
| Cheese Soufflé (Scott Chen's) | 1/2 recipe | 466 | 21 | 21 | 33 | 64% | 365 | 289 | 0 |
| Chicken in Pearl Onions (Aldo's) | 1 serving | 547 | 33 | 20 | 33 | 55% | 126 | 510 | 1 |
| *Modified Recipe | 1 serving | 410 | 32 | 21 | 18 | 39% | 99 | 319 | 1 |
| Chicken Marsala (Cavatore) | 1 serving | 298 | 31 | 5 | 16 | 47% | 102 | 143 | 1 |
| *Modified Recipe | 1 serving | 283 | 35 | 7 | 11 | 36% | 85 | 222 | 1 |
| Chicken Pernod Soup (La Tour) | 1 serving | 234 | 14 | 5 | 17 | 66% | 76 | 676 | 0 |
| *Modified Recipe | 1 serving | 145 | 18 | 8 | 3 | 21% | 35 | 517 | 0 |
| Chicken Salad Monte Cristo (Rivoli) | 1 serving | 817 | 35 | 15 | 68 | 75% | 172 | 423 | 2 |
| *Modified Recipe | 1 serving | 394 | 36 | 23 | 17 | 39% | 102 | 544 | 2 |
| Chicken Tenderloin with Broccoli & Black Pepper (Scott Chen's) | 1 serving | 414 | 28 | 7 | 31 | 66% | 67 | 809 | 2 |
| *Modified Recipe with 1 cup Rice | 1 serving | 477 | 33 | 51 | 15 | 29% | 67 | 93 | 5 |
| *Chilled Cherry Soup (Chez Nous) | 1 serving | 251 | 2 | 62 | 2 | 6% | 0 | 2 | 4 |
| Chocolate Chip Bourbon Pecan Pie (Brennan's) | 1 serving | 593 | 6 | 81 | 30 | 43% | 87 | 208 | 3 |
| Chocolate Terrine with Mocha Vanilla Sauce (Chez Nous) | 1 serving | 319 | 9 | 26 | 21 | 58% | 167 | 118 | 1 |
| *Chocolate Waffles (Rancho Tejas) | 1 waffle | 598 | 11 | 89 | 22 | 33% | 256 | 635 | 1 |
| Coquina Cookies (La Tour) | 1 cookie | 113 | 1 | 14 | 6 | 48% | 0 | 8 | 0 |
| Crab Salad Brennan's (Brennan's) | 1 serving | 419 | 19 | 13 | 35 | 71% | 47 | 611 | 6 |
| *Modified Recipe | 1 serving | 241 | 18 | 11 | 16 | 55% | 47 | 477 | 5 |
| Crabmeat Florentine (Rivoli) | 1 serving | 461 | 30 | 20 | 31 | 58% | 149 | 545 | 6 |
| *Modified Recipe | 1 serving | 269 | 28 | 20 | 10 | 31% | 95 | 544 | 6 |
| *Creamy White Grits with Greens & Mushrooms (Cafe Annie) | 1 serving | 245 | 7 | 44 | 3 | 12% | 8 | 906 | 3 |
| Creole Onion Soup (Brennan's) | 1 serving | 152 | 4 | 12 | 10 | 56% | 0 | 826 | 2 |
| *Modified Recipe | 1 serving | 92 | 4 | 12 | 3 | 28% | 0 | 776 | 2 |
| Crisp Poblano Crab Cakes with Tomato Coulis (St. Regis) | 1 serving | 660 | 56 | 37 | 32 | 44% | 427 | 973 | 5 |
| *Modified Recipe with 1 cup Pasta | 1 serving | 857 | 63 | 76 | 33 | 35% | 427 | 974 | 8 |
| Double Lamb Chops with Sauce & Spinach (Cafe Annie) | 1/2 recipe | 1063 | 107 | 32 | 56 | 48% | 346 | 2757 | 6 |
| *Modified Recipe | 1/4 recipe | 489 | 52 | 15 | 24 | 45% | 206 | 158 | 3 |
| Duck Gumbo (Rainbow Lodge) | 1/12 recipe | 369 | 17 | 10 | 29 | 71% | 61 | 316 | 1 |
| *Modified Recipe | 1/16 recipe | 203 | 13 | 8 | 13 | 59% | 46 | 237 | 1 |
| Eggplant Parmesan (Cavatore) | 1 serving | 880 | 21 | 48 | 69 | 69% | 319 | 838 | 8 |
| *Modified Recipe | 1 serving | 307 | 14 | 41 | 11 | 31% | 0 | 634 | 8 |
| Eggplant Patties in Ginger & Garlic Sauce (Scott Chen's) | 1 serving | 559 | 15 | 34 | 41 | 65% | 38 | 726 | 2 |
| *Modified Recipe with 1 Cup Rice | 1 serving | 655 | 20 | 79 | 30 | 40% | 38 | 445 | 6 |
| Eggplant Sandwich (River Oaks) | 1 sandwich | 1146 | 28 | 92 | 74 | 58% | 257 | 415 | 8 |
| *Modified Recipe | 1 sandwich | 601 | 23 | 73 | 25 | 37% | 129 | 468 | 8 |
| Fettuccine "Favorite" (Rotisserie) | 1 serving | 1009 | 34 | 103 | 51 | 45% | 150 | 451 | 6 |
| *Modified Recipe | 1 serving | 778 | 28 | 103 | 27 | 31% | 68 | 239 | 6 |
| Fillet of Beef with Brandy Sauce (Cavatore) | 1/2 recipe | 1115 | 59 | 3 | 93 | 76% | 303 | 255 | 1 |
| *Modified Recipe | 1/4 recipe | 308 | 23 | 2 | 22 | 64% | 85 | 104 | 0 |
| Fillet of Beef with Coffee Beans in Broth & Grits (Cafe Annie) | 1/4 recipe | 693 | 55 | 48 | 29 | 39% | 153 | 1649 | 3 |
| *Modified Recipe | 1/6 recipe | 420 | 37 | 32 | 14 | 32% | 102 | 785 | 2 |
| Fillet of Flounder with Dill Sauce (La Tour) | 1 serving | 443 | 34 | 2 | 33 | 68% | 93 | 187 | 0 |
| *Modified Recipe | 1 serving | 202 | 34 | 2 | 6 | 27% | 93 | 187 | 0 |

| | Portion | Calories | Protein (g) | Carbohydrate (g) | Fat (g) | % Fat Calories | Cholesterol (mg) | Sodium (mg) | Dietary Fiber (g) |
|---|---|---|---|---|---|---|---|---|---|
| Flourless Chocolate Cake (Simposio) | 1/8 recipe | 785 | 23 | 111 | 32 | 35% | 200 | 916 | 0 |
| *Modified Recipe | 1/12 recipe | 524 | 16 | 74 | 21 | 35% | 133 | 610 | 0 |
| Fresh Berries with Meyer Lemon Curd (Aldo's) | 1 serving | 618 | 7 | 29 | 55 | 78% | 479 | 39 | 2 |
| *Fresh Thyme & Brie Cheese Grits (Sabine) | 1 serving | 395 | 15 | 70 | 6 | 13% | 18 | 253 | 1 |
| Frittata with Sweet Onion, Bacon & Fontina (Riviera) | 1 wedge | 350 | 23 | 7 | 25 | 65% | 553 | 510 | 1 |
| *Modified Recipe | 1 wedge | 182 | 18 | 13 | 6 | 29% | 18 | 231 | 1 |
| *Frozen Sangria (Rancho Tejas) | 3/4 cup | 227 | 0 | 31 | 0 | 0% | 0 | 16 | 0 |
| Greek Shrimp Salad with Lemon Vinaigrette (Olivette) | 1 serving | 370 | 13 | 22 | 26 | 62% | 46 | 2646 | 7 |
| *Modified Recipe | 1 serving | 226 | 11 | 20 | 12 | 47% | 39 | 507 | 7 |
| *Grilled Chicken with Carrot-Cranberry Chutney (Riviera) | 1 serving | 708 | 115 | 22 | 14 | 19% | 315 | 374 | 2 |
| Grilled Vegetable & Chicken Soup (Pignetti's) | 1 serving | 388 | 41 | 22 | 16 | 36% | 99 | 668 | 4 |
| *Modified Recipe | 1 serving | 348 | 41 | 22 | 11 | 28% | 99 | 668 | 4 |
| Gulf Blue Crab Nachos (Rancho Tejas) | 1 serving | 234 | 10 | 9 | 18 | 67% | 55 | 457 | 1 |
| *Modified Recipe | 1 serving | 138 | 10 | 10 | 7 | 45% | 24 | 438 | 1 |
| Gulf Red Snapper Fillet Meunière (Rivoli) | 1 serving | 497 | 35 | 1 | 39 | 71% | 125 | 126 | 0 |
| *Modified Recipe | 1 serving | 233 | 35 | 3 | 8 | 32% | 78 | 124 | 0 |
| Hibiscus Salad with Goat Cheese Cakes & Dressing (Rainbow Lodge) | 1 serving | 463 | 13 | 42 | 27 | 52% | 9 | 444 | 5 |
| *Modified Recipe | 1 serving | 198 | 6 | 24 | 9 | 38% | 4 | 231 | 4 |
| Italian Pear Tart (Rainbow Lodge) | 1 slice | 420 | 7 | 36 | 28 | 59% | 142 | 157 | 2 |
| Italian Salad (Aldo's) | 1 serving | 266 | 13 | 15 | 19 | 61% | 13 | 382 | 6 |
| *Modified Recipe | 1 serving | 168 | 9 | 14 | 10 | 50% | 6 | 231 | 6 |
| Jumbo Crab Cakes with Mango Salsa & Cream (River Oaks) | 1 serving | 1656 | 55 | 179 | 81 | 44% | 460 | 911 | 10 |
| Key Lime Cheesecake (Rotisserie) | 1 slice | 314 | 5 | 26 | 22 | 61% | 105 | 168 | 0 |
| King Ranch Casserole (Rancho Tejas) | 1/6 recipe | 665 | 29 | 54 | 39 | 52% | 124 | 791 | 5 |
| *Modified Recipe | 1/8 recipe | 388 | 22 | 41 | 16 | 37% | 93 | 593 | 5 |
| *Linguine with Clam Sauce (Cavatore) | 1 serving | 598 | 32 | 89 | 10 | 16% | 41 | 76 | 8 |
| Marbled Fudge Brownies (Brennan's) | 1 serving | 381 | 5 | 46 | 22 | 49% | 98 | 144 | 2 |
| Marinated Seared Tuna with Charred Fruit Salsa (Ruggles) | 1 serving | 476 | 53 | 11 | 22 | 43% | 83 | 773 | 2 |
| *Modified Recipe | 1 serving | 396 | 53 | 11 | 13 | 31% | 83 | 488 | 2 |
| Mercer's Warm Comfort Strudel (La Réserve) | 1 serving | 628 | 5 | 43 | 50 | 70% | 128 | 238 | 2 |
| New World Shrimp with Tomato, Vanilla & Chili (Olivette) | 1 serving | 171 | 10 | 15 | 9 | 46% | 59 | 440 | 4 |
| *Modified Recipe | 1 serving | 141 | 10 | 15 | 6 | 35% | 59 | 440 | 4 |
| New York Strip alla Robespierre (Simposio) | 1 serving | 534 | 38 | 2 | 43 | 74% | 101 | 158 | 1 |
| *Modified Recipe | 1 serving | 304 | 38 | 2 | 14 | 43% | 115 | 128 | 1 |
| Normandy Brie Soup with Truffles & Croutons (La Réserve) | 1 serving | 996 | 16 | 19 | 93 | 82% | 279 | 924 | 0 |
| Olive Crusted NY Strip with Arugula & Potatoes (Riviera) | 12 oz steak | 1077 | 81 | 44 | 61 | 52% | 201 | 2151 | 5 |
| *Modified Recipe | 6 oz steak | 424 | 40 | 19 | 19 | 42% | 100 | 593 | 2 |
| Orange Papaya Mojo (Ruggles) | 1/2 cup | 126 | 1 | 17 | 7 | 47% | 0 | 2 | 3 |
| *Modified Recipe | 1/2 cup | 97 | 1 | 17 | 4 | 31% | 0 | 2 | 3 |
| Orange Scented Chicken (River Oaks) | 1/4 recipe | 565 | 52 | 27 | 26 | 42% | 180 | 224 | 3 |
| *Modified Recipe | 1/6 recipe | 291 | 35 | 18 | 8 | 24% | 94 | 90 | 2 |
| Oven Roasted Salmon (Simposio) | 1 serving | 322 | 35 | 6 | 17 | 48% | 80 | 87 | 2 |
| *Modified Recipe | 1 serving | 259 | 35 | 6 | 10 | 35% | 80 | 87 | 2 |

| | Portion | Calories | Protein (g) | Carbohydrate (g) | Fat (g) | % Fat Calories | Cholesterol (mg) | Sodium (mg) | Dietary Fiber (g) |
|---|---|---|---|---|---|---|---|---|---|
| Pan Seared Tuna Loin with Slaw & Wonton Crisps (Pignetti's) | 1 serving | 716 | 57 | 26 | 40 | 51% | 103 | 2368 | 2 |
| *Modified Recipe | 1 serving | 400 | 56 | 20 | 7 | 18% | 103 | 449 | 2 |
| *Pasta with Chicken, Tomatoes, Peppers & Arugula (La Griglia) | 1 serving | 832 | 79 | 71 | 23 | 26% | 168 | 288 | 5 |
| *Pasta with Frisée, Mushrooms, Corn & Truffle Oil (Tasca) | 1 serving | 331 | 11 | 52 | 11 | 27% | 0 | 199 | 7 |
| Pecan Crusted Pork Chop (Sabine) | 1/6 recipe | 1055 | 50 | 52 | 72 | 61% | 340 | 500 | 4 |
| *Modified Recipe | 1/8 recipe | 492 | 36 | 36 | 22 | 40% | 209 | 358 | 2 |
| Plantain Crusted Pork Loin (Ruggles) | 1 serving | 686 | 31 | 46 | 43 | 56% | 68 | 1061 | 2 |
| *Modified Recipe | 1 serving | 417 | 28 | 43 | 15 | 32% | 68 | 1061 | 2 |
| Poached Chicken Salad with Confit & Vinaigrette (Tasca) | 1 serving | 461 | 39 | 20 | 26 | 50% | 90 | 196 | 6 |
| *Modified Recipe | 1 serving | 341 | 38 | 19 | 13 | 33% | 90 | 189 | 6 |
| Poblano Dip (Olivette) | 1/4 cup | 114 | 3 | 4 | 10 | 76% | 24 | 217 | 1 |
| *Modified Recipe | 1/4 cup | 85 | 4 | 6 | 6 | 56% | 18 | 228 | 1 |
| *Pork Tenderloin Calvados (La Tour) | 1 serving | 293 | 38 | 5 | 11 | 34% | 102 | 142 | 2 |
| Portobello Fries with Mushroom Tea Vinaigrette (Pignetti's) | 1 serving | 865 | 29 | 68 | 54 | 56% | 167 | 1041 | 6 |
| Potato Gnocchi with Spinach & Gorgonzola (Simposio) | 1 serving | 563 | 13 | 43 | 39 | 61% | 170 | 1807 | 4 |
| *Modified Recipe | 1 serving | 352 | 15 | 43 | 13 | 34% | 87 | 680 | 3 |
| Putt Thai Korat (Nit Noi) | 1 serving | 915 | 36 | 132 | 26 | 25% | 169 | 2536 | 2 |
| *Modified Recipe | 1 serving | 911 | 35 | 132 | 26 | 25% | 169 | 651 | 2 |
| Quick Marinated Grilled Swordfish (Vallone's) | 9 oz fillet | 386 | 51 | 1 | 18 | 43% | 100 | 237 | 0 |
| *Modified Recipe | 6 oz fillet | 257 | 34 | 1 | 12 | 43% | 66 | 158 | 0 |
| Raspberry Chicken Salad with Raspberry Vinaigrette (Riviera) | 1 serving | 320 | 28 | 13 | 18 | 49% | 69 | 267 | 5 |
| *Modified Recipe | 1 serving | 255 | 26 | 13 | 11 | 38% | 64 | 182 | 5 |
| Raspberry Soufflé with Raspberry Sauce (Rivoli) | 1 soufflé | 697 | 16 | 77 | 33 | 42% | 411 | 157 | 3 |
| Red Baron's Linguine (Damian's) | 1 serving | 868 | 37 | 102 | 34 | 36% | 56 | 454 | 11 |
| *Modified Recipe | 1 serving | 601 | 24 | 100 | 12 | 17% | 16 | 275 | 11 |
| *Red Snapper Court-Bouillon (Brennan's) | 1 serving | 232 | 34 | 11 | 2 | 10% | 80 | 764 | 2 |
| Reese's Peanut Butter Cup Cheesecake (Ruggles) | 1 serving | 1247 | 26 | 105 | 84 | 59% | 212 | 830 | 5 |
| Ribeye Poblano (Rancho Tejas) | 14 oz steak | 926 | 86 | 11 | 58 | 57% | 262 | 1193 | 0 |
| *Modified Recipe | 7 oz steak | 394 | 42 | 3 | 23 | 53% | 124 | 349 | 0 |
| Roast Lamb on Bread Pudding & Red Wine Sauce (Tony Ruppe's) | 1 rack | 1639 | 128 | 43 | 103 | 57% | 394 | 1302 | 6 |
| *Modified Recipe | 1/2 rack | 790 | 66 | 28 | 45 | 51% | 197 | 679 | 5 |
| Roasted Corn & Lamb Soup (Sabine) | 1 serving | 461 | 55 | 20 | 17 | 34% | 161 | 988 | 3 |
| *Modified Recipe | 1 serving | 417 | 53 | 20 | 13 | 29% | 153 | 662 | 3 |
| Salad 2000 (Damian's) | 1 serving | 546 | 13 | 40 | 38 | 61% | 34 | 240 | 4 |
| *Modified Recipe | 1 serving | 238 | 6 | 21 | 15 | 54% | 17 | 123 | 2 |
| San Angelo Sauce (Rancho Tejas) | 1 cup | 769 | 21 | 23 | 66 | 76% | 202 | 1770 | 1 |
| *Modified Recipe | 1/2 cup | 184 | 9 | 13 | 11 | 50% | 36 | 270 | 1 |
| Seafood Antipasto (Cavatore) | 1 serving | 253 | 31 | 10 | 9 | 31% | 204 | 1203 | 2 |
| *Modified Recipe | 1 serving | 227 | 31 | 9 | 6 | 24% | 204 | 790 | 1 |
| Sesame Fillet Mignon (Scott Chen's) | 1 serving | 419 | 21 | 7 | 34 | 74% | 81 | 68 | 0 |
| *Modified Recipe | 1 serving | 255 | 24 | 7 | 14 | 50% | 70 | 66 | 0 |
| Shredded Pork with Scallions (Scott Chen's) | 1 serving | 487 | 25 | 10 | 39 | 71% | 68 | 1419 | 1 |
| *Modified Recipe with 1 cup Rice | 1 serving | 614 | 30 | 54 | 30 | 44% | 68 | 266 | 5 |

| | Portion | Calories | Protein (g) | Carbohydrate (g) | Fat (g) | % Fat Calories | Cholesterol (mg) | Sodium (mg) | Dietary Fiber (g) |
|---|---|---|---|---|---|---|---|---|---|
| *Shrimp Pasta with Fresh Tomato (Aldo's) | 1 serving | 493 | 17 | 69 | 15 | 27% | 36 | 52 | 7 |
| Shuu-Shee Sea Shells by the Sea Shore (Nit Noi) | 1 serving | 413 | 33 | 16 | 26 | 55% | 69 | 815 | 2 |
| *Modified Recipe | 1 serving | 252 | 34 | 19 | 5 | 16% | 79 | 171 | 2 |
| Smoked Salmon Salad (La Tour) | 1 serving | 287 | 18 | 7 | 21 | 65% | 20 | 724 | 5 |
| *Modified Recipe | 1 serving | 211 | 18 | 6 | 13 | 53% | 20 | 717 | 5 |
| Smoked Salmon Tartare (Rotisserie) | 1 serving | 178 | 15 | 11 | 8 | 41% | 142 | 1241 | 1 |
| Smoked Thyme Mushroom Risotto (Tasca) | 1 serving | 602 | 9 | 50 | 40 | 60% | 53 | 912 | 2 |
| *Modified Recipe | 1 serving | 392 | 12 | 50 | 14 | 34% | 20 | 680 | 2 |
| Smoked Trout Cakes with Remoulade (Rainbow Lodge) | 1 serving | 692 | 44 | 49 | 35 | 45% | 231 | 781 | 3 |
| *Modified Recipe | 1 serving | 610 | 43 | 49 | 26 | 38% | 125 | 736 | 3 |
| Southern Corn Chowder (Rivoli) | 1 serving | 411 | 13 | 34 | 27 | 56% | 93 | 553 | 4 |
| *Modified Recipe | 1 serving | 185 | 10 | 25 | 6 | 28% | 25 | 202 | 3 |
| *Spinach with Orzo & Sun-Dried Tomatoes (Damian's) | 1 serving | 393 | 12 | 67 | 8 | 19% | 0 | 76 | 4 |
| Steak au Poivre (Rotisserie) | 8 oz steak | 575 | 70 | 1 | 25 | 41% | 202 | 818 | 0 |
| *Modified Recipe | 6 oz steak | 376 | 52 | 1 | 14 | 35% | 152 | 200 | 0 |
| Summer Swordfish (La Réserve) | 1 serving | 491 | 32 | 14 | 32 | 57% | 53 | 355 | 3 |
| *Modified Recipe | 1 serving | 312 | 32 | 14 | 12 | 33% | 53 | 355 | 3 |
| *Sweet Potato Cobbler (Sabine) | 1 serving | 335 | 3 | 60 | 10 | 27% | 27 | 172 | 2 |
| Thai Chicken Curry (Nit Noi) | 1 serving | 405 | 19 | 31 | 25 | 53% | 33 | 757 | 3 |
| *Modified Recipe | 1 serving | 248 | 21 | 35 | 4 | 13% | 43 | 808 | 3 |
| The King & I (Nit Noi) | 1 serving | 733 | 53 | 92 | 17 | 21% | 99 | 1018 | 3 |
| *Modified Recipe | 1 serving | 730 | 52 | 92 | 17 | 21% | 99 | 324 | 3 |
| Tortellini Pasta with Cream Sauce (Cavatore) | 1 serving | 556 | 23 | 22 | 42 | 68% | 247 | 808 | 1 |
| *Modified Recipe | 1 serving | 296 | 18 | 27 | 13 | 39% | 147 | 989 | 1 |
| Turbot with Tomatoes & Basil (Chez Nous) | 1 serving | 358 | 27 | 9 | 23 | 58% | 69 | 286 | 1 |
| *Modified Recipe | 1 serving | 241 | 27 | 10 | 9 | 35% | 96 | 269 | 1 |
| *Tuscan Beans (Damian's) | 1 serving | 459 | 24 | 72 | 9 | 17% | 0 | 97 | 12 |
| *Upside Down Fig Cake with Whipped Cream (Tony Ruppe's) | 1 slice | 461 | 4 | 77 | 17 | 32% | 78 | 285 | 3 |
| Veal Cutlet Vienna Style (Rivoli) | 1/4 recipe | 1351 | 82 | 63 | 83 | 56% | 405 | 681 | 2 |
| *Modified Recipe | 1/8 recipe | 564 | 41 | 32 | 29 | 48% | 187 | 340 | 1 |
| Veal Scaloppini with Lemon Butter Sauce (La Tour) | 7 oz portion | 929 | 39 | 4 | 82 | 79% | 271 | 140 | 1 |
| *Modified Recipe | 6 oz portion | 298 | 33 | 4 | 13 | 41% | 141 | 117 | 1 |
| Vegetable Musmun (Nit Noi) | 1 serving | 662 | 13 | 56 | 47 | 60% | 0 | 1461 | 7 |
| *Modified Recipe | 1 serving | 299 | 10 | 53 | 6 | 18% | 5 | 78 | 7 |
| Venetian Risi e Bisi (Olivette) | 1 serving | 378 | 13 | 64 | 8 | 19% | 6 | 1398 | 7 |
| *Modified Recipe | 1 serving | 378 | 13 | 64 | 8 | 18% | 5 | 581 | 7 |
| *Venison Backstrap with Blackberry Reduction (Sabine) | 1 serving | 436 | 46 | 31 | 12 | 24% | 171 | 578 | 4 |
| *Warm Apple Galette with Syrup & Lemon (Olivette) | 1/4 recipe | 701 | 4 | 124 | 24 | 30% | 24 | 251 | 4 |
| *Modified Recipe | 1/8 recipe | 350 | 2 | 62 | 12 | 30% | 12 | 126 | 2 |
| Warm Chocolate Cakes with Meringue (Cafe Annie) | 1 serving | 957 | 16 | 114 | 53 | 48% | 315 | 139 | 2 |
| White Chocolate Crème Brûlée (St. Regis) | 1 serving | 586 | 7 | 44 | 43 | 66% | 301 | 118 | 1 |
| Wild Mushroom Risotto with Asparagus Sauce (Anthony's) | 1 serving | 379 | 12 | 67 | 6 | 14% | 3 | 1071 | 3 |
| *Modified Recipe | 1 serving | 354 | 10 | 66 | 4 | 10% | 3 | 81 | 3 |

# INDEX

# ABOUT ANN CRISWELL – AUTHOR

Ann Criswell has been employed at the Houston Chronicle for 38 years, as food editor since the Food section's inception in 1966. She has written freelance food articles, authored nine cookbooks and edited several others. As food editor of the Chronicle she contributed most of the recipes in the original "Texas the Beautiful Cookbook" published in October 1986.

She is a member of the Association of Food Journalists, Houston Culinary Guild and Houston Culinary Historians.

In 1987, she was named the first honorary member of the South Texas Dietetic Association and received an award of excellence from the American Heart Association, American Cancer Society and Texas Restaurant Association. In 1992, the Texas Dietetic Association named her Media Person of the Year.

Scholarships have been established in her name at the Houston Community College and the School of Culinary Arts at the Art Institute of Houston. In 1999 she received the Hearst Eagle award, Hearst Newspapers' highest service recognition. She was one of 20 recipients from 6000 employees at the 10 Hearst Newspapers.

Because of a special interest in wine, she wrote a wine column for many years in the Chronicle and has made several wine tours to Europe and California. She also has judged Texas wine competitions and national cooking contests including the National Beef Cook-Off, Pillsbury BAKE-OFF and the National Chicken Cooking Contest.

Among her major interests are the End Hunger Network, Houston Food Bank and the annual Share our Strength Taste of the Nation benefit for anti-hunger projects.

She is an honor graduate of Texas Woman's University. Her late husband, Jim, was a Houston newspaperman. She has a daughter, Catherine; son, Charles; and four grandchildren, Ryan and Christopher Criswell and James and Ann Claire Lester.

# ABOUT FRAN FAUNTLEROY – PUBLISHER

Fran Fauntleroy was inspired to begin her own company, Houston Gourmet Publishing, after writing and marketing two successful cookbooks, "Six Flew Over The Cuckoo's Kitchens" and "Cuckoo, Too," with six lifelong friends.

She is responsible for eight Houston restaurant cookbooks and 12 Houston Gourmet menu guides. Fran has published and sold more than 200,000 of these books in the past 22 years!

Her high energy and great interest in Houston's fine restaurants is the springboard that keeps her busy thinking of new ways to spotlight the ever-changing dining scene of which she is so proud. Houston has arrived and excelled in the culinary arena!

Following the success of "Dallas Is Cooking!," a cookbook highlighting the restaurants for which that city has become famous, Fran then initiated "Houston Is Cooking" with Ann Criswell. They have now joined together to create "Houston Is Cooking *2000*" after their success with "Houston Is Cooking The Best" and "Houston Is Cooking At Home." This special gourmet collector's item cookbook showcases the city's most popular restaurants and chefs going into the new millennium who have successfully brought Houston recognition on a national level.

In addition to being a wife to John, mother of three grown children — Glenda, Shelley and Parker — their special spouses Robby, Mitch and Lara — and grandmother to Ginny, Rob, Parker, Mitchell and Matthew Garrett. They are all the blessings of her life.

# WHO'S WHO

*Key to Back Cover Photograph*

*Photographed at Rienzi, The Museum of Fine Arts Houston, former home of Carroll and Harris Masterson III.*

1  **Ann Criswell,** *Author*
2  **Fran Fauntleroy,** *Publisher*
3  **Ann Steiner,** *Editor*
4  **Linda McDonald,** *Nutritionist*
5  **Tommy Leman,** *Damian's*
6  **Jimmy Mitchell,** *Rainbow Lodge*
7  **Melissa Piper,** *Brennan's*
8  **Robert Del Grande,** *Cafe Annie*
9  **Joey Vallone,** *Vallone Restaurant Group*
10  **Hessni Malla,** *La Tour d'Argent*
11  **Sonny Lahham,** *La Tour d'Argent*

12  **Gregory Torres,** *Cavatore*
13  **Jim Mills,** *Olivette, The Houstonian*
14  **Joe Mannke,** *Rotisserie for Beef and Bird*
15  **Charles Dash,** *St. Regis*
16  **Danielle Noble-Brach,** *Chez Nous*
17  **Stephen Gasaway,** *Chez Nous*
18  **Denman Moody,** *Wines*
19  **Aaron Guest,** *Sabine*
20  **Michelle LeBleu,** *River Oaks Grill*
21  **Tony Rao,** *River Oaks Grill*

22  **Bruce McMillian,** *Tony's*
23  **John Sheely,** *Riviera Grill, Radisson Suite*
24  **Alice Vongvisith,** *Nit Noi*
25  **Carl Walker,** *Brennan's*
26  **Charles Clark,** *Tasca*
27  **Pierre Gutknecht,** *Rivoli*
28  **Tony Ruppe,** *Tony Ruppe's*
29  **Pedro Castro,** *Aldo's*
30  **Pat McCarley,** *Rancho Tejas*
31  **Mercer Mohr,** *La Réserve, Omni*
32  **Alberto Baffoni,** *Simposio*

# Notes

## ORDER FORM

Name _____

Address_____

City _____State _____Zip _____

Telephone_____

### Houston Is Cooking *2000*

$21.95 per copy plus $3.00 handling and postage per book.

*Make checks or money orders payable to* Houston Is Cooking *and mail to:*

Houston Gourmet
2 Pine Forest
Houston, Texas 77056

*Texas residents, also add applicable state sales tax*

### OTHER BOOKS AVAILABLE
### *Houston Is Cooking At Home*

A Cookbook featuring the Recipes from 24 Houston Restaurants with Color Photographs, *Nutritional Information and Wine Suggestions.*

**$21.95** per copy plus $3.00 handling and postage per book.

| QUANTITY | PRICE | SHIPPING | TAX | SUBTOTAL |
|----------|-------|----------|-----|----------|
|          |       |          |     |          |
|          |       |          |     |          |

**TOTAL THIS ORDER** _____

*Wholesale orders are welcome!*
*Buyers please contact Fran Fauntleroy at*
**713-621-3230** *to place an order.*

---

## ORDER FORM

Name _____

Address_____

City _____State _____Zip _____

Telephone_____

### Houston Is Cooking *2000*

$21.95 per copy plus $3.00 handling and postage per book.

*Make checks or money orders payable to* Houston Is Cooking *and mail to:*

Houston Gourmet
2 Pine Forest
Houston, Texas 77056

*Texas residents, also add applicable state sales tax*

### OTHER BOOKS AVAILABLE
### *Houston Is Cooking At Home*

A Cookbook featuring the Recipes from 24 Houston Restaurants with Color Photographs, *Nutritional Information and Wine Suggestions.*

**$21.95** per copy plus $3.00 handling and postage per book.

| QUANTITY | PRICE | SHIPPING | TAX | SUBTOTAL |
|----------|-------|----------|-----|----------|
|          |       |          |     |          |
|          |       |          |     |          |

**TOTAL THIS ORDER** _____

*Wholesale orders are welcome!*
*Buyers please contact Fran Fauntleroy at*
**713-621-3230** *to place an order.*

# Notes